A Forgotten Campaign

The British Armed Forces in France 1940 – From Dunkirk to the Armistice

Paul Fantom

Helion & Company Limited

Helion & Company Limited
Unit 8 Amherst Business Centre
Budbrooke Road
Warwick
CV34 5WE
England
Tel. 01926 499 619
Email: info@helion.co.uk
Website: www.helion.co.uk
Twitter: @helionbooks
Visit our blog at blog.helion.co.uk

Published by Helion & Company 2021
Designed and typeset by Mary Woolley (www.battlefield-design.co.uk)
Cover designed by Paul Hewitt, Battlefield Design (www.battlefield-design.co.uk)

ISBN 978-1-914059-01-8

British Library Cataloguing-in-Publication Data.
A catalogue record for this book is available from the British Library.

This book is dedicated to the memory of my father, Derek Fantom (1939-2017)

Contents

List of Illustrations vi
List of Maps vii
List of Abbreviations and Terms viii
Acknowledgements xii
Foreword xiii
Prologue xv

Part I: After Operation Dynamo: 5 to 9 June 1940 19
1 The British Armed Forces in France after Dunkirk 21
2 *Fall Rot:* Phase 2 of the German Conquest of France 35
3 Offensive on the Somme and Aisne 47

Part II: Operation Cycle: 10 to 13 June 1940 79
4 An Increasingly Desperate Situation 81
5 Le Havre and St Valery-en-Caux 92

Part III: Operation Aerial: 14 to 18 June 1940 121
6 Withdrawal 123
7 Final Evacuations 135

Part IV: The Anglo-French Relationship 145
8 Haddock Force: Air Operations Against Mussolini's Italy 147
9 Anglo-French Military Co-operation 154
10 The Anglo-French Political Relationship 167

Conclusion 175
Epilogue 195

Appendices:
I BEF Order of Battle, 5 to 18 June 1940 201
II BAFF Order of Battle, 5 to 18 June 1940 206
III *Heer* Order of Battle, June 1940 208

Bibliography 211
Index 215

List of Illustrations

Lieutenant General Sir Alan Brooke. 113
Lieutenant General James Marshall-Cornwall. 113
Major General Victor Fortune (GOC 51st Division) with *Generalmajor* Erwin Rommel at St Valery-en-Caux. (Imperial War Museum RML 342) 114
Acting Major General Archibald Beauman. 114
Admiral Sir William James. 115
Admiral Sir Martin Dunbar-Nasmith, VC. 115
Air Vice Marshal P.H.L. Playfair. 116
Air Marshal A.S. Barratt. 116
Vickers Light Tank Mk VI B. 117
A13 Cruiser Mk IV. 117
Hawker Hurricane Mk I, France 1940. 118
Bristol Blenheim Mk I. 118
Vickers Wellington Mk I. 119
HMT *Lancastria*. (Private Collection) 119
7th Panzer Division column near Abbeville, June 1940. 120
Evacuated British Troops on a transport during Operation Aerial. 120

List of Maps

Case Red 37
Rouen 68
Drive south 74
St Valery 99

List of Abbreviations and Terms

1/Nth	First line Battalion of the Nth Battalion
2/Nth	Second line Battalion of the Nth Battalion
AASF	Advanced Air Striking Force of the RAF
ADM	Admiralty papers (TNA)
AFV	Armoured fighting vehicle
AIR	Air Ministry papers (TNA)
AOC-in-C	Air Officer Commanding-in-Chief
Armée de l'Air	French Air Force
Ausf	*Ausführung* (Variant)
BAFF	British Air Forces in France
BEF	British Expeditionary Force
Bde	Brigade
Bn	Battalion
CAB	Cabinet papers (TNA)
Capt	Captain
CIGS	Chief of the Imperial General Staff
Col	Colonel
Coy	Company
Cpl	Corporal
C/Sgt	Colour Sergeant
CSM	Company Sergeant Major
DCM	Distinguished Conduct Medal
DCR	*Divisions Cuirassées de Reserve* (French Army Reserve Tank Division)
DFC	Distinguished Flying Cross
DFM	Distinguished Flying Medal

Div	Division
DLC	*Divisions Légère de Cavalerie* (French Army Light Cavalry Division)
DLM	*Divisions Légères Mécaniques* (French Army Light Mechanised Division)
DSO	Distinguished Service Order
Eds	Editors
Fall Gelb	Case Yellow: Code name of phase 1 of the German invasion of France, commencing 10 May 1940
Fall Rot	Case Red: Code name of phase 2 of the German invasion of France, commencing 5 June 1940
Fliegerkorps	Air Corps of the German Air Force
Général d'armée	French Army rank of General of an army (British Army rank equivalent is General)
Général d'armée aérienne	French Air Force rank of General of the Air Force (RAF rank equivalent is Air Chief Marshal)
Général de corps d'armée	French Army rank of General of an army corps (British Army rank equivalent is Lieutenant General)
Général de division	French Army rank of General of an army division (British rank equivalent is Major General)
Général de brigade	French Army rank of General of an army brigade (British Army rank equivalent is Brigadier)
General der Artillerie	*Wehrmacht* rank of General of Artillery (British Army rank equivalent is Lieutenant General)
General der Infanterie	*Wehrmacht* rank of General of Infantry (British Army rank equivalent is Lieutenant General)
General der Kavallerie	*Wehrmacht* rank of General of Cavalry (British Army rank equivalent is Lieutenant General)
General der Panzertruppen	*Wehrmacht* rank of General of Armoured troops (British Army rank equivalent is Lieutenant General)
General der Pioniere	*Wehrmacht* rank of General of Engineers (British Army rank equivalent is Lieutenant General)
Generalfeldmarschall	*Wehrmacht* rank of Field Marshal (British Army rank equivalent is Field Marshal)
Generalleutnant	*Wehrmacht* rank of Lieutenant General (British Army rank equivalent is Major General)
Generalmajor	*Wehrmacht* rank of Major General (British Army rank equivalent is Brigadier)

Generaloberst	*Wehrmacht* rank of Colonel General (British Army rank equivalent is General)
GOC	General Officer Commanding
Heer	German Army
HLI	Highland Light Infantry
HMSO	His Majesty's Stationery Office
HQ	Headquarters
IWM	Imperial War Museum
KOSB	King's Own Scottish Borderers
KOYLI	King's Own Yorkshire Light Infantry
Kampfgeschwader	*Luftwaffe* Bomber Squadron
Kriegsmarine	German Navy
L of C	Line of Communication
L/Cpl	Lance Corporal
1/Lt	First Lieutenant
2/Lt	Second Lieutenant
Lt-Col	Lieutenant Colonel
Luftwaffe	German Air Force
Maréchal de France	Marshal of France
MC	Military Cross
MM	Military Medal
NCO	Non-Commissioned Officer
OKH	*Oberkommando des Heeres* (High Command of the German Army)
OKW	*Oberkommando der Wehrmacht* (High Command of the German armed forces)
Panzerkampfwagen	German AFV (abbr. *Panzer or PzKpfw)*
PREM	Premier's (or Prime Minister's) papers (TNA)
Pvt	Private
RA	Royal Artillery
RAC	Royal Armoured Corps
RAF	Royal Air Force
RE	Royal Engineers
Regia Aeronautica	Italian Air Force
Regt	Regiment

RSM	Regimental Sergeant Major
RN	Royal Navy
RTR	Royal Tank Regiment
Sgt	Sergeant
TA	Territorial Army
TNA	The National Archives, Kew (formerly the Public Record Office)
TS	Treasury Solicitor papers (TNA)
VC	Victoria Cross
Vice Amiral	French Navy rank of Vice Admiral
Wehrmacht	Unified armed forces of Germany, 1935-45
WO	War Office papers (TNA)

Stylistic Convention

Individuals are described by the rank and/or title that they held during June 1940.

Acknowledgements

The planning, researching and writing up of this book has been undertaken alongside the daily challenges and demands of employment and life in general, whilst endeavouring not to neglect family members and friends. Indeed, during the time which this has taken to complete, it has become a significant part of my life. Therefore, I would like to express my sincere appreciation and gratitude to a number of people and institutions who have been most generous with their advice, assistance, intellectual stimulation and support. In terms of the content, the opinions expressed and the preparation of a manuscript that is suitable for publication, however, I alone am responsible; including for any errors of fact, or of interpretation.

First, I owe a considerable debt of thanks to Emeritus Professor John Bourne of the University of Wolverhampton for his taking the time to provide constructive feedback on the preliminary proposal, for giving invaluable advice in terms of arranging publication and for writing the Foreword to this volume. Similarly, at Helion & Co., Duncan Rogers and Dr Michael LoCicero have offered practical assistance, guidance and support throughout the completion of this project.

Second, my appreciation must be extended to The National Archives at Kew, the Archives of the Tank Museum at Bovington, Dorset and the Imperial War Museum. All members of their professional staffs were unfailingly courteous, knowledgeable and extremely accommodating in their efforts to locate and provide for me when needed the relevant documents and images that I required, and also by the making of a number of useful suggestions for further lines of enquiry.

Third, for their continued friendship, encouragement and interest in this undertaking, I am very grateful to the following people: Carl Craney, Nigel Easom (and for his assistance by providing me with relevant articles from *The Times*), Dereck Francis, Dr Spencer Jones of the University of Wolverhampton (and for his assisting me to obtain copies of pertinent articles from various journals), Dr Ruth Harrison, Stephen Roberts and Mark Terrett. I am obliged to Councillor Rose Martin of Walsall Council for the information that she kindly gave me about the wartime service of her late father, Thomas Patrick Smith, who had witnessed the sinking of the Cunard liner *HMT Lancastria* during his evacuation from the port of St Nazaire on 17 June 1940. For their support and understanding throughout the four years that it has taken me to complete this enterprise, I would also like to thank my colleagues at Walsall Council, Craig Goodall, Nikki Gough, Fred Hancock, Deborah Longley, Beverley Mycock, Helen Owen, Neil Picken and Matthew Powis.

Finally, this book would never have been completed had it not been for the love, patience, support and understanding of my wife, Kristina Fantom, and my mother, Edith Fantom. My debt of gratitude to them is incalculable. This book has been dedicated to the memory of my late father, Derek Fantom, who was able to see this work commence but who sadly passed away before it could reach fruition.

Foreword

France's Great War was a triumphant epic of national resistance. France's Second World War was a humiliating ordeal of defeat, occupation and collaboration. This remarkable transformation in the space of a generation has often been described, never better perhaps than by Sir Alistair Horne in *To Lose a Battle: France 1940* (1969), which begins with the Victory Parade down the Champs Elysées on Bastille Day 1919 and ends with a column of German troops goose-stepping through the Arc de Triomphe on 14 June 1940. The familiarity of this fall should not disguise how utterly shocking it was at the time. That 'Our Great Ally France' would collapse in a matter of weeks in the face of a German army numerically inferior, no better armoured and less mechanised was unthinkable. The British, of course, shared the humiliation of 1940 in full measure, but – characteristically, some might claim – managed to pluck the flower safety out of the nettle danger through the 'Miracle of Dunkirk', a miracle made possible by the heroic defence of the Dunkirk perimeter by French, Belgian (and some British) troops. This was where the matter seemingly ended. The Battle of France was over. The British readied themselves for the Battle of Britain. Only when I read this book did I realise that the familiar British narrative was not the whole story. The Battle of France was not over. For the first time, I understood the significance of the opening words of Churchill's peroration to his immortal speech to the House of Commons on 4 June 1940, the final day of the Dunkirk evacuation. It begins 'We will fight in France ...'. Given that the British army had just been evacuated from France, less the beleaguered 51st (Highland) Division, what did Churchill mean? As a historian of the Great War who grew up in the shadow of the Second World War, his meaning had entirely escaped me. Having withdrawn one army, the British intended to re-embark another. Two divisions, the 52nd (Lowland) and the 1st Canadian, would land in France and join up with the 51st (Highland) Division and two brigades of the 1st Armoured Division, to form a 'second BEF'. The justification for this decision was to express 'political solidarity' with the French and attempt to keep them in the fight. The man charged with implementing the scheme, Lieutenant General Sir Alan Brooke, was in no doubt that it was militarily insane and said so. It is difficult to see the decision as an example of hard-headed *realpolitik*, but more a sentimental Churchillian gesture to be set alongside his offer to form a political union between Britain and France. If this story has a hero, other than the ordinary British soldiers, many of them lightly armed odds and sods from the lines of communication, it is Alan Brooke. As Dr Paul Fantom points out, Brooke began his relationship with Churchill down a phone line when he made it clear that another evacuation was imperative, declaring 'You've lost one Scottish division. Do you want to lose another?' If Dunkirk was a damn close run thing, the second evacuation was even closer and could easily have ended in disaster. For once, the familiar publishing trope of describing some historical event as 'forgotten' is entirely justified. These events have been forgotten. They deserve to be remembered. Read this book and be amazed.

John Bourne
University of Wolverhampton

Prologue

In modern British history, few years have received such extensive scrutiny as that which has been given to 1940, and to the events that occurred during the course of its 366 days. It was the year when the conflict that began in September 1939 was transformed from being the so-called 'Phoney War' into a very real one, with Adolf Hitler's Germany achieving with an unprecedented rapidity its military domination over a substantial portion of Continental Europe. And, until Germany's invasion of the Soviet Union in June 1941 and Japan's attack on Pearl Harbour in December 1941, which brought both the USSR and the USA into the conflict on the side of the Allies, Great Britain and its Empire stood as the only source of opposition to the tyranny of Nazi Germany not to have been vanquished and then subdued.

Carried out between 27 May and 4 June 1940, Operation Dynamo was the evacuation of the largest component of the British Expeditionary Force that had been despatched to the Continent following the outbreak of the war. This withdrawal came to pass when many of the formations of the BEF and the other Allied armies were forced to retreat and were cut off and swiftly surrounded as a consequence of *Fall Gelb*, the first phase of the German *Wehrmacht's* invasion of France. In total, some 338,226 Allied troops were successfully rescued from the beaches and the harbour of the French port of Dunkirk, to be embarked onto a variety of Royal Navy and other civilian vessels and returned to Great Britain. Indeed, so well-known has the *Dunkirk spirit* become in Britain that it is now synonymous with indomitable determination and a resilience in the face of an overwhelming adversity.

But the past is not always what it may seem and it is the responsibility of the historian to try to discover the truth of what actually happened. For instance, it has been the conventional view that with the departure from Dunkirk of the last of the little ships and then the rounding-up by the victorious German armed forces of those British and Empire troops who were unable to be evacuated, and who would spend the next five years as captives held in various prisoner of war camps spread across occupied Europe, it was the end of this chapter in the history of the Second World War. Yet, despite the impression that following the conclusion of Operation Dynamo the British Army ceased to have any further presence in France until 6 June 1944, this was most definitely not the case. What is certain though is that the enormous drama of the Dunkirk evacuation still continues to overshadow those events that took place in France during the subsequent days of June 1940.

This is because between 5 and 18 June, several formations of the British and Empire armed forces remained in France with the avowed intention of fighting on to retain a foothold on the Continent. This included not only the residual infantry and armoured brigades and divisions of the BEF, but also the rear echelon Line of Communication troops who were responsible for logistics and stores, and a Royal Air Force contingent and its support services. Furthermore, it was also the aim of the British Government to bolster, encourage and support a beleaguered, demoralised and exhausted French Army that was being comprehensively overwhelmed by the *blitzkrieg* tactics of the German *Wehrmacht*, and two further divisions of British Army and Empire troops were despatched to France to assist in this endeavour.

Hence, an important aspect of this overlooked episode in the history of the campaign was the creation of what would be termed the 'second BEF'. This was to be led by a British commander who had already been recognised as one of the most capable senior general officers in the British Army at this time, the recently knighted Lieutenant General Sir Alan Brooke. As the General Officer Commanding the BEF's II Corps, Brooke had previously served in France and, having been evacuated from Dunkirk, he was tasked to return to the Continent to take charge of those British formations still there and those waiting to be sent out. Therefore, this new force was to be comprised of the 51st (Highland) Infantry Division, the 2nd and 3rd Brigades of the 1st Armoured Division, and the various units of the Line of Communication troops, all of which were still in France. These were to be reinforced by the other divisions that were due to be sent out from Britain, namely the 52nd (Lowland) Infantry Division and the 1st Canadian Division. The intended mission of this second BEF was to support the French forces in the attempt to halt the German invasion.

However, before all of these fresh divisions could be brought into action on the front line, and despite the numerous heroic efforts of individual servicemen and their battalions and companies, the Allied forces in France proved unable to stem the unrelenting advance of the German *Wehrmacht's* armoured panzer divisions and its mechanised infantry. Codenamed Operation Cycle, an evacuation by the Royal Navy was planned and intended to be carried out from the port of Le Havre. Disaster struck when a considerable portion of the 51st Division was cut off and prevented from reaching this anchorage, and the attempt to embark these troops onto ships at the smaller fishing port of St Valery-en-Caux could not be completed. This was due to a combination of the well-positioned artillery of the German Army, which was bombarding St Valery's beach and harbour with shellfire and harassing any visible targets with machine gunfire, and the adverse weather conditions. Both of these conspired to prevent the Royal Navy's ships from entering the port. Although finding themselves to be short of ammunition, suitable weapons and food, and still unable to be evacuated by the vessels waiting just beyond the range of the German guns, the soldiers of the 51st Division continued to fight on with great valour and fortitude. Nevertheless, as their situation became increasing desperate, and with the enemy's panzers and well-armed infantry closing in on them before overrunning their defences, they were left with no choice but to ground their arms and surrender.

The extent of the catastrophe that would ensue for Britain and the wider Allied cause should what remained of the British and Empire troops in France be forced to suffer the same humiliating fate as the 51st Division did not bear contemplation. Moreover, the implications that this would have if a German invasion of the British mainland were to be attempted led inevitably to the fateful decision by the British political and military leadership to withdraw its remaining troops from France.

There had also been some discussions with their French counterparts regarding the creation of a British-Franco redoubt, or stronghold, in Brittany that it was considered might be furnished with supplies sent out from Britain. However, whilst the military leadership of both Britain and France recognised the unfeasibility of the redoubt plan and in practical terms it progressed no further, this was a time when all such decisions were constrained and often became muddled by the overriding political considerations of the moment. In the expectation that the capitulation of the French armed forces was imminent, especially once the French Government had begun to seek the negotiation of an armistice with Germany, the British Government decided that no further British troops should be despatched to France and a crucial rear-guard campaign was organised to extricate and evacuate the remaining formations to prevent them from being captured and having to endure years of enemy captivity.

Through Operation Aerial, this would allow further Allied troops (even including some of the Czech and Polish units) to be rescued from several ports and harbours on the French coastline and returned safely to Britain by Royal Navy and other vessels. Just as had occurred during Operation Dynamo, the beaches, harbours and ports where the troops of the BEF were situated whilst awaiting their escape from the Continent were frequently bombed by *Luftwaffe* aircraft that had evaded the patrols being mounted by the RAF Fighter Command. These were flown mainly from airfields and bases in the Channel Islands and from the British mainland.

On 17 June 1940, a tragedy occurred when the *HMT Lancastria*, a former vessel of the Cunard Line, which had been converted into a troopship earlier in the year, was fatally damaged by the bombs dropped from a *Luftwaffe* Junkers Ju 88 bomber. Consequently, the *Lancastria* was sunk in the estuary of the River Loire, near to the port of St Nazaire. This enemy action resulted in an appalling loss of life, as thousands of British Army and RAF servicemen, and even some civilians, were on board at the time and thousands died dreadful deaths as a consequence, either by being trapped on the ship when it sank or whilst adrift in the sea and unable to be rescued. This was the greatest loss of life ever to have resulted from the sinking of a single British vessel and, upon direct orders from Prime Minister Winston Churchill, the Government suppressed the news of this event for some weeks thereafter, until it emerged through publication in the press of the United States.

An examination of the British official records indicates that the total number of military and civilian personnel who were returned to Great Britain in the aftermath of the Battle of France through Operations Dynamo, Cycle and Aerial was 558,032, of whom some 368,491 were from the British Army and the RAF. Were it to have occurred, these were the troops who would have been called upon to defend the country should Operation Sea Lion, the proposed German invasion of the British mainland, have been launched from the French ports and with the possible collusion of those ships of the French Navy that had sided with the Vichy regime in 1940. When the anticipated enemy invasion did not occur, it was these men and the units rescued from France in 1940 which, when re-equipped, re-organised and in some cases re-constituted, would go on to make critical contributions in other theatres of war, and eventually to those Allied armies which participated in Operation Overlord, and the landings on the Normandy beaches four years later, on D-Day, 6 June 1944.

Therefore, the motivation for writing this book has been to examine and evaluate what is believed to be an important yet considerably under-appreciated aspect of the campaign of the British armed forces in France during 1940. In it are described the engagements fought, not only by the regular troops of the Brigades and Divisions of the British Army, but also the frequently desperate and fierce struggles of the various improvised formations of rear echelon and territorial soldiers. Although usually short of arms and ammunition, equipment and organisation, they were never lacking in courage, determination and steadfastness, and their adversaries frequently had to pay a heavy price for whatever successes they gained on the battlefield. This account also provides the detail of the further evacuations of Army and RAF personnel that were carried out during very difficult circumstances by the Royal Navy and other civilian vessels during Operation Cycle and Operation Aerial, respectively.

This research underpinning this book has been completed by making use of the extensive holdings of The National Archives at Kew and of the Tank Museum's Archives at Bovington, together with numerous other resources, which are as detailed in the bibliography. The main aim has been to offer to the reader an objective account of the contributions that were made by the respective British armed forces in France during this period and an evaluation of their significance to the overall campaign. Accordingly, it has also sought to explore the political dimension and the dynamics and key relationships existing between the British forces, their commanding officers in the field and at home, and the principal British politicians and their French counterparts. In this manner, the intention has been to provide some of the context for the decisions that were made at the time and the impact these had on operations. An example of this being the implementation of the British plan for the aerial assault on key industrial targets on the Italian mainland by the bombers of the RAF's Haddock Force following Italy's entry into the war on 10 June 1940.

It is therefore necessary to point out that this is an area of research that has received somewhat limited scholarly attention to date. Where it has been featured within the numerous publications on Operation Dynamo and the Dunkirk evacuation, for example, there has been a tendency to treat it as being rather tangential, and in a manner sometimes to be viewed as perfunctory instead of with any real enthusiasm. The men of the BEF were contending with a determined enemy, whose highly mobile armoured and mechanised forces had swept through the Low Countries and France in an unparalleled manner and given that these later naval evacuations were undertaken by the officers and men involved with the highest degree of professionalism, resolve and skill, all of those who served deserve better recognition.

Thus this volume sets out to offer an account of the staunch resistance against German forces that were frequently superior in equipment, tactics and technology, and in their daring, flexibility and stamina on the battlefield. This book is also intended to be an assessment of the actions and operations carried out, the successes and tragedies, and the legacy for the remainder of the war and in the longer term. This is a story that has been largely overlooked by many historians and others, both in the days that followed the events which will be described and subsequently. It deserves to be told and for full acknowledgement to be given to the heroism and the sacrifices made by those members of the British armed forces who were there.

Part I

After Operation Dynamo: 5 to 9 June 1940

1

The British Armed Forces in France after Dunkirk

The Composition of the BEF and the BAFF

The British Expeditionary Force was initially comprised of four regular infantry divisions (1st, 2nd, 3rd and 4th Divisions), an incomplete 5th Division and one partial armoured brigade of two battalions. Despatched from 9 September 1939 onwards, by the end of that month there were more than 152,000 British troops in France.[1] These formations were subsequently afforded artillery, engineering, medical and transport support units, so that by March 1940 the number of British troops increased to 316,000.

This force was variable in extent and in provision, however. Even though it included battalions of such prestigious regiments as the Grenadier Guards and the Coldstream Guards, its battlefield effectiveness was hindered by poor equipment and training. The 48th, 50th and 51st Territorial divisions arrived on the Continent during January 1940 to augment the regular units and were assigned to positions below the River Seine, in the BEF's southern district. Further to the Army Council's meeting held on 1 December 1939, it was noted that, 'on the outbreak of war, 65 per cent of the territorial infantry had less than one year's service, and 50 per cent less than six months'.[2] In view of the BEF's comparatively small size and structure, the larger French Army determined and directed Allied strategy, which had as its primary objective the defence of France, and it relied extensively on the fortifications of the Maginot line.

Prior to 10 May 1940 and the commencement of *Fall Gelb* (Case Yellow), namely the first phase of the German *Wehrmacht's* invasion of France, the war in the west had essentially been a rather limited one. Indeed, and given that at this time the principal war aim of the British Government that was headed by Neville Chamberlain was to seek a guaranteed peace, the operation of the BEF was constrained as much by the restrictions imposed on it as by the availability of a sufficient number of military personnel who were fully trained and equipped, and whether the arms and equipment issued to them were suitable for their purposes.

1 L.F. Ellis, *The War in France and Flanders 1939-40* (London: HMSO, 1953), p.15.
2 P. Caddick-Adams, 'Phoney War and Blitzkrieg: The Territorial Army in 1939-40', *RUSI Journal*, 1998, Vol. 143 (2), p.68.

However, on 19 May, Chamberlain's successor, the recently installed British Prime Minister, Winston Churchill, had instructed the Committee of the Chiefs of Staff to investigate and assess whether Great Britain would be able to fight on alone should France be lost during the German invasion and a substantial element of the BEF prove itself to be incapable of being evacuated from the Continent.[3] In their conclusions, the Chiefs of Staff argued that it was a question of whether, should the British nation be called upon to fight on single-handedly, immediate survival was possible and, in the longer term, whether in these circumstances the war could be brought to a victorious conclusion by Britain and its overseas Empire.

Between 31 May and 4 June 1940, a total of 338,226 Allied troops, of whom 224,318 were British servicemen, were evacuated from the beach and the harbour of the French port of Dunkirk.[4] This remarkable feat was achieved because of the Royal Navy's overwhelming superiority over, and freedom from any interference by, the German Navy (*Kriegsmarine)*, which had suffered heavily during the invasion of Norway with the loss of one heavy cruiser, two cruisers, ten destroyers and other types of craft. Moreover, there were enough civilian volunteers in Britain's coastal communities who were able to be found at very short notice to undertake the crucial role of ferrying the evacuated troops from the beach and the harbour out to the larger ships of the Royal Navy to be taken back to Britain. The Royal Air Force's Fighter Command was also able to provide sufficient air cover, with the Hawker Hurricanes and Supermarine Spitfires being sent on sorties from their bases in southern England.

The very nature of the evacuation meant it was unavoidable that a huge amount of military resource was left behind at Dunkirk. According to the minutes of the War Cabinet held on 5 June 1940, this included 475 armoured fighting vehicles (AFVs) and 30,000 other vehicles, 12,000 motorcycles, 1,000 heavy guns, 400 anti-tank guns, 90,000 rifles, 8,000 Bren light machine guns, 8,000 telephones, 1,855 radio sets and 7,000 tons of all types of ammunition.[5] The loss of such arms and equipment had a considerable impact, not only on the forces that had been evacuated from the Continent and which were being re-formed in Britain in preparation for the expected German invasion; it also affected those British divisions and other units still fighting in France. British industry would take several months to recoup the deficiency.

Although the number of British military personnel rescued during Operation Dynamo, which was formally concluded at 2.23 pm on 4 June by an announcement from the British Admiralty, represented the majority of the BEF, on 5 June there were approximately 136,000 British troops still remaining in France. This included two brigades of an armoured division, one infantry division and several other territorial formations, together with a significant number of military personnel who had been posted to the Line of Communication (L of C) units, base depots and other establishments. Therefore, this was contrary to the widespread view that 'after Dunkirk, there was hardly any British Army presence on the Continent, except for a Highland Division which was still in France after retreating from the Saarland'.[6] The units that remained in France following the Dunkirk evacuation were especially diverse and the following

3 The National Archives (TNA) CAB 66/7: War Cabinet Memoranda.

4 D. Newbold, 'British planning and preparations to resist invasion on land, September 1939 - September 1940' (Unpublished PhD thesis, University of London, 1988), p.167.

5 TNA CAB 65/7: War Cabinet Minutes.

6 J. Jackson, *The Fall of France: The Nazi Invasion of 1940* (Oxford: OUP, 2003), p.97.

paragraphs represent an attempt to summarise the British Army's order of battle in terms of the battalions and brigades concerned.[7]

The 51st (Highland) Infantry Division was commanded by Major General Victor Fortune.[8] It was comprised of the 152nd, 153rd and 154th Brigades, which were commanded by Brigadiers H.W.V. Stewart, G.T. Burney and A.C.L. Stanley-Clarke respectively. The 152nd Brigade consisted of the 2nd and 4th Seaforth Highlanders and the 4th Queen's Own Cameron Highlanders; the 153rd Brigade was comprised of the 4th Black Watch and the 1st and 5th Gordon Highlanders; and the 154th Brigade contained the 1st Black Watch and the 7th and 8th Argyll and Sutherland Highlanders. In addition, there were other divisional troops from the Royal Artillery, the Royal Engineers and from other units that were to provide the support in their respective areas of expertise or operation. During the First World War, the 51st Division had deservedly earned for itself a high reputation as a well-trained and efficient fighting infantry division. Prior to the end of May 1940, and to gain practical experience, it was assigned to operate near to the Maginot Line in the Lorraine area. After this, it was relocated to the north of Rouen, where it was to hold a front line of 15 miles in length, from the left bank of the River Somme, south-east of Abbeville to the sea, with all three brigades and other units from the cavalry being placed into the line.

As a component part of Major General Roderic Petre's 12th (Eastern) Division, the 35th Brigade was commanded by Brigadier V.L. de Cordova and contained the 2/5th, 2/6th and 2/7th Battalions of the Queen's Royal Regiment. Brigadier G.R.P. Roupell's 36th Brigade contained the 5th Royal East Kent Regiment (The Buffs), and the 6th and 7th Queen's Own (Royal West Kent) Regiment. Commanded by Brigadier R.J.P. Wyatt, the 37th Brigade contained the 6th and 7th Royal Sussex Regiment and the 2/6th East Surrey Regiment. Following its arrival on the Continent, this Division was situated in Normandy and was employed at the docks in Le Havre and at Fécamp, as well as in assisting with the construction and maintenance of the railway lines in the area.

The 23rd (Northumbrian) Division was led by Major General Arthur Herbert and it contained the 69th Brigade, which was commanded by Brigadier, The Viscount Downe. Within this formation was the 5th East Yorkshire Regiment, together with the 6th and 7th Green Howards. Also included within the 23rd Division was Brigadier P. Kirkup's 70th Brigade, and this was made up of the 10th and 11th Durham Light Infantry and the 1st Tyneside Scottish. Divisional troops also included the Royal Engineers and the 8th and 9th Royal Northumberland Fusiliers. Placed in the rear area to the north of the River Somme, this Division was mainly tasked with airfield construction and the building of access roads, mostly in the vicinity of St Pol.

7 See Appendices I and II for a more comprehensive description.

8 Sir Victor Morven Fortune (1883-1949) had commanded the 1st Battalion of the Black Watch and fought with considerable distinction during the First World War. During the Battle of France, he was a Major General and the General Officer Commanding (GOC) the 51st (Highland) Infantry Division. After being forced to surrender to Rommel's 7th Panzer Division at St Valery-en-Caux, he spent the remainder of the war as the most senior British officer to be held in German captivity. During this time, he worked to improve the conditions experienced by the British prisoners of war. Major General Fortune was very well-liked by the troops of the 51st Division but during the 1940 campaign, several of the French commanders, and especially Maxime Weygand, began to refer to him in the most professionally discourteous, disrespectful and unjustified manner, as 'General Misfortune'.

Major General Henry Curtis was in overall command of the 46th (North Midland and West Riding) Division that contained the 137th Brigade, which was under the command of Brigadier J.B. Gawthorpe, and Brigadier E.J. Grinling's 138th Brigade and Brigadier R.C. Chichester-Constable's 139th Brigade. The 137th Brigade was made up of the 2/5th West Yorkshire Regiment and the 2/6th and 2/7th Duke of Wellington's Regiment. The 138th Brigade comprised the 6th Lincolnshire Regiment, the 2/4th King's Own Yorkshire Light Infantry (KOYLI) and the 6th York and Lancaster Regiment. The 139th Brigade contained the 2/5th Leicestershire Regiment, and the 2/5th and the 9th Sherwood Foresters. Arriving in April 1940, these troops were allocated to the unloading of ships, stacking of ammunition and assisting with the construction of railway lines in Brittany, around St Nazaire and Rennes.

The 52nd (Lowland) Infantry Division began to arrive in France on 8 June and was to be concentrated at Rennes. It was under the command of Major General James Drew.[9] The Division was comprised of the 155th, 156th and 157th Brigades that were commanded by Brigadier T. Grainger-Stewart, Brigadier J.S.N. Fitzgerald and Brigadier Sir J.E. Laurie respectively, together with Divisional troops of the Royal Artillery and Royal Engineers. The 155th Brigade consisted of the 7/9th Royal Scots and the 4th and 5th King's Own Scottish Borderers (KOSB); the 156th Brigade was comprised of the 4/5th Royal Scots Fusiliers, and the 6th and 7th Cameronians (Scottish Rifles); the 157th Brigade was made up of the 1st Glasgow Highlanders and the 5th and 6th Highland Light Infantry. As with the other Divisions, there were also various support units provided by the Royal Artillery and Royal Engineers.

The 1st Canadian Infantry Brigade (a component unit of Major General Andrew McNaughton's 1st Canadian Infantry Division) was also ordered to embark for France in June 1940. It was comprised of units from the Royal Canadian Regiment, the Hastings and Prince Edward Regiment, the 48th Highlanders of Canada and the 1st Field Regiment Royal Canadian Horse Artillery. This Brigade remained in France until it was evacuated to Britain on 16 June 1940.

The Line of Communication (L of C) troops were under the command of Major General Philip de Fonblanque.[10] Their purpose was to give logistical support, as they ensured that the units in the forward positions were adequately and promptly supplied with the necessities of ammunition, fuel and rations. They also worked in the various depots and repair workshops that were used by the BEF. Often known by the other troops as 'the grocers' but, given what they were responsible for supplying, this was a rather disparaging nickname when considering the importance of what they did. The main L of C headquarters was situated in Le Mans, with a northern region HQ on the Seine, at Rouen. In addition to the various companies of the Royal Engineers, the L of C also included the men of the 4th Royal East Kent Regiment (the Buffs), the 14th Royal Fusiliers, the 12th Royal Warwickshire Regiment, the 4th Border Regiment and the 1/5th Sherwood Foresters.

9 James Syme Drew (1883-1955) was a Major General and the GOC of the 52nd (Lowland) Division during the Battle of France. Following the evacuation of this Division from Cherbourg during Operation Aerial, Major General Drew was appointed to be the GOC responsible for Combined Operations, following which he was appointed to be the Director-General with responsibility for the Home Guard.

10 Philip de Fonblanque (1885-1940) was a Major General and, until the arrival of Sir Henry Karslake, he was responsible for the BEF Lines of Communications.

Due to the threat which had developed to the British Army's base at Rouen, as created by the *Wehrmacht's* rapid advance, Major General de Fonblanque was ordered to establish an improvised force that could be called upon for local defence purposes. This order had come from his superior, the General Officer Commanding (GOC) the Line of Communication troops, Lieutenant General Sir Henry Karslake.[11] In turn, the responsibility for this was passed to the officer who had been responsible for the Northern District's Line of Communication and was in charge of the security arrangements for the 13 airfields that had been constructed for the RAF, the recently promoted Acting Major General Archibald Beauman.[12] In this capacity, he had called upon troops drawn from the Royal Engineers, Royal Army Ordnance Corps, Royal Corps of Signals, other garrison troops and several of the Territorial Battalions to create what was termed the 'Beauforce'. Supposedly, this was comprised of nine infantry battalions; in reality, it actually consisted of the largely untrained second-line Territorial and reinforcement units that had been used mainly for pioneer duties, together with any other composite and miscellaneous units that could be found.

There were two other notable improvised formations. The 'Digforce' was established from the 2,500 troops of the Auxiliary Military Pioneer Corps, which had been assigned for construction and labour duties in the rear echelon because it contained men who were typically reservists and who were not fit enough or sufficiently ready for front line service. Several of these battalions were placed under the command of Lieutenant Colonel J.B.H. Diggle. The 'Vicforce' was a brigade-sized formation, which was named after its commander, Colonel C. E. Vickary, who had taken over the command of the five provisional battalions that had been created from those reinforcement troops then in the BEF's infantry and general base depots.

From the end of May 1940, the men in these three formations were placed under the command of Acting Major General Beauman and were subsequently to be known as the Beauman Division, with Beauforce, Digforce and Vicforce becoming the A, B and C Brigades of this Division. Although containing a sizeable number of men, there was very little in the way of armament and other useful arms and equipment for them to make use of. Their weaponry was typically bolt-action rifles and a few anti-tank rifles and Bren light machine guns, which most of the men had never fired before, even in practice. Indeed, they lacked not only any decent means of transport or signalling equipment but also artillery support, apart from a small number of 2-pounder anti-tank guns appropriated from various ordnance depots.

11 Sir Henry Karslake (1879-1942) was a Lieutenant General and was appointed GOC Line of Communication in May 1940. In this capacity he had been dug out of retirement and appointed by the former Chief of the Imperial General Staff (CIGS), General Sir Edmund Ironside, with Major General de Fonblanque then becoming his subordinate. There remains some confusion over what had been a verbal appointment made by Ironside for Karslake to become the Corps commander with overall control of the British troops then remaining in France, but when General Sir John Dill replaced Ironside as the CIGS on 27 May, it was significant that he declined to ratify his predecessor's decision.

12 Archibald Bentley Beauman (1888-1977) won the Distinguished Service Order (DSO) during the First World War and had been promoted to the rank of Brigadier at the age of 27, making him the youngest holder of this rank at the time. Following his recall from early retirement, he was made Acting Brigadier and the Commanding Officer of the BEF's Northern District, with responsibility for managing logistics within the Lines of Communication area. He subsequently raised and commanded an improvised force of second-line troops that became known as the *Beauman Division*, and he was promoted to the rank of Acting Major General in May 1940.

In his report on the operations conducted by these units during the period May-June 1940, Beauman described his men as being 'one of the most complete improvisations which even the British Army has carried out when in face of the enemy'.[13] It was rather unfortunate that this disparate collection of rather hurriedly gathered together infantry battalions became known as the Beauman Division because it might have caused confusion to their French allies, who believed it to be a fighting division complete with the ancillary services that were to be expected of a division. However, this was subsequently disputed and demonstrated that the French commanders, *Général d'armée* Robert Altmayer and *Général d'armée* Alphonse-Joseph Georges, were aware of the reasons for its creation and its limitations.[14] Assisted by a few tanks spared from the 1st Armoured Division, the Beauman Division was given the task of holding the line along the Rivers Béthune and Andelle. Whilst good work was done by it in organising this position and putting up a courageous defence in the face of superior opposition, it was eventually forced to retreat back to Rouen.

Turning to the British Army's armoured contingent, following the 1st Armoured Division's rushed arrival in France on 14 May 1940, no further British tanks would be sent to the Continent.[15] This was the British Army's first true armoured division and was commanded by Major General Roger Evans.[16] Having as its emblem a white rhinoceros on a black background, it contained the 2nd and 3rd Armoured Brigades, commanded by Brigadier R.L. McCreery and Brigadier J.G. Crocker respectively, with the 1st Support Group commanded by Brigadier F.E. Morgan, and with the divisional troops of the Royal Engineers 1st Field Squadron.

The 2nd Brigade was comprised of the Queen's Bays, the 9th Royal Lancers and the 10th Royal Hussars and was initially equipped with Light tanks; whereas the 3rd Brigade contained the 2nd Royal Tank Regiment, 3rd Royal Tank Regiment and the 5th Royal Tank Regiment, and 2 RTR, 3 RTR and 5 RTR were equipped with the various models of the Cruiser tank. Intended to fight alongside these armoured formations was the 1st Support Group, but this formation no longer had any motorised infantry support (due to this being transferred in order to form the 30th Infantry Brigade and being deployed for the defence of Calais). Hence, it was short of units and also lacked artillery support, since its only divisional unit was the 101st Anti-tank and Anti-aircraft Regiment, and this was instructed to join the Line of Communication units that were south of the River Somme. Many of these constituent elements would eventually be re-organised into such improvised units as the Beauman Division.

It had been decided that both of the Armoured Brigades would be reconfigured by a swapping of tanks, in order to have a more equal spread of the numbers of light and cruiser tanks. The outcome of this was predictably two-fold. Each Brigade attempted to foist its most unreliable vehicles onto the other, and many of the crews had to be given hasty retraining to acquaint themselves with the driving and gunnery requirements of these unfamiliar vehicles. By 28

13 TNA WO 167/1412: Beauman Division, Headquarters.

14 B. Karslake, *1940, The Last Act* (London: Cooper, 1979), p.128.

15 The 1st Armoured Division was the only division of this type in the British Army at this time. By comparison, during the Battle of France, the French Army had three armoured divisions, whilst the German Army had ten armoured (panzer) divisions.

16 Roger Evans (1886-1968) was a Major General and in 1938 became the GOC of the 1st Armoured Division. Following the Division's evacuation from France, he was appointed GOC for the Aldershot area before retiring from army service in 1944.

May, due to battle damage and breakdowns, the 10th Hussars and the Queen's Bays could only muster enough tanks to form a composite armoured regiment. Working tank transporters were in short supply and what was left of the 1st Armoured Division was placed under the command of Major General Fortune and the 51st Division, which had to this point been holding the Maginot Line and had then been transferred to the Bresle area. On 3 June, the 2nd and 3rd Armoured Brigades were refitting in the area to the east of Rouen but in spite of this they remained short of at least one hundred tanks.

The British Air Forces in France (BAFF) had been established on 15 January 1940. The purpose being in order to provide the unified overall command of those RAF squadrons that had been sent to France and which were placed under the command of Air Marshal Sir Arthur Barratt.[17] The BAFF was comprised of two elements, the Air Component of the BEF and the Advanced Air Striking Force (AASF). The BAFF was also able to request additional support from the medium and heavy bomber squadrons of the RAF's Bomber Command that operated from the airfields and bases located in Britain.

The BEF's Air Component was commanded by Air Vice Marshal Charles Blount.[18] It was equipped with the Hawker Hurricane fighter and Bristol Blenheim light/medium bomber, with the aim of giving air support to the BEF's ground forces. The AASF was commanded by Air Vice Marshal Patrick Playfair.[19] This also used Hawker Hurricane fighters and Bristol Blenheim bombers, together with Fairey Battle light bombers, was established on 24 August 1939, and was accountable directly to the Air Ministry, whilst being independent of the BEF. Initially, the intention was for the AASF to be used to attack strategic targets inside Germany but, following French objections, this aim was revised with it undertaking independent bomber operations against the German Army and its lines of communications. The Air Component was later re-designated as the Back Component and it left France in order to co-ordinate RAF support from British air bases at the time of the Dunkirk evacuation; in the meantime, the AASF remained in France but retreated from its initial base at Troyes to Orléans, and then to Le Mans before finally moving to bases around the Loire, and it then began to return to Britain between 15 and 18 June 1940.

Air Vice Marshal Blount's Air Component contained the No. 60 Fighter Wing (85 and 87 Squadrons), No. 61 Fighter Wing (607 and 615 Squadrons), No. 70 Bomber Reconnaissance Wing (18 and 57 Squadrons), No. 52 Bomber Wing (53 and 59 Squadrons), No. 50 Army Co-operation Wing (4, 13 and 16 Squadrons) and No. 51 Army Co-operation Wing (2, 26

17 Sir Arthur Sheridan Barratt (1891-1966) was appointed as Air Marshal in July 1939 and was the principal RAF's Liaison Officer to the *Armée de l'Air* (the French air force) and then the Air Officer Commanding-in-Chief (AOC-in-C) the British Air Forces in France (BAFF), following which he became, respectively, the AOC-in-C, Army Co-operation Command, then the AOC-in-C, Technical Training Command and finally the Air Chief Marshal and Inspector General of the RAF.

18 Charles Hubert Boulby Blount (1893-1940) was an RAF Air Vice Marshal and during the Battle of France was the AOC-in-C of the Air Component of the BEF, a part of British Air Forces France which provided RAF reconnaissance and fighter cover to the BEF's ground forces. Blount died in an air accident in October 1940.

19 Sir Patrick Henry Lyon Playfair (1889-1974) was an RAF Air Vice Marshal and during the Battle of France he was the AOC-in-C of the Advanced Air Striking Force (AASF), following which he was appointed to be the RAF's AOC-in-C, Air Forces in India, and he was subsequently promoted to the rank of Air Marshal.

and 81 Squadrons). Within Air Vice Marshal Playfair's AASF were the No. 71 Bomber Wing (105, 114, 139 and 150 Squadrons), No. 75 Bomber Wing (88, 103 and 218 Squadrons), No. 76 Bomber Wing (12, 142 and 226 Squadrons) and No. 67 Fighter Wing (1, 73 and 242 Squadrons).

In terms of the RAF's presence in France, whilst the BAFF's Air Component was withdrawn to Britain following the BEF's evacuation from Dunkirk, the AASF was intended to remain whilst British grounds troops continued to fight on in France. Its squadrons had been moved to the area between Orléans and Le Mans during the period of lull before the commencement of *Fall Rot* on 5 June. Air Marshal Barratt was well aware that this force was inadequate for what was to be expected of it and he advised the British Air Ministry on 3 June that the number of fighter squadrons in France should either be brought up to a total strength of ten, or that all of the British Air Forces should be withdrawn from the Continent.[20] Both of these options were impossible, for to take any more of the squadrons from RAF Fighter Command would increase the vulnerability of Britain's home defence and to remove those that were then in France was, at this stage, clearly politically unacceptable.

It was intended that from these air bases, the AASF would have the freedom to be able to operate anywhere along the front line, but following the German Army's breakthrough on 11 June, the British Air Ministry advised the AASF that it needed to be ready to make a prompt departure from France if it was called upon to do so. In turn, its squadrons were moved to the west, to Angers, Saumur, Rennes and Nantes, and were expected to operate from congested bases that were already being used by the French Air Force (the *Armée de l'Air*). On 15 June, Air Marshal Barratt determined that the Fairey Battle bomber squadrons should return to Britain, which left just five fighter squadrons to cover the evacuations then underway from the ports on the Atlantic coast. The most important of these ports were covered by 1, 73 and 242 Squadrons, with St Malo and Cherbourg being protected by 17 and 501 Squadrons, which would eventually operate from the Channel Islands until the remainder of the BEF returned to Britain.[21] Aircraft from the RAF's Coastal Command and Fighter Command squadrons (the latter operating from RAF Tangmere) would also provide the sorties to escort those ships returning to Britain from France during the evacuation operations.

The Doctrine, Strategy and Tactics of the British Armed Forces

It is the overall direction of a nation's military endeavours, in order that it may achieve its political objectives during wartime, that will shape the strategy and policies being pursued by its armed forces. Hence, given the set of circumstances that are faced, this will determine whether it is an offensive or a defensive stance that should be adopted. The military doctrine is the way in which an army is operationally and tactically structured to fight its enemies, or, in other words, what its methods of organisation, procedures and techniques are, and how they should be applied during combat conditions. Military doctrine has even greater importance when

20 J. Terraine, *The Right of the Line: The Royal Air Force in the European War, 1939-1945* (Ware: Wordsworth Editions, 1997), p.160.

21 Notable members of the 501 Squadron were the then Sergeant Pilot (later Squadron Leader) James Harry 'Ginger' Lacey, who became one of the highest scoring RAF fighter aces of the Second World War, and the then Sergeant Pilot (later Wing Commander) Paul Caswell Powe Farnes, who was the last surviving Battle of Britain RAF fighter ace, and who died aged 101 years on 28 January 2020.

there are multiple branches of an armed force that require co-ordination, as is the case when an army's ground forces are provided with close support by an air force. Therefore, the successful application of military doctrine relies, in turn, on the extent of the professionalism and of the training that is provided to the armed forces in question.[22]

During the inter-war years, the British Army's doctrine, strategic and tactical thinking, and its troop training had been fashioned mainly by the experiences of the First World War. Accordingly, it still centred on the importance of defence, holding defensive positions and a rigid and unfavourable view was held of flexible responses and strategic withdrawals. In the late 1930s, even as the possibility of another war grew increasingly likely, with the Munich agreement in 1938 being to all intents and purposes only a temporary postponement of armed struggle in Europe, it had become increasingly evident that the British Army was unprepared for the possibility of such a conflict. The Committee of Imperial Defence asserted that 'Great Britain was quite incapable of waging any type of war – let alone a Continental war'.[23] The doctrine of the territorial units was also still essentially that of the First World War and their equipment, including armaments, transport and uniforms, was equally as outdated.

One of the reasons for this was that there was a lack of suitable equipment. The provision of inadequate, inappropriate or insufficient arms and equipment was a part of the failure of successive British Governments to come to any firm conclusions on the role that the British Army was intended to play. In terms of the manufacture of weaponry, and especially of medium and heavy guns for the artillery, this was inadequate to meet the needs of the Army even at this stage, let alone when it had been expanded to the numbers that would eventually be needed. Hence, much valuable time and resource that could have been otherwise used to better effect, was wasted on experimentation that proved of little value and was due to indecisiveness.

Turning to its armoured forces, Britain had been the first nation to design and pioneer the use of truly workable AFVs during the First World War. With its vehicles being used in battle for the first time at Flers-Courcelette on 15 September 1916, the British Army could claim with some justification to have pioneered tank warfare. In spite of this, and primarily due to the financial constraints and political uncertainties of the inter-war years, a succession of experimental and short-lived AFVs had seen service with the British Army. Hence, in a case of armoured doctrine having to try to conform to manufacturing and technological limitations, rather than the contrary, the British Army did not have available to it the well-designed, mass manufactured and reliable tanks that perhaps could have given it a more realistic chance of combatting the *Wehrmacht's* panzer divisions during May and June 1940.

By the late 1930s, the British Army was equipped with what were termed as light tanks, cruiser tanks and infantry tanks. The choice of the tanks in service derived from what was essentially a trade-off between the vehicle's speed and its armour and weapons. Therefore, whilst light tanks might be faster, their crews were less robustly protected due to the limitations of their thinner armour and less able to inflict damage on the tanks of enemy forces, especially if armed only with machine guns.

According to British inter-war armoured doctrine, the light tanks were afforded a specification for rapid movement and greater manoeuvrability in order to undertake reconnaissance and

22 D. Porch, 'Military Culture and the Fall of France in 1940: A Review Essay', *International Security*, April 2000, Vol. 24 (4), p.168.
23 B. Karslake, *1940, The Last Act*, p.19.

fire support roles. The cruiser tank concept was originally developed by Brigadier Giffard Le Quesne Martel.[24] This was that these tanks should essentially act as a form of mechanised cavalry to exploit any gaps in an enemy's defences. Hence, those in the British Army's senior hierarchy with a more traditionalist view deemed that these factors would in some way be able to restore the cavalry charge to its rightful place on the battlefield, with these vehicles being able to use their higher speeds and longer range to take advantage of weaknesses in enemy positions and sever lines of communication and supply during open warfare.

Infantry tanks were more heavily armoured but slower, and their job was to support the infantry to break through the enemy's lines and create the gap to be opened up by the cruiser tanks. There were two types of infantry tanks in use at the time of the battle of France. These were the Matilda I and Matilda II but, whilst they might have shared a name, they were completely different in terms of their specification and overall battlefield effectiveness. In fact, only a handful remained in service in France after 5 June 1940, as virtually all of those that had been sent to the BEF were either destroyed during combat or were abandoned by their crews as they made their way towards Dunkirk and evacuation.

By 1940, the Air Ministry and the War Office had still not agreed what type of air support was to be provided by the RAF to the ground forces of the BEF. At the end of the First World War and during the early inter-war years, there had been successful co-operation between the RAF and the British Army, but this had diminished over time. Inter-service rivalries had undoubtedly played their part in this. Consequently, unlike their counterparts in the *Luftwaffe*, which had squadrons trained for direct co-operation with ground troops, the RAF units sent to France were untrained for and did not possess aircraft that could undertake the close support role that the British Army and its Allies on the ground would need so desperately.

The air strategy of the RAF and the French *Armée de l'Air* was at this time reliant on its fighter aircraft to achieve zonal air superiority whilst the separate bomber forces were to operate against strategic targets, many of which were located within Germany, and particularly in the industrial area of the Ruhr. These bombing missions were also carried out in the belief that they would be of assistance to the Allied ground forces by diverting the *Luftwaffe's* squadrons from the front line in order to carry out the air defence against such incursions. As such, Allied air strategy was reactive rather than a proactive, and giving due consideration to the limitations of the available aircraft and the difficulties of communications and command structures, it was not able to react especially well to the rapidly changing circumstances of the campaign that was being fought. Both the RAF and the *Armée de l'Air* were still engaged in the process of catching up with some of the technological developments that had by that stage been better harnessed by their adversaries in the *Luftwaffe.*

Air operations conducted between 10 May and 4 June revealed that the RAF's bomber squadrons sustained far fewer losses when they were accompanied by a fighter escort. Unfortunately, there was an insufficient number of operational fighter aircraft in France to achieve this on all missions. As previously mentioned, in order to rectify this deficiency, Air Marshal Arthur Barratt informed the British Air Ministry that either the fighter squadrons needed reinforcement or that the bombers should be returned to their bases in Britain. In

24 Sir Giffard Le Quesne Martel (1889-1958) was notable as a pioneering British military engineer and tank strategist. During the Battle of France, he held the rank of Major General and was the GOC of the 50th (Northumbrian) Infantry Division.

political terms, the latter was clearly impossible, but then so was the former, as the British Government refused to send more fighter squadrons to France because this would only serve to weaken Britain's domestic air defences. This limited what steps could be taken practically and, for example, Air Marshal Barratt determined that the six AASF squadrons which were equipped with the Fairey Battle light bomber aircraft should be used principally on night raids and that when tasked with daytime missions, they should be provided with fighter escort.

According to the RAF's report on the AASF in France from September 1939 to June 1940, from 10 May, the operations of the AASF fell into four phases. Phase 1 occurred from 10 to 16 May, when the AASF operated from bases in the Reims area. Its bombers were able to operate by day and fighter squadron operations were intensive and aerial combat was frequent. Phase 2 was from 17 May to 10 June, when both the bomber and fighter squadrons were operating from bases now situated in southern Champagne and the AASF's headquarters was based at Troyes. Both the bomber and fighter squadrons were withdrawn to bases in the Loire basin on 2 June but they continued to be operational until 18 June, with the bomber squadrons now operating by day and night. Phase 3 was from 10 to 16 June, during which the bomber squadrons performed sorties against targets in the vicinity of the Rivers Seine and Somme, and the fighter squadrons were also deployed to the Somme area. Refuelling was now carried out in the Rouen area. Finally, phase 4 took place during the final days of the British campaign in France, from 16 to 18 June. The bomber squadrons had by now started to return to their bases in Britain, and the AASF's fighter squadrons, which had been reinforced by 17 and 224 Squadrons, were covering the embarkation of the British ground forces that was taking place in the western ports of France, especially at St Nazaire, Le Havre and Cherbourg.[25]

Therefore, during the early months of the war, and throughout the Battle of France, little account appeared to have been taken by the British military commanders (or for that matter by their French allies) of the rapid speed of advance achieved by the highly mobile German ground forces and the air supremacy swiftly gained by the *Luftwaffe* during the 1939 offensive in Poland. In relation to this limited level of awareness of the *Wehrmacht* and its disposition, reference can be made to the intelligence summaries that were circulated within the 48th Division during March 1940 that 'grossly over-estimate the numbers of German aircraft and infantry divisions'.[26]

Moreover, elsewhere there was an under-estimation of the enemy's capabilities that in effect served to disregard them. In some cases, this was an attempt to maintain a high level of morale for the British troops. Even after their first clashes with the German armed forces, which should have disabused the British commanders of this, the enemy's air and armoured power was not in itself quite enough to subdue the BEF's morale, and it was demonstrated that in the face of such events the British troops generally retained their resilience and willingness to fight. This was despite the roads being increasingly jammed with slow-moving columns of hundreds of thousands of refugees who had fled the fighting in what was termed by the French *L'Exode* (the Exodus), a situation which led to the BEF's progress being hindered at all times.

Another factor that had and would continue to hamper the BEF's effectiveness after 5 June was the complex chain of command and the lack of clarity and confusion that ensued. Indeed,

25 TNA AIR 35/255: Report on the AASF in France, September 1939 - June 1940.
26 P. Caddick-Adams, 'Phoney War and Blitzkrieg: The Territorial Army in 1939-40', p.70; TNA WO 167/244: 48th (South Midland) Division War Diary.

until Lieutenant General Sir Alan Brooke reached France and assumed command of all the British troops there, all British divisions were under the orders of various French commanders.[27] The 51st Division was under the orders of *Général d'armée* Robert Altmayer of the French 10th Army; the French High Command had taken responsibility for the 1st Armoured; and the Beauman Division was receiving its orders from Lieutenant General Sir Henry Karslake, who had arrived in France on 23 May and had taken charge of the L of C troops. Hence, it was the case that only through the work of the Military Missions attached to the headquarters of these French Generals and the other, unofficial, means that British units were able to liaise and keep in contact with each other and their allies.

The Arms and Equipment of the BEF and BAFF

In terms of the arms and equipment supplied to them, the majority of the British Army's infantry units were not dissimilar to their French ally and their German adversary. Although the German Army had by now started to issue its squad leaders, such as junior officers and some of the more senior NCOs, with the MP 38 and then the MP 40 machine pistol, all of these armies still equipped most of their rank-and-file troops with single shot bolt-action rifles. In the British Army's case, this was with the tried-and-tested 0.303-inch Lee-Enfield SMLE Mark III, which had proven its accuracy and reliability ever since its introduction, and especially during the First World War. The availability of other forms of higher-rate firepower, including the portable Bren light machine gun or the Vickers water-cooled heavy machine gun, was by June 1940 for most of the British Army's units dictated by scarcity of supply. Indeed, the troops of the Beauman Division probably had as many rifles and almost as many Bren and Lewis machine guns as their First World War counterparts, but what they lacked was anti-tank weapons and artillery support. An absence of proficient signallers also made command and control on the battlefield quite difficult to achieve successfully.

The British Army's light tanks during this stage of the campaign were the Vickers Mark VI B and VI C, both of which had entered into service in 1936. The Mark VI B weighed 4.93 tons, was 13 feet in length and 6 feet ten inches wide, and it had a three-man crew of a commander, gunner and driver. Its armour was between 4 and 14 mm thick and its armament was comprised of two Vickers machine guns, of 0.5-inch and 0.303-inch calibres respectively. Powered by a Meadows 6-cylinder petrol engine, its maximum speed was 35 mph and 25 mph off-road. The Mark VI C differed insofar as it had an engine with improved performance and the Vickers machine guns had been replaced by BESA 7.92 mm and 15 mm machine guns.

Several models of cruiser tank were in service with the 1st Armoured Division in France. From the earliest A9 Cruiser I to the later A13 Cruiser IV (Mark II), the basic specification was not fundamentally different, and all of the models were for the time reasonably well armoured and armed. Hence, when engaged in a one-on-one confrontation with an enemy, they should

27 Sir Alan Francis Brooke (1883-1963) was a Lieutenant General who had commanded II Corps in France prior to the BEF's evacuation from Dunkirk. He returned to France with orders for the creation of a second BEF but, fully appreciating the reality of the situation at the stage in the campaign, oversaw the evacuation of all the remaining British forces. He later succeeded General Sir John Dill as the CIGS, was promoted to the rank of Field Marshal in 1944 and was then created Baron Alanbrooke, of Brookeborough in the County of Fermanagh, in 1945.

have been capable of dealing with the equivalent German tanks of the period and if there had been sufficient numbers of them made available, with adequately trained crews, this account might have been very different.

The Cruiser I was designed in 1936 by Sir John Carden, manufactured by Vickers and it was introduced into service with the British Army during 1939. It weighed 13 tons, was 19 feet in length and 8 feet four inches in width, and it was equipped with the AEC 179 6-cylinder petrol engine that produced a maximum speed of 25 mph and 15 mph off-road. With armour protection ranging between 6 to 14 mm, it was vulnerable to the German artillery's anti-tank guns and the medium tanks of the panzer divisions, such as the Panzer III. It had a six-man crew (commander, gunner, loader, driver, two machine gunners) and its main weapon was the Ordnance QF 2-Pounder gun and a secondary armament of three 0.303-inch Vickers machine guns, one being located in the main turret and two mounted in smaller turrets situated in the hull on either side of the driver's central position. Although a number of these tanks went on to see some service during the early stages of the North African campaign, their performance continued to be hamstrung by the problems of mechanical unreliability.

With its manufacture carried out by various firms such as Nuffield Mechanizations and Aero, English Electric, Leyland and the London, Midland and Scottish Railway Company, the A13 Cruiser IV (Mark II) came into initial service with the British Army in 1940. It was notable for using a type of suspension pioneered by the American engineer J. Walter Christie to create faster vehicles with an improved ride quality over rough terrain. Weighing 14 tons, it was 19 feet nine inches long and 8 feet four inches wide. Armour was from 6 to 30 mm in thickness and faceted armour was mounted on the original turret sides and rear, which gave the tank a far more modern appearance and better protection than the earlier cruisers. A Nuffield Liberty V12 petrol engine afforded the tank a maximum speed of 30 mph and an off-road 14 mph. Armed with the same 2-Pounder armament as the other cruiser tanks and one turret-mounted 0.303-inch Vickers machine gun, it had a crew of four (commander, gunner, loader and driver). Unfortunately, of those tanks that were sent to France in 1940, many were in poor condition on arrival, having been rushed into service, and their crews had not been adequately trained. Used in North Africa during 1940-41, this AFV performed well against the Italian opposition but it lost combat effectiveness against the improved German Panzer III and Panzer IV tanks.

All cruiser tanks were equipped with the Vickers Ordnance QF 2-Pounder gun as their principal armament. This was a quick firing weapon of 40 mm calibre, and it was of a reasonable specification and performance given the standards of 1940, at a time when the German army's main battle tank, the Panzer III, was only armed with a 37 mm gun (although that vehicle was progressively up-armed after the 1940 campaign, firstly to a short-barrelled and then to a long-barrelled 50 mm gun, and finally to a short-barrelled 75 mm gun). However, unlike the German machines, British tanks were only supplied with anti-tank ammunition rather than a mix of both anti-tank and high explosive shells. Thus, by not providing these vehicles with any HE rounds, they were effectively preventing them from undertaking any satisfactory support role for the infantry, wherein they might be required to assault enemy strong points such as machine gun or artillery emplacements and troop concentrations.

The Fairey Battle was introduced in 1937 as a single-engine light bomber capable of carrying either 1,000 lb (4x250 lb) of bombs internally or 1,500 lb of bombs mounted externally on underwing racks. Manned by a crew of three (pilot, bomb-aimer and air gunner), its meagre protection from attack by enemy aircraft was limited to one forward-firing wing-mounted

Browning 0.303-inch machine gun and one rearward firing Lewis 0.303-inch machine gun. With its relatively slow maximum speed of 257 mph and this inadequate defensive capability, the Battle quickly became very easy prey for the German fighters of the day, particularly the fast and very manoeuvrable Messerschmitt Bf 109, which in its E series boasted a top speed of 342 mph. Furthermore, by June 1940, with 323 Hurricanes having been lost or damaged in combat during May and only 226 new replacements being delivered, there were far too few British fighters in France to provide the depth of fighter coverage that would have reduced the losses then being experienced by the Fairey Battle squadrons.

Designed by Sidney Camm, the Hawker Hurricane first saw service with the RAF's Fighter Command during December 1937 and it was the AASF's principal single-engine fighter aircraft during the Battle of France. In 1940, its Mark I series was powered by a Rolls-Royce Merlin III V12 engine with a constant speed metal propeller that gave it a maximum speed of 318 mph, a range of 460 miles and a ceiling of 36,000 feet. It was 32 feet long, with a wing span of 40 feet and when fully loaded it weighed 6,600 lb. The aircraft's armament consisted of eight 0.303-inch Browning machine guns that were mounted in each of the wings in two banks of four guns, each supplied with 333 rounds of ammunition. It was notable that the thickness of the wings ensured that when in-flight the aircraft provided a stable gun platform for the pilot. During the Battle of France, it was still able to out-gun its primary adversary, the Messerschmitt Bf 109 E1, at least whilst that German aeroplane was still only fitted with four 7.92 mm machine guns. By the time of the Battle of Britain, this deficit in armament had been recognised by the *Luftwaffe* and addressed for the E3 model, as the Bf 109's two wing-mounted machine guns were replaced by a 20 mm cannon in each wing. In time this would lead to the RAF's fighters eventually being up-gunned as well with cannon weapons of a similar type.

The Bristol Blenhein was a twin-engine bomber that was also introduced into RAF service in 1937. It was developed from the type 142 civilian airliner that had been designed to meet Lord Rothermere's challenge to produce the fastest commercial aircraft in Europe and at that time it was faster than most of the fighter aircraft then in service. During the Battle of France, it was the main light/medium bomber used by the AASF and by RAF Bomber Command. Powered by two Bristol Mercury VII engines that gave it a maximum speed of 285 mph, a range of 1,125 miles and ceiling of 31,500 feet, the Blenheim Mark I was 39 feet 9 inches in length and had a wing span of 56 feet 4 inches. When fully loaded with its bomb load of 1,000 lb, it weighed 8,700 lb. For defence, it had a single 0.303-inch machine gun forward mounted in the aircraft's nose and in a rearward dorsal turret was a single 0.303-inch Vickers K machine gun. This wholly inadequate armament was unable to deter German fighters in 1940 and when the Blenheim squadrons were sent on missions in France and the Ruhr, a significant number were damaged or lost over enemy territory.

2

Fall Rot: Phase 2 of the German Conquest of France

Case Red: Aims and Objectives

In August 1939, the majority of the divisions of the *Heer* (the German Army), including its armoured formations, and squadrons of the *Luftwaffe* (the German Air Force) were concentrated in eastern Germany in readiness for the intended invasion of Poland. These forces remained there, or in occupied Poland, for some months thereafter. Consequently, along the Franco-German border there were only a mere 42 German infantry divisions without armoured support. At this time, these *Wehrmacht* forces were opposed by 70 of France's divisions of infantry and tanks, but the French Army just sat and waited.

Following Germany's rapid conquest of Poland, partition arrangements were agreed with the Soviet Union, which provided an assurance that the number of divisions stationed in the east could be reduced considerably. Accordingly, much of the *Heer* and the *Luftwaffe* was able to return to the western front in preparation for the planned onslaught on France and the Low Countries in the spring of 1940. Then they would face a combined Allied opposition of 135 armoured and infantry divisions, consisting of formations of the British, Belgian, Dutch and French Armies. Had this force been adequately equipped and trained, and organised and led properly, then it ought to have been able to have brought the German campaign to a halt.

Fall Gelb (Case Yellow) was the plan for the first phase of the German invasion of France that commenced on 10 May 1940, and it entailed an assault on Belgium, the Netherlands and northern France. In the latter, the highly mobile and well-organised panzer and motorised infantry divisions were directed through those forests of the Ardennes which had been deemed by the Allies to be impenetrable. The German forces picked their moment well and with the intention of cutting off and pushing back towards the sea those divisions of the BEF and the French Army which had been purposefully lured into Belgium in the expectation of the German invasion taking place there. Once the German forces had smashed their way through the weakly-held French sector on the River Meuse, between Dinant and Sedan, six of their panzer divisions had forced their way through this gap and followed the valley of the River Somme until reaching the Channel coast. This culminated in the encirclement of the Allied armies and the evacuation of British troops, firstly from Calais and Boulogne, and then at the port of Dunkirk between 31 May and 4 June 1940.

In order to act as the spearhead during the attack on the poorly organised French Army, the *Heer* had assembled its best premium divisions containing the elite and best trained formations. The artillery, infantry, engineering and tank formations were integrated into the panzer divisions and these had received extensive preparation for mobile warfare via combined arms operations with the *Luftwaffe*. By making the best possible use of surprise and confusion, they were able to attack with daring and speed before their opponents could react and organise. Hence, the German commanders targeted their forces to strike with overwhelming force, encircle and take full advantage of the disorientation created in the Allied command arrangements.

Following the conclusion of this first phase of the Battle for France, and in preparation for the second offensive, the *Heer* conducted a re-organisation and redeployment of its forces. The adroit manner in which this was carried out provided an opposite apt demonstration of the high levels of competence, efficiency, flexibility and logistical skill of its General Staff, the corps commanders and their staff officers. For example, the panzer divisions of *General der Panzertruppen* Heinz Guderian had raced to reach the Channel coast, cutting off the majority of the Allied forces to prevent them from retreating southwards, and trapping them so that their only escape was by evacuation from Dunkirk. Once this was successfully executed, Guderian's panzers were redeployed over 150 miles to the east, to a position west of Sedan.

At midnight on 4 June 1940, the German Führer, Adolf Hitler, had issued the command that throughout all of Germany the church bells should be rung for three days in celebration of the achievements of the armed forces and, in his Order of the Day on 5 June, he referred to this as 'the greatest battle in world history'.[1] Earlier, on 21 May, the plan that would conclude the campaign and lead to the conquest and final defeat of France was presented to Hitler by the Chief of Staff of the High Command of the German Army, the *Oberkommando des Heeres* (OKH), *General der Artillerie* Franz Halder.[2] Codenamed *Fall Rot* (Case Red), this would follow on from *Fall Gelb* as the second phase of the Battle of France. Furthermore, on 31 May, the following order was issued by the Head of the OKH and the *Heer's* Commander-in-Chief, *Generaloberst* Walther von Brauchitsch.[3]

> Operational enemy reserves in considerable numbers need no longer be expected. It will therefore be possible first to break down under heavy assault the hastily constructed enemy front south of the Somme and the Aisne and then, by rapid, deep penetration, to prevent the enemy from carrying out an ordered retreat or from forming a defence line in the rear.[4]

1 G. Stewart, *Dunkirk and the Fall of France* (Barnsley: Pen & Sword, 2008), p.119.

2 Franz Halder (1884-1972) had been promoted to the rank of *General der Artillerie* (General of Artillery) in 1938 and was appointed as *Chef des Generalstabes des Heeres* (Chief of the General Staff of the Army) of the *Oberkommando des Heeres* (German Army High Command) on 1 September 1938, a position he held until 1942. He was promoted to the rank of *Generaloberst* (Colonel General) in July 1940.

3 Walther Heinrich Alfred Hermann von Brauchitsch (1881-1948) was promoted to the rank of *Generaloberst* in February 1938 and then to *Generalfeldmarschall* (General Field Marshal) in July 1940. He had been the German Army's Commander-in-Chief from 1938 but in the aftermath of the failure of the *Wehrmacht's* assault on Moscow during December 1941, he was dismissed from this office by Hitler and was to spend the remainder of the war in enforced retirement.

4 L.F. Ellis, *The War in France and Flanders 1939–40*, p.274.

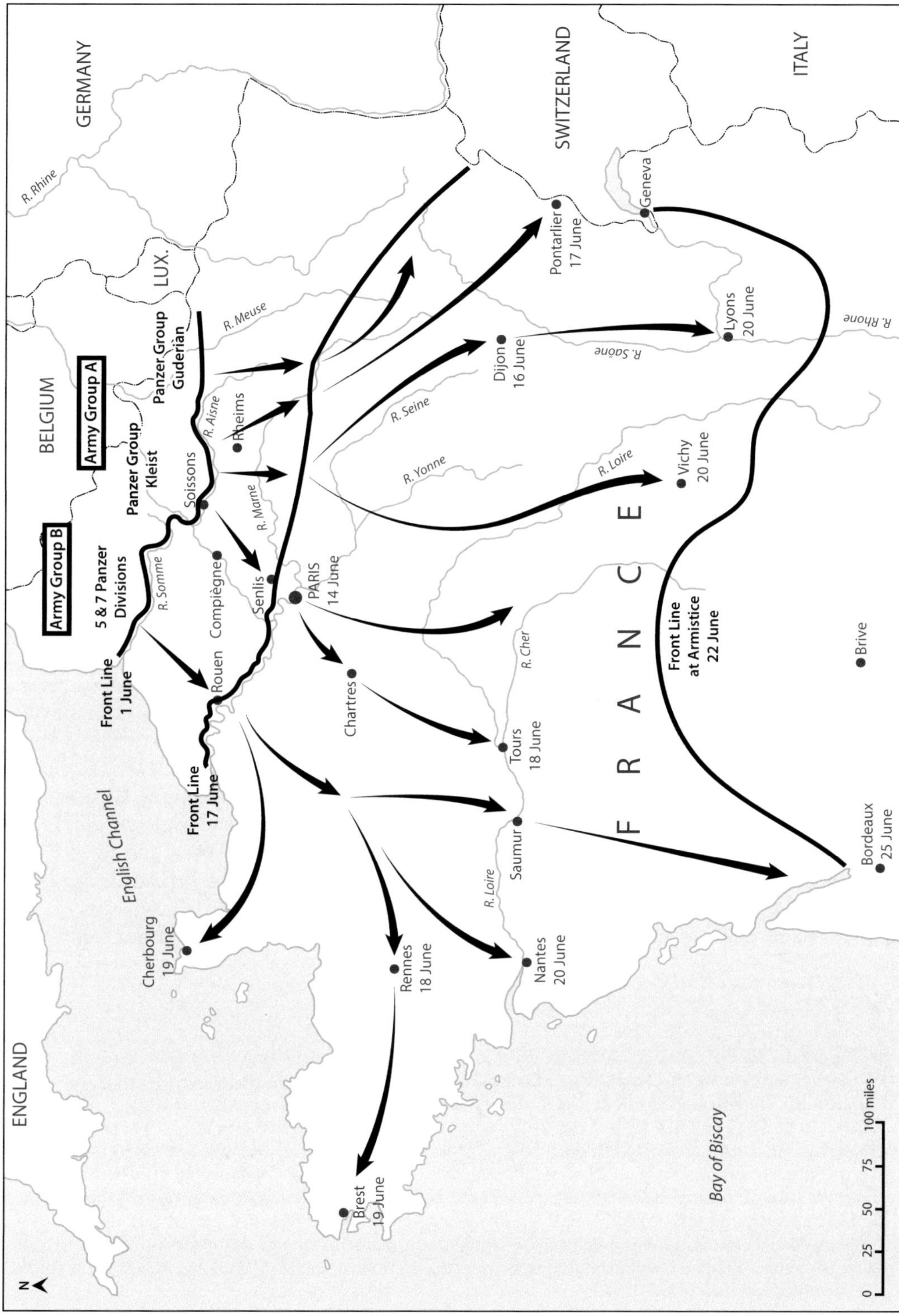
GERMANY
BELGIUM
LUX.
SWITZERLAND
ITALY
ENGLAND
FRANCE
English Channel
Bay of Biscay
R. Rhine
R. Meuse
R. Aisne
R. Marne
R. Somme
R. Seine
R. Yonne
R. Loire
R. Cher
R. Saône
R. Rhone
Army Group A
Army Group B
Panzer Group Guderian
Panzer Group Kleist
5 & 7 Panzer Divisions
Front Line 1 June
Front Line 17 June
Front Line at Armistice 22 June
Soissons
Rheims
Compiègne
Senlis
PARIS 14 June
Rouen
Chartres
Tours 18 June
Saumur
Nantes 20 June
Rennes 18 June
Brest 19 June
Cherbourg 19 June
Dijon 16 June
Pontarlier 17 June
Geneva
Lyons 20 June
Vichy 20 June
Bordeaux 25 June
Brive
N
0 25 50 75 100 miles

Case Red

Fall Rot was to commence on 5 June. It was planned to quickly overwhelm the French Army and the remaining British divisions and, given the superiority in numbers and equipment now enjoyed, 143 of the *Heer's* divisions were to be employed in the three Army Groups A, B and C.[5] In fact, 104 of these divisions were positioned between the sea and the River Meuse, advancing along the line of the Rivers Somme and Aisne. The orders from the OKH specified:

> The intention of the Supreme Command is to annihilate the allied armies remaining in France as rapidly as possible... Operational enemy reserves need no longer be expected. It will therefore be possible first to break down the enemy's hastily constructed front south of the Somme and the Aisne by heavy assault and then, by rapid and deep penetration, prevent the enemy retreating in good order or from forming another defence line in the rear.[6]

Army Group B was to make an opening attack over the River Somme and in the direction of the River Seine, together with a thrust between the coast and the River Oise to secure the flank. The main offensive, which was to begin on 9 June, and would be over the River Aisne, was to be carried out by Army Group A. Attacking southwards, on either side of Reims, it was intended that the Allied forces should be destroyed and the Maginot Line subjected to a subsidiary onslaught that would engineer a breakthrough at its most vulnerable points between St Avold and Sarreguemines.

Army Group A was commanded by *Generaloberst* Gerd von Rundstedt.[7] It was facing the French from the east of Laon to the north of the Maginot Line and would attack on either side of Paris and towards the River Seine. Army Group A consisted of elements from *Generaloberst* Günther von Kluge's 4th Army, *General der Infanterie* Ernst Busch's 12th Army and *Generaloberst* Wilhelm List's 16th Army, and it was comprised of 45 divisions of which 39 were infantry, two were motorised infantry and four were panzer divisions. Army Group B was under the command of *Generaloberst* Fedor von Bock.[8] Still standing on the right of the German line, its main attack was to drive south, beginning east of Paris and advancing towards Rheims on 9 June. Army Group B was comprised of elements of the 4th, 6th and 9th Armies, and it had 47 Divisions of which 36 of them were infantry, four were motorised infantry, and there was one cavalry division and six panzer divisions, together with two motorised infantry brigades. Army Group C was commanded by *Generaloberst* Wilhelm Ritter von Leeb.[9] It consisted of 24 infantry divisions and was to attack the French forces by penetrating the Maginot Line from

5 See Appendix III for a more detailed description of the German formations.

6 M. Glover, *The fight for the Channel ports: Calais to Brest 1940* (London: Leo Cooper, 1985), p.147.

7 Karl Rudolf Gerd von Rundstedt (1875-1953) commanded Army Group A during the Battle of France. In November 1938, he had retired from the German Army with the rank of *Generaloberst* but was recalled to active service by Hitler in 1939. He was promoted to *Generalfeldmarschall* in July 1940.

8 Moritz Albrecht Franz Friedrich Fedor von Bock (1880-1945) was a *Generaloberst* and the commander of Army Group B during the Battle of France and was promoted to the rank of *Generalfeldmarschall* in the German Army in July 1940.

9 Wilhelm Josef Franz Ritter von Leeb (1876-1956) was the commander of Army Group C during the Battle of France. He had been promoted to *Generaloberst* in November 1939 and was raised to the rank of *Generalfeldmarschall* in July 1940.

the Upper Rhine. These three Army Groups would then converge on the Plateau de Langres, to the south-east of Paris, and to the rear of the Maginot Line.

The panzer and motorised infantry divisions were concentrated into the five armoured Corps, each of which was comprised of two panzer divisions and one motorised infantry division. Two of these Corps were assigned to Army Group A and were to be known as the *Panzergruppe Guderian*. They contained the XXXIX Corps (the 1st and 2nd Panzer Divisions and the 29th Infantry Division) and the XLI Corps (the 6th and 8th Panzer Divisions and the 20th Infantry Division). Similarly, two of these Corps were assigned to Army Group B and they were known as the *Panzergruppe Kleist*. They contained the XIV Corps (the 9th and 10th Panzer Divisions and the 9th and 13th Infantry Divisions) and the XVI Corps (the 3rd and 4th Panzer Divisions, the 4th and 33rd Infantry Divisions, and included units drawn from the *SS-Verfügungstruppe* and the *Leibstandarte Adolf Hitler* Regiment). Also assigned to Army Group B was the XV Corps which was known as *Panzergruppe Hoth*. This contained within it the 5th and 7th Panzer Divisions and the 2nd Infantry Division.

Wehrmacht Doctrine, Strategy and Tactics

In 1940, the *Wehrmacht* possessed a cadre of resourceful and well-trained officers who led highly motivated troops.[10] They were able to make the most of a military doctrine and tactics, the foundations of which had been established during the 1920s by *Generaloberst* Hans von Seeckt. In his capacity as the *Chef der Heeresleitung* (Commander-in-Chief) of the *Truppenamt* (Troops Office) for the *Reichswehr* (the armed forces of the Weimar Republic), von Seeckt had drawn heavily on the lessons learnt by the German armed forces during the First World War, particularly those from the eastern front where there had been greater operational mobility.

Hence, the *Wehrmacht's* strategic offensive aims were derived from a doctrine that was in turn dependent upon the fundamentals of daring, speed and surprise, together with those tactics that were designed to fracture morale and generate disorganisation amongst the units of the opposing armies in order to win decisive and swift victories. This was carried out most successfully through the use of fast, highly mobile forces that made effective use of communications technology (and especially the radio) and which were supported by concentrated artillery firepower and aerial close support from the *Luftwaffe*, with its bombers acting as airborne artillery.

This approach proved to be most profitable when implemented during the shorter military campaigns, such as the spectacular victories against armies such as those of Poland, which were relatively small and therefore much easier to overcome quickly. It soon came to be widely known as *blitzkrieg*, the German term for 'lightning war'. Yet some of these tactics had actually been developed and employed during the First World War by the British Army and the Royal Flying Corps, such as the most effective use of AFVs and the provision of close support from the air.

10 When considering the achievements of the *Wehrmacht* during the Battle of France, it should be noted that many of those serving in the panzer divisions and other front-line units made regular and often habitual use of Pervitin, a powerful methamphetamine produced by the Berlin pharmaceutical company of Temmler. This drug was effective in reducing fatigue and raising morale and stamina, making those who were taking it feel almost super-human and able to continue to march and fight for days without sleep or food. However, it also increased their propensity for risk-taking and reduced any feelings of empathy that these soldiers might have had.

Unfortunately, for the British a tactical amnesia now appeared to be in evidence, together with poisonous inter-service rivalries and the disastrous longer-term consequences for the armed forces of the spending reductions of successive Governments in the 1930s.

The *Wehrmacht's* planning for *Fall Rot* had as its basis the key aspects of traditional German military thinking, including the theory of *Vernichtungsgedanke* (annihilation theory), where *Bewegungskrieg* (the battles of manoeuvre) would result in the rapid encirclement and destruction of the opposition's armed forces. Consequently, the panzer divisions were not to be used in independent or individual operations; despite having the same size and equal importance of the *Wehrmacht's* others units, they were subordinated to the three Army Groups which had been designated to execute the plan.

The tactics typically employed by the panzer divisions were to advance across country at high speed and to avoid any roads that had been blocked or barricaded, and to bypass those positions and villages that had been fortified. Such obstacles could then be left to be tackled by the infantry, as they followed in the wake of the tanks. The mechanised units carried out reconnaissance missions, often using armoured cars and the faster, smaller light tanks, and would then advance and assault the positions which had been identified as weak spots in their opponent's defences. Having been seized, this ground would be claimed by the German infantry and artillery so that it could be utilised as the launching point for the next wave of attacks.

Effective communication by radio also enabled the exploitation of opportunities as they occurred, and much faster than the Allied armies were able to respond. Being aware that the lighter of the German tanks, such as the Panzer I and Panzer II, rather than the Panzer III and Panzer IV, could be outgunned by their adversaries, these smaller machines were often used as bait, to entice the Allied tanks onto prepared positions where the German artillery's anti-tank guns would be able to trap and efficiently despatch the Allied AFVs. This also helped to conserve the numbers of panzers that would be available to the *Panzerwaffe* for future operations by limiting what would otherwise have been costly tank-on-tank engagements.

Prior to the commencement of the western offensive, very little analysis of the operational techniques of the *Wehrmacht* had been carried out by any of the Allied armies. However, one example was a study that had been conducted by the British 48th Division based on what was known about the tactics of the German armed forces from the Polish campaign. This had accurately concluded that the:

> General principles of German tactics in Poland seem to have been: to make minute preparations concerning the ground to be attacked with the help of a well-organised intelligence service; to select and define sectors to be attacked in order to isolate and outflank them; to penetrate enemy positions by the savage and mass use of artillery, aircraft and tanks operating in close liaison; to bypass sectors of resistance; to destroy communications and liaison, thus paralysing HQs …[11]

During the 51st Division's assault on the Abbeville bridgehead on 4 June, a number of German prisoners from the 199th Regiment of the 57th Infantry Division were captured. An important insight into one of the tactics being used by the *Heer* was described by Lieutenant General James

11 P. Caddick-Adams, 'Phoney War and Blitzkrieg: The Territorial Army in 1939-40', p.70.

Marshall-Cornwall.[12] This was presented in a report to the Chief of the Imperial General Staff, General Sir John Dill.[13] The German captives revealed that their infantry had been instructed not to resist when attacked by Allied armour, but to let the tanks pass through their positions to carry on to the rear, where they could then be dealt with by anti-tank weapons situated in pre-prepared positions. Hence, once such a trap had been sprung and the Allied tanks were thus engaged, it was the German infantry's duty to oppose the Allied infantry.[14] A further report to the CIGS on 14 June further elaboration:

> The great numerical superiority of the enemy both on the ground and in the air has, of course, given him a great advantage. The crushing effect of his armoured attacks has been overwhelming, delivered as they were in close co-operation with his dive bombers, acting as a very mobile and flexible artillery support.
>
> Turning to the German offensive methods, the outstanding feature is the way in which they maintained their objective. There was no thought of exposed flanks, there was no waiting to gain touch with neighbouring units. Every formation pushed straight ahead to the appointed goal regardless of the losses or exhaustion. Success was invariably achieved. How maintenance of vehicles and replenishment with petrol and ammunition was effected is still a mystery to me. The fact remains that every advance resulted in a victory.[15]

These observations were borne out by an entry made in the 1st Armoured Division's War Diary, in which a reference is also made to the *Wehrmacht's* tactics for attacking Allied defensive positions. This stated that in the early phases of the German offensive on 5 June, during the commencement of *Fall Rot*, and following on from what had been an intense artillery bombardment and an attack on the Allied positions by the bombers of the *Luftwaffe*, the German infantry units had advanced initially unsupported by their tanks, although the armoured forces subsequently came into action later in the day and in great numbers.[16] The difference between this and the Allied approach was that rather than the tanks having to reduce the speed of their advance to allow for the slower pace of the infantry, the German motorised infantry was able to keep up with the panzer divisions and to lead the attack when required.

Whilst the *Luftwaffe* was not tied directly to the *Heer*, it played an essential role in the operations of the ground forces, although even with its more modern equipment and the crucial experience gained during the Spanish Civil War, it was only slightly more prepared for the

12 James Handyside Marshall-Cornwall (1887-1985) was promoted to Lieutenant General in 1938 and, in May 1940, he was sent to France to assist with the evacuation of British troops from Cherbourg. He waited to board what would be the last ship to leave that port.

13 Sir John Greer Dill (1881-1944) was a General and had commanded the I Corps in France, before being appointed as Vice-Chief of the Imperial General Staff. However, following the replacement of Chamberlain by Churchill as Prime Minister, Dill succeeded General Sir Edmund Ironside as the Chief of the Imperial General Staff (CIGS), the professional head of the British Army. Promoted to Field Marshal in November 1941, he was posted to Washington as the Prime Minister's personal representative, where he was Chief of the British Joint Staff Mission.

14 TNA WO 32/9388: Overseas: Europe (Code O (V)), Despatches from BEF 12-19 June 1940.

15 Ibid.

16 TNA WO 167/334: 1st Armoured Division War Diary.

1940 campaign as it evolved. In contrast, the French Air Force, the *Armée de l'Air*, was poorly organised and rigidly dogmatic, making it largely unwilling to adapt and when it was placed under pressure, it collapsed; whilst the RAF was still operating under a number of constraints, in terms of its equipment and tactics. The consequence of this was that air superiority was quickly ceded to the *Luftwaffe*.

The *Luftwaffe's* doctrine was not exclusively to act as airborne artillery for the *Heer* but to win superiority in the air and then to achieve air supremacy. Its contribution to the victories gained in Poland, the Low Countries and in the first phase of the invasion of France was due to the successful accomplishment of realistic aims and objectives. This was especially so when compared with the Allies, and a practical approach and flexibility ensured that it was able to cope with rapidly changing circumstances, to make the most effective use of resources and to harness the initiative demonstrated by the lower echelons of the command structure.

From 1-4 June, the *Luftwaffe* had been engaged on strategic missions that had targeted the French aircraft industry based in and around Paris and the fuel depots which surrounded Marseilles. Thereafter, and with the commencement of *Fall Rot*, it resumed its responsibilities for providing close support to the *Heer's* ground forces, especially when they were confronted with a fortification or the French artillery's concentrated gun emplacements needed to be dealt with. Furthermore, and determined to prevent any further Allied evacuations from occurring after Dunkirk, the *Luftwaffe* had assigned *Fliegerkorps I* to the Normandy and Brittany sectors. It also sought to ensure that whenever possible, the more capable of the Allied aircraft, and especially the Hawker Hurricane, were outnumbered by *Luftwaffe* aircraft during combat and kept in constant action. The intention of this was to prevent the Allied fighters from being deployed in the areas where they were really needed and it would also have a negative effect on the battle-worthiness of these aeroplanes, should their ground crews be unable to be carry out the essential maintenance required for them.

Wehrmacht Arms and Equipment

Just as it had been during the 1939 invasion of Poland, in the 1940 campaign in the Low Counties and in France the backbone of the German *Panzerwaffe*, or armoured force, was still having to make use of some comparatively poorly specified AFVs. These were the Panzer I and Panzer II light tanks that had been developed during the early to mid-1930s.[17] The heavier and better armed and armoured vehicles, such as the Panzer III and Panzer IV, were available but only in relatively limited numbers, and hence the Panzer divisions had to resort to using those tanks that had been appropriated by the *Wehrmacht* following its occupation of Czechoslovakia during 1938-39.

Tracing its origins to the British Carden Loyd tankette and intended as a training vehicle due to its paltry armament of two 7.92 mm MG 13 machine guns and its limited protection of between 7 and 13 mm of armour, the Panzer I was designed in the year before Hitler came to power and its production commenced in 1934. Manufactured by Henschel, MAN, Krupp and Daimler, and weighing 5.4 tons, with dimensions of 13.2 feet in length by 6.8 feet wide,

17 The term *Panzer* was in fact a truncation of the German word *Panzerkampfwagen* (Armoured Fighting Vehicle) and was often further abbreviated to PzKpfw.

and a top speed of 23 mph, it had a two-man crew of a commander/gunner and a driver. There were two variants of the Panzer I, which were the Ausf A and Ausf B respectively, and by the time of the Battle of France this AFV had already seen service with the ground forces of the German Condor Legion during the Spanish Civil War and in the campaigns in Poland, Denmark and Norway, and the Low Countries. By 1940, it was quite simply outclassed by many of its opponents and best utilised in an infantry suppression capacity.

The Panzer II was created to replace the Panzer I and to act as a stop-gap until the better specified and larger AFVs, such as the Panzer III and Panzer IV, were ready to enter front line service. The Panzer II was designed in 1934 and went into production the following year. Several models had been developed during the lead up to the war, and by 1940 the Ausf C variant weighed 8.9 tons, had between 5 and 16 mm of armour, and was armed with a 20 mm KwK 30 L/55 auto-cannon and a 7.92 mm coaxial MG 34 machine gun. With a top speed of 25 mph, it was 15 foot 9 inches long and 7 foot 3 inches wide, and was operated by a three-man crew of commander/gunner, loader/radio operator and driver. The Panzer II did not see action in the Spanish Civil War but it was used during the invasions of Poland, Denmark and Norway, and the Low Countries and France. It was typically employed on reconnaissance and scouting duties. Thereafter, it was increasingly relegated from front line service, and was eventually replaced by the Panzer III and Panzer IV.

Intended to be main battle tank of the panzer divisions and capable of engaging and destroying the enemy's AFVs in tank-on-tank combat, the Panzer III was a medium tank designed during 1934-35 and the first prototypes were created in 1937. By 1940, production of the Daimler-Benz manufactured Ausf E and Ausf F variants had commenced and these vehicles saw service during the Battle of France. Weighing 23 tonnes and having a length of 18 feet 3 inches and a width of 9 feet six inches, its 12-cylinder Maybach engine provided a top speed of 25 mph (12 mph off-road) and a range of 103 miles. Armour protection was 15 mm all round and the five-man crew (commander, gunner, loader, driver, and radio operator/bow machine gunner) had at their disposal either two or three 7.92 mm MG 34 machine guns together with the 37 mm main armament. During the war, this tank was progressively up-gunned with the short-barrel 50 mm, the long-barrel 50 mm and then, in its final Ausf N variant, with the short-barrel 75 mm gun. By this time, the roles of the Panzer III and the Panzer IV had effectively been exchanged, as the Panzer IV increasingly became the main German battle tank whilst the Panzer III steadily evolved into a close support AFV.

The Panzer IV was originally intended for an infantry support role and the destruction of enemy strong points and anti-tank guns but it was refined and regularly up-gunned to become a main battle tank. It was the most numerous of all the German tanks of the war, with 8,500 of them being built. Development had begun during 1934, leading to production being carried out by Krupp from 1936 onwards and, by 1939, there had been successive variants with each of them incorporating improvements to the vehicle's armour, engine and suspension. The Ausf D variant had entered into service by the time of the Battle of France. Weighing 25 tonnes, with a length of 19 feet 5 inches and width of 9 feet five inches, and 20 to 30mm of armour, its Maybach HL120 TRM 12-cylinder engine provided a top speed of 24 mph (9.9 mph off road) and gave the vehicle an operational range of 120 miles. As with the Panzer III, the tank had a crew of five (commander, gunner, loader, driver, radio operator/bow machine gunner) but had as its main armament the short-barrelled low velocity 75mm gun and the secondary armament of two 7.92 mm MG 34 machine guns.

To supplement the panzer divisions when necessary, the German Army used a number of Czech-made tanks as substitutes, especially for the Panzer III. These vehicles had been re-designated as the Panzer 35(t) and the Panzer 38(t), with the (t) denoting tschechisch, or the German word for Czech.[18] Following the annexation and occupation of Czechoslovakia in 1938-39, a total of 244 of the Panzer 35(t) tanks were seized and 132 of them participated in the Battle of France. However, this model proved to be limited by its shortcomings and spare parts, as these became increasingly difficult to obtain by 1940 thereby preventing its maintenance.

At the time of the occupation of Czechoslovakia, 150 of the vehicles that the Germans would eventually rename as the Panzer 38(t) had been ordered by the Czech Government although none of them saw service with that country's military. The German authorities rated this AFV very highly and, due to its reliability and ease of maintenance, 1,400 had been manufactured by the end of its production in 1942 (although its chassis continued to be built and employed for various other vehicles, including several tank destroyers). Weighing up to 9.85 tonnes, it was 15 feet 1 inch long by 7 feet wide, had between 8 and 30 mm of armour, and its Praga TNHPS/II engine provided an operational range of 160 miles and a top speed of 26.1 mph (9.3 mph off-road). The tank was manned by crew of four (a commander/gunner, loader, driver and bow machine gunner/radio operator) and its armament was comprised of a 37mm gun supplemented by two 7.92 mm ZB-53 (MG 37(t)) machine guns.

The aircraft employed by the *Luftwaffe* on the western front during 1940 were, with the notable exception of the RAF's Hawker Hurricane, superior to most then in operation within the Allied air forces. Furthermore, the failure of the Allies to take the German aerial threat seriously, and to provide their armies with appropriate anti-aircraft support, left their unprotected ground troops largely vulnerable to and at the mercy of the strafing attacks carried out by the *Luftwaffe*, which became a hallmark of the aerial element of *Blitzkrieg*.

Following the achievement of air superiority by its fighter aircraft, the *Luftwaffe's* Junkers Ju 87 dive bombers (universally known as the Stuka, derived from *Sturzkampfflugzeug*, the German term for a dive bomber) could then be unleashed on the slow-moving columns of refugees and soldiers. Psychologically, even before its bombs had been released, the Stuka could readily provoke sheer panic and terror, especially when a column's transport was horse-drawn. This was due to the loud wailing sound generated when diving towards a target by the sirens known as the 'Jericho Trumpets' fitted to the underside of the aircraft's inverted gull wings.

Indeed, and whilst within a matter of weeks this aircraft would be brutally savaged by RAF Fighter Command's Hurricanes and Spitfires during the Battle of Britain, it nevertheless gained a fearful reputation during the campaigns in France and the Low Countries. The Ju 87 B series (as flown during the Battle of France), had a two-man crew (a pilot and a rear gunner), was 36 feet 5 inches in length with a wingspan of 45 feet 3.5 inchs, and its Junkers Jumo 211 Da V-12 inverted liquid-cooled piston engine gave the aircraft a maximum speed of 211 mph. It carried one 550 lb bomb mounted directly beneath the fuselage and four 110 lb bombs under its wings, and for defence against enemy fighters it had two wing-mounted 7.92 mm MG 17 machine guns and one 7.92 mm rearward firing MG 15 machine gun.

18 The Panzer 35(t) had been developed and built in Czechoslovakia by Skoda and the Panzer 38(t) was designed and built there by the company of Praga.

The *Luftwaffe's* two principal fighter aircraft during 1940 were manufactured by the Bayerische Flugzeugwerke (BFW) (the Bavarian Aircraft Works, which had been reconstituted as Messerschmitt AG in 1938). Respectively, these were the single-engine Messerschmitt Bf 109 and the twin-engine Messerschmitt Bf 110. Each of these aircraft had been designed to perform a specific combat role. The Bf 109 was intended to be a high speed, short-range interceptor aircraft; the Bf 110 could function either as a long-range heavy fighter (termed by the *Luftwaffe* as a *Zerstörer* or destroyer) or as a fighter-bomber (described as a *Jabo* or *Jagdbomber*).

The design stage for the Messerschmitt Bf 109 was undertaken during 1934, when it was agreed that it should be the successor to the *Luftwaffe's* earlier biplane fighter aircraft, which were now obsolete. The first prototypes commenced trialling during 1935, production began in 1937 and a number of the Bf 109 A series saw some action with the *Luftwaffe's* Condor Legion during the Spanish Civil War. Thereafter, and until the introduction of the Focke Wulf Fw 190 later during the Second World War, the Bf 109 maintained its position as the principal single engine fighter of the *Luftwaffe*. Coming into operation in late 1938, it was the E (*Emil*) series (E1 and E3 models) that saw front line service during the Battle of France.

The Bf 109 E1 was 28 feet 4.5 inches in length with a wing span of 32 feet 4.5 inches. The Daimler-Benz DB-601A engine enabled it to reach a maximum speed of 348 mph and maximum height of 34,450 feet, and its operational range was 410 miles. The armament of the E1 model was comprised of four 7.92 mm MG 17 machine guns (one fitted in each wing and two mounted along the top of the fuselage and synchronised to fire through the propeller) and it carried 3,000 rounds of ammunition. The main improvement to the E3 was that the two wing mounted machine guns were replaced with 20 mm MG FF cannons to boost the aircraft's hitting power against the RAF's fighters with their eight Browning machine guns.

The Messerschmitt Bf 110 was developed during 1935 and the first machines were delivered to the *Luftwaffe* in 1937. The specification of the C series, which had reached service during 1940, was that it had a length of 39 feet 7.25 inches, a wingspan of 53 feet 3.75 inches and it had a twin-tail configuration. Powered by two Daimler-Benz DB 601A-1 engines, its maximum speed was 336 mph, the maximum height obtainable was 32,810 feet, with a range of 481 miles. It could boast a heavy armament mounted in its nose of either four 7.92 mm MG 17 machine guns or with two 20 mm MG FF/M cannons replacing two of the four machine guns. A single 7.92 mm MG 15 machine gun was located at the rear of the cockpit for defence against enemy fighters attacking from the rear. Depending on its role, the aircraft had either two or three crew members. The combat experience of this aircraft during the Battle of France (and even more so during the Battle of Britain) revealed its vulnerability to attack from the faster fighters of the RAF, due mainly to its size and overall lack agility, and especially when it was undertaking a defensive close support role.

Throughout the early years of the war, for bombing missions the *Luftwaffe* was reliant on three main aircraft, all of which were twin-engine medium bomber designs: These were the Dornier Do 17, the Heinkel He 111 and the Junkers Ju 88.

The idea for the Dornier Do 17 was originally conceived in 1932 as a high-speed twin-engine mail plane for the *Lufthansa*, Germany's civilian airline. However, following the Nazi Party's rise to power in 1933, this concept was modified and the *Fliegender Bleistift* (or flying pencil, as it became known) was recast as a *Schnellbomber* (fast bomber) or, in other words, a light bomber that was fast enough to outrun any defending fighter aircraft. The overall design was further revised following the lessons learnt by the *Luftwaffe* during the aircraft's service in the Condor

Legion during the Spanish Civil War. By 1940, the Do 17 Z series was in operation and was 51 feet 10 inches in length with a wingspan of 59 feet 1 inch. Powered by two Bramo 323P 9-cyl. air-cooled radial piston engines, its maximum speed was 255 mph, maximum height was 26,900 feet and it could carry 2,205 lb of bombs (either twenty 110 lb or four 551 lb bombs). Defence was achieved by six 7.92 mm MG 15 machine guns in the front upper/lower, rear upper/lower and beam positions (all firing from its crew in the cockpit area). The aircraft was operated by a crew of four (pilot, bombardier and two gunners). Production of this aeroplane as a bomber was concluded in 1940, but following further design revisions, thereafter, it continued to be manufactured for and utilised by the *Luftwaffe* as a night fighter.

Initially designed in 1934, during the Spanish Civil War the early models of the Heinkel He 111 were pressed into service with the *Luftwaffe's* Condor Legion. Due to its continuous modification and use in a variety of roles from medium/heavy bomber to torpedo bomber to airborne platform for the launching of the V1 flying bomb, this twin-engine aeroplane became perhaps the best-known German bomber of the war. It was a large aircraft, being 53 feet 10 inches in length, with a wingspan of 74 feet 2 inches, and having by the outbreak of war the trademark glazed cockpit known as the 'greenhouse'. Powered by two Junkers Jumo 211 F-1 engines, its maximum speed was 270 mph, the maximum height attainable was 21,300 feet and its maximum range was 1,400 miles. The internal bomb bay could hold 4,400 lb of bombs and up to 7,900 lb could be carried on external bomb racks but such a large load impeded performance. Up to seven 7.92 mm machine guns (MG 15 or MG 81) were provided for defence via the nose, dorsal, side and ventral positions. A 20 mm MG FF cannon could also be mounted in the forward ventral location. The aeroplane was operated by a complement of five crew members (pilot, navigator/ bombardier/nose gunner, ventral gunner, dorsal gunner/radio operator, side gunner).

Manufactured from 1936 onwards, one of the *Luftwaffe's* most versatile aeroplanes was the Junkers Ju 88, which saw varied service as a medium bomber, dive bomber, heavy/night fighter, torpedo bomber and reconnaissance aircraft. Manned by a crew of four (pilot, bombardier/front gunner, radio operator/rear gunner, navigator/ventral gunner), it was 47 feet 2 inches in length with a wingspan of 65 feet 7.5 inches and was powered by two Junkers Jumo 211 J-1 engines. These provided the Ju 88 with a respectable maximum speed of 290 mph, a range of 1,223 miles and a maximum altitude of 17,700 feet. An internal bay could accommodate up to 3,100 lb of bombs; alternatively, up to 6,600 lb could be carried on external bomb racks, although the extra drag would diminish the aircraft's performance. Four 7.92 mm MG 81 machine guns situated in the cockpit's forward and aft positions and to the rear of the ventral position provided the aircraft's defence. During the Battle of France, the Ju 88 A series enjoyed success in its role as a dive bomber and in the making of precision attacks on logistical targets that helped to paralyse the French transport network. Indeed, and as will be described in Chapter 7, it was a Junkers Ju 88 that was responsible for dropping the bombs that sank the HMT *Lancastria* on 17 June 1940.

3

Offensive on the Somme and Aisne

Overview: Initial British Response

By 5 June 1940, the Commander-in-Chief of the Allied armies in France was *Général d'armée* Maxime Weygand (who despite being 73 years of age had replaced the younger *Général d'armée* Maurice Gamelin on 20 May).[1] Weygand had to make what use he could of the forces at his disposal to defend a frontline that ran for 225 miles, from Sedan and along the Aisne and Somme rivers to Abbeville. Facing the Allies were 143 divisions of the *Heer* (of which 104, including all ten panzer divisions, would be employed in this offensive) and a *Luftwaffe* that now enjoyed air superiority on the Continent, apart from the occasions when it clashed with the RAF over the English Channel. Weygand had at his command 68 infantry divisions (of which 25 had been diverted from the defence of the Maginot Line), three armoured divisions and three light cavalry divisions, together with the formations of the BEF that had remained in France or were being sent south of the River Somme with a view to establishing what was by then beginning to be called the second BEF.

Weygand's first course of action, therefore, was to form a defensive line which ran along the River Somme, and inevitably became known as the Weygand line. This was intended to prevent the enemy from achieving further penetration towards the south of France. Unlike the German divisions, which were concentrated where their commanders selected for maximum impact; by contrast, the Allied armies had to stretch their limited forces to run along the whole of the front because they did not know where the Germans would launch their next offensive.

The intention was not, however, an attempt to hold a rigid line or even a defensive belt. Instead, it was to organise a defence in greater depth so that should the enemy's mobile armoured forces succeed in penetrating the line, it would be made more difficult for the infantry divisions to follow up and consolidate the position. Formed around physical obstacles, such as villages and woods, the French forces were concentrated into strongpoints that were known as 'hedgehogs'

1 Maxime Weygand (1867-1965) was a *Général d'armée* who retired from the French Army in 1935, but was recalled to service in 1939, and replaced *Général d'armée* Maurice Gamelin as supreme Allied Commander on 17 May 1940. Following Paul Reynaud's resignation as Prime Minister, and *Maréchal de France* Philippe Pétain's appointment as his successor, Weygand was appointed Minister for Defence.

because they bristled with guns. These were supported with anti-tank guns, arranged in order to be able to stall the attacks of the panzer divisions, tie up and drain their resources. It was thought that Allied counter-attacks could then be attempted to try to re-connect with any pockets of British or French units that had been isolated to the north. With limited numbers, there were no arrangements for secondary lines of resistance and, should the German forces succeed in breaking through, it could lead to the collapse of the French Army and end the Allied struggle with the enemy in France.

The first offensive of *Fall Rot* commenced at 0400 hours on 5 June and was carried out by Army Group B's 4th Army, which was under the command of *Generaloberst* Hans Günther von Kluge.[2] It involved the 5th and 7th Panzer Divisions, the 6th, 12th, 27th, 31st, 32nd, 46th, 57th Infantry Divisions, the 1st Cavalry Division, the 2nd Motorised Division and the 11th Motorised Brigade. The advance was to be from the south of Abbeville, between Longpré and Picquigny, and it would be on a line from Abbeville to Amiens, along a 125-mile front, which ran from Amiens to the sea. This would allow the *Heer's* armoured and mechanised units to work past the Allied troops situated along the River Bresle and River Béthune, both of which ran parallel to the River Somme. These positions were being held by Major General Fortune's 51st Division and the French 7th and 10th Armies, commanded by *Général d'armée* Aubert Frère and *Général d'armée* Robert Altmayer respectively.[3]

The main assaults took place at Amiens, where the Germans had gained a significant foothold on the southern bank of the River Somme and on the Oise-Aisne canal.[4] The enemy forces were then to make an advance towards the lower Seine with the aim of capturing Le Havre and the bridgeheads at Rouen, Les Andelys and Vernon. The attack executed on the River Aisne had been planned by *Generaloberst* List to be an operation carried out by the infantry, with the panzer divisions being deliberately held back in order for them to exploit the breakthrough when it came, despite the loud protests about this made by *General der Panzertruppen* Guderian.[5]

The intention was also to drive a wedge between the French IX and X Corps, which could then be opened up by the XV Corps of *Generalleutnant* Hermann Hoth.[6] The Corps' spearheads would be the 5th and 7th Panzer Divisions that were commanded by *Generalmajor* Joachim Lemelsen (who had recently replaced *Generalleutnant* Max von Hartlieb-Walsporn)

2 Günther Adolf Ferdinand von Kluge (1882-1944), known as Hans Günther von Kluge, commanded the German 4th Army, which was the formation to achieve the first breakthrough at Amiens and reach the River Seine on 10 June. He was promoted to *Generalfeldmarschall* by Hitler on 19 July 1940.

3 Marie-Robert Altmayer (1875-1959) was a *Général d'armée* who had retired from the French Army in 1937 but, on 21 May 1940, was recalled to active service following *Général d'armée* Weygand's orders and commanded the French 10th Army. Captured by the Germans on 19 June, he remained a prisoner of war until 23 December 1941, then retired from military service on 26 February 1942.

4 *Manchester Guardian*, 6 June 1940.

5 Heinz Wilhelm Guderian (1888-1954) was a *General der Panzertruppen* and he played a key role in the development of the *Panzerwaffe* and had been the Inspector of Motorized Troops before commanding *Panzergruppe Guderian*. He was promoted to *Generaloberst* in July 1940.

6 Hermann Hoth (1885-1971) was a *Generalleutnant* and the commander of XV Motorised Corps, which contained the 5th Panzer and 7th Panzer Divisions, had been on *General der Panzertruppen* Heinz Guderian's right flank during their advance through the Ardennes. He was promoted to *Generaloberst* in July 1940.

and *Generalmajo*r Erwin Rommel.[7] Units of the German infantry were to take control of the railway bridges across the Somme at Flixecourt and Hangest-sur-Somme, so that engineers could remove the rails from the track for the tanks of the 7th Panzer Division to cross the bridges without hindrance. Hence, by that evening the 7th Panzer Division had reached a position south of Montagne-Fayel, where it defeated a counter attack from the French 2nd *Division Cuirassées de Reserve* (DCR). The swift-thinking Rommel took the 7th Division, with the 5th Division following in its wake, across country.

Consequently, the German mechanised forces could easily avoid many of the French 'hedgehogs' that were left to be dealt with by the infantry which was following behind them. Effectively, this enabled the Panzer divisions to make progress without meeting any significant opposition. Rommel would subsequently be ordered to turn to the north-west, to swing around Rouen and make for Fécamp. If successfully executed, this would cut off *Général d'armée* Altmayer's left wing. Able to reach this destination within days, the 7th Division could then work back towards Dieppe, thereby trapping Altmayer's 10th Army, including the 51st Division.

During the opening stage of the *Fall Rot* offensive, it was felt that the enemy had perhaps reverted to the type of attack being made by the German Army in 1918. Given that it involved the ground that had been contested by the original BEF during the First World War, the *Manchester Guardian* considered this latest German offensive to be rather reminiscent of the 1914 Schlieffen Plan. This newspaper reported that the German offensive, as was to be expected, was directed against two of the weaker spots in the French line. These were at Amiens, where the Germans had established a bridgehead on the southern bank of the River Somme, and west of Laon, where the French line ran along the canal between the Rivers Oise and Aisne.[8]

For example, a heavy preliminary bombardment was made by the *Wehrmacht's* heavy artillery, and often from the air by the *Luftwaffe's* Stuka dive bombers, to soften up the Allied positions. This would be followed successively by the armoured divisions and then by the infantry, whose task it would be to hold onto the gains that were made by the panzers. Initially the enemy's progress was limited by the latter, especially when resistance proved particularly stubborn, with Kleist's two Panzer Corps being held up south of Amiens and heavy casualties were inflicted. As noted by the *Manchester Guardian*, there was believed to have been reduction in the number of German AFVs due to the losses suffered by the Panzer divisions during the earlier battles in Flanders and northern France.[9] Certainly, this part of the offensive meant that an extensive re-deployment of German resources was therefore necessary, which had an impact on the troops and their vehicles. *General der Kavallerie* Erich Hoepner's XVI Panzer Corps, which consisted of two panzer divisions and a motorised infantry Division, lost 80 of its 500 tanks during the course of this first German attack.

On 5 June, the 1st Armoured Division and the 51st Division were the principal British fighting formations still in France, the latter having through no fault of its own been separated from the rest of the BEF. Both were placed under the control of the French IX Corps, commanded by

7 Johannes Erwin Eugen Rommel (1891-1944) was a *Generalmajor* who successfully commanded the 7th Panzer Division during the Battle of France. In February 1941, he was given command of the *Deutsches Afrika Korps* and promoted to *Generalleutnant*, and in June 1942 to *Generalfeldmarschall*. He committed suicide following his being implicated in the 20 July 1944 plot to kill Adolf Hitler.

8 *Manchester Guardian*, 6 June 1940.

9 Ibid.

Général de corps d'armée Marcel Ihler.[10] In turn, this was part of the 10th Army of *Général d'armée* Robert Altmayer. The 10th Army held the left sector of the Somme front, from Abbeville to the sea, and was comprised of the IX Corps, X Corps and the 3rd *Divisions Légères Mécaniques* (DLM), a French Light Mechanised Division. All British troops located south of the Somme were placed under Altmayer's overall command, and this was to be co-ordinated and overseen by the British Military Mission, situated at the 10th Army headquarters.[11]

By this time, the British approach to the offensive was essentially to reinforce those French forces that were still fighting in the attempt to prevent their total collapse. The men of the 51st Division had already been in action on the Saar front, and they had undergone a long journey to bring them to this new sector. On 4 June, the Division had been part of an offensive intended to eliminate the German bridgeheads along the River Somme at Abbeville, due to the vulnerability of the western extent of the *Weygand line*. Together with two of the two French Army's formations, the 31st Infantry Division (the Pyrenean Chasseurs) and the remaining tanks of the 2nd Armoured Division, the 51st Division was ordered to assault and take the two ridges of the Monts de Caubert and Mareuil-Caubert, near to Abbeville. Crucially, this was on a wide front that was well protected by the German forces. Major General Fortune had sought to postpone this action due to the non-arrival of sufficient ammunition for the French artillery. Assurances were given to him that it would arrive, although it never did.[12]

Lacking the necessary artillery support, all that could be provided was a rather feeble and badly directed barrage of only ten minutes duration, and with the French tanks that were promised having also failed to arrive in sufficient time, the assault had to begin without them. Advancing well ahead of the tanks that had now begun to arrive, instead of behind them for cover, the 2nd Seaforth Highlanders attempted to clear the German infantry's forward positions on the edge of the woods. Due to a lack of intelligence information and reconnaissance, the Highlanders did not know where the enemy's strongpoints were until they actually reached them and by then it was too late and they came under fire. When the French AFVs did appear, they drove into an undetected minefield before coming under heavy fire from the well positioned German anti-tank and field artillery, with both the minefield and the German guns exacting heavy losses on the French armour.[13]

The 4th Seaforth Highlanders had been told to follow up this assault but they were confronted with sustained heavy machine gun fire from Mont de Caubert. The 4th Queen's Own Cameron Highlanders were ordered to capture an objective to the south of Caubert but also encountered heavy fire from the crews of the German machine guns who were dug into defensive positions. On the left flank, the 1st Black Watch advanced to the Petit Bois to provide cover for the 1st Gordon Highlanders, who were driving the Germans out of the Grand Bois, but it proved difficult to hold this objective even when the required position had been gained.

10 Marcel Ihler (1880-1975) was a *Général de corps d'armée* and from 21 May 1940 he was appointed as the commander of the French IX Corps and remained so until forced to surrender to the German Army at St Valery-en-Caux on 12 June 1940.

11 In the absence of a unified Allied headquarters, communication between the British and French armies was carried out via liaison officers based at the headquarters of the commanders of armies or the army groups. For the BEF, these were the Military Missions, and they were typically commanded by a Major General or a Lieutenant General.

12 TNA WO 32/9388: Overseas: Europe (Code O (V)), Despatches from BEF 12-19 June 1940.

13 L.F. Ellis, *The War in France and Flanders 1939–40*, p.266.

Neither of the Allied air forces had participated in his unsuccessful operation. Unsurprisingly, therefore, the British troops made limited progress, were subjected to concentrated enemy artillery and machine gun fire, and were eventually forced to withdraw.[14] The attack failed, and at the close of the day that part of the line held by the 51st Division was probably not dissimilar to that which was held on the evening of the 3 June but the cost in terms of casualties was considerable, with 152nd Brigade having 20 officers and 243 other ranks either killed or wounded during the day.[15]

By 5 June, since its troops were spread thinly between the villages that were being used as strongpoints, the 51st Division's condition was that there were insufficient troops on the ground to prevent infiltration by the enemy. The frontage on the Somme sector allocated to this Division was also very wide. Some 40 miles in length, this was many times longer than that which a fully equipped and manned infantry division might be expected to hold. The conventional deployment was one division per four miles of suitably entrenched positions.[16] The Highlanders were outnumbered and lacking in ammunition and the other necessities, but this was comparable to conditions experienced elsewhere by the French Army due to the lack of resources at this time.

The 154th Brigade was on the left to the south of St Valery-sur-Somme, the 153rd Brigade were in the centre, and the 152nd Brigade was on the right and occupying an area lying to the south of Abbeville. When due consideration is given to its well-equipped and professional enemy, which was able to make full use of its artillery and the *Luftwaffe*'s Stuka dive bombers to apply immense pressure, this was an impossible task.[17] Consequently, it was only possible to hold the strong points and, because each of the respective British companies was situated in villages or similar locations that were at least one mile apart, the distance between them was too great for the realistic provision of support to their neighbours. Accordingly, this allowed the enemy forces to bypass them with ease and to attack and penetrate the gaps that had been left in the line. Communication was by telephone lines, but these could be cut by the enemy, either by hand or as a result of shellfire, and so contact had to be maintained by the use of despatch riders where possible, and when not, by runners.

In terms of the British Army's armoured formations, and as was pointed out in his subsequent report on the operations that had taken place during the Battle of France, when what remained of the 1st Armoured Division was placed under the overall command of Major General Fortune of the 51st Division, Major General Evans confirmed to him that the Division's tanks were now in a very poor mechanical condition.[18]

This was a consequence of the combination of battle damage and the long distances that they had been required to travel on roads and without any facilities to carry out the essential maintenance that these vehicles so badly needed. Furthermore, there was little or no artillery support, reserves, bridging equipment or spare parts available, and some of the vehicles were missing crucially important items of equipment such as radio sets and the full complement of weapons, because this had arrived after embarkation was ordered and there had been insufficient

14 B. Karslake, *1940, The Last Act*, pp.138-41.
15 P. Warner, *Battle of France, 1940* (Simon & Schuster, 1990), p.212.
16 S. David, *Churchill's Sacrifice of the Highland Division, France 1940* (London: Brassey, 1994), p.76.
17 H. Sebag-Montefiore, *Dunkirk: Fight to the Last Man* (London: Penguin, 2006), p.458.
18 TNA WO 167/334: 1st Armoured Division War Diary.

time to distribute and fit the equipment to the tanks upon arrival in France.[19] As such, not more than the equivalent of one armoured regiment could be mustered from the limited resources of the 2nd and 3rd Armoured Brigades at this time. In an attempt to rectify the deficient or under-equipped vehicles, from 1 June British units were withdrawn so that they could be re-fitted to the south of the River Seine. Hence, the 1st Armoured Division was scarcely in any position to participate effectively in any offensive operations.

Furthermore, and as was recorded on 5 June by 2nd Armoured Brigade's War Diary, discussions were held regarding the re-organisation of this Brigade (but not of the improvised armoured composite regiment). Those tank crews that found themselves without vehicles were to be converted to infantry, conveyed in motorised transport, and so they were to be known as dismounted parties.[20] This response was made upon the insistence of the French commanders, and these parties of British tanks and dismounted troops were deployed in a piecemeal way against what were fundamentally unsuitable objectives and situations. As a consequence, these British units sustained heavy battle casualties, reducing yet further their effectiveness.

Turning to the participation of the respective Allied air forces, and reiterating the earlier requests made by *Général d'Armée Aérienne* Joseph Vuillemin, the Commander-in-Chief of the French air force, to the British Government, the French authorities again pleaded for ten RAF fighter squadrons to be sent to France immediately, to be followed by a further ten squadrons as soon as they could be made available.[21] The British Government's response had been to send to France two squadrons of Hawker Hurricanes, which were to join the AASF, and for a further four squadrons to be allocated from Fighter Command to make use of the French airfields near to Rouen but to return to Britain at the conclusion of each day's operations. This meant that from 6 to 8 June, a total of 144 RAF fighter aircraft had been committed to the air battle being waged over France. In the first three days of the *Fall Rot* offensive, and despite the extremely limited number of fighters available to provide the RAF's bombers with escorts, the Fairey Battle light bomber squadrons flew 42 daylight missions for the loss of only three aircraft. The sorties flown by the RAF's bomber forces were to targets that had been specifically identified for them by the French High Command.

5 June 1940

On 5 June, *The Times* provided a reminder to its readership that 'The BEF attached to the main French Army is still in being and very much alive' and that 'at any moment in this war of swift surprise and swifter action they may be called upon to undertake tasks of extreme importance'.[22] This was prophetic because on that day, the German offensive on the Somme was made in opposition to the 51st Division's position at St Valery-sur-Somme. By this time, after twelve days of continual movement and battle, including being ordered on 4 June to mount an assault on the Abbeville bridgehead, the 51st Division's condition was one of near exhaustion.

The German 12th Infantry Division, with support from the 11th Motorised Brigade, moved forward against the positions held by the 7th and 8th Argyll and Sutherland Highlanders at the

19 Bovington Tank Museum Archives: Report on the operations of the 1st Armoured Division in France.
20 TNA WO 167/419: 2nd Armoured Brigade War Diary.
21 S. David, *Churchill's Sacrifice of the Highland Division, France 1940*, p.114.
22 *The Times*, 5 June 1940.

St Valery-sur-Somme bridgehead, from Saigneville, Mons, Catigny, Pendé, Tilloy to Sallenelle. As pointed out, the Argylls were too far apart for them to realistically give any support to each other and, although the troops fought with great determination and valour, their positions were overwhelmed and fell to the enemy during the course of the afternoon.

At Franleu, the 7th Argylls were surrounded by the enemy's infantry and some of their armoured cars, whilst at Mons and Arrest, German forces also successfully infiltrated the defensive positions.[23] At 0300 hours, a despatch rider who had been attached to No. 12 Platoon of C Company arrived at 7th Battalion's headquarters at Franleu and reported that the Platoon's positions were under attack. In response, a section of Bren Gun Carriers commanded by Second Lieutenant Robert Powell was despatched immediately to assist C Company. At 0345 hours, the telephone lines to C and D Companies of the 7th Argylls fell silent. Parties of signallers were sent out to find out what had happened but the firing of automatic weapons was heard and believed to be an enemy patrol. Taking three men with him, the most senior Non-Commissioned Officer, Regimental Sergeant Major W.S.I. Lockie, went out to investigate. Upon his return he reported that there were a large number of enemy troops who had taken up positions on both sides of the road that led to Arrest and to Quesnoy-le-Montant, and that his party had exchanged shots with them.[24]

Captain Irvine Robertson had organised the defence of the 7th Argyll's Battalion headquarters and he had ordered that the Bren machine guns be taken from the universal carriers and that machine gun posts be set up at points around the village. RSM Lockie took charge of the left-hand posts and Company Sergeant Major Dyer took those on the right, while Sergeant Robins led a patrol to seek out enemy snipers. The 7th Battalion's War Diary records that RSM Lockie was magnificent right to the end, despite being wounded, and that CSM Dyer also sustained gunshot wounds in his arms and legs.[25] By this time, the telephone line to Brigade headquarters had been cut and Second Lieutenant Spens was ordered to connect a line to Valines or, should this not be possible, to head directly to Brigade Headquarters and report the situation.

With the latter being the case, a report was made by Spens to Major Rowley-Orr and to Brigadier A.C.L. Stanley-Clarke. Lieutenant Colonel E. Buchanan had ordered the A Company to move back to Franleu to assist with the defence of the village, which had been surrounded by enemy troops who were subjecting the buildings to bombardment with their 5-inch mortars. This fire was accurate and concentrated on the Battalion HQ, leading the 7th Argylls to conclude that the Germans must have identified this position before the attack had commenced.[26] Heavy casualties were inflicted on the Argylls and many wounded were taken down into the cellar of the building used as the HQ, which had previously been a school.

Captain Logan suspected that the enemy was gathering its forces in a ravine one kilometre from the village and contacted Lt-Col Buchanan to request that this location be brought under artillery fire. This was done but it was not possible to observe whether the shellfire had been accurate and even if the enemy had been there at all; however, it was recorded that everything went quiet, leading to the conclusion that it was indeed successful and that a possible attack had

23 TNA WO 167/711: 4th Black Watch War Diary.
24 TNA WO 167/704: 7th Argyll & Sutherland Highlanders War Diary.
25 RSM W.S.I. Lockie was awarded the Distinguished Conduct Medal for his action but inexplicably, and in spite of his wounds, CSM Dyer was to receive no such recognition.
26 TNA WO 167/704: 7th Argyll & Sutherland Highlanders War Diary.

effectively been prevented. German cavalry attacked D Company of the 7th Argylls at 0400 hours.[27] These assaults were twice repelled but, shortly after this, the enemy brought some of its light tanks and motorcyclists up to give assistance to their cavalry units.

At 0445 hours, the German troops were seen to be advancing from the west. Approximately 1,000 strong, the enemy infantry was divided in order to surround on three sides the position then being held by C Company of the 7th Argylls and to advance on to Franleu. This was then subjected to an intensified bombardment, the mortars having been brought up on horse-drawn wagons, with the fire directed especially towards the positions in the hedgerows where the Company's Bren gun posts were situated. At this time, Major Young gave orders for the forward platoons to be withdrawn, with Second Lieutenant Green holding the crossroads at Arrest. The Company arrived at St-Bliment, which was held by D Company of the 8th Argylls and took up a position on the right flank of the village. By 1100 hours, the Germans had consolidated their position in the Catigny-Ochancourt valley and this village came within range of their artillery, and the shells began landing increasingly closer to the centre and then hitting the Argyll's headquarters. While visiting a forward observation post, Major Tress was wounded in the leg by shrapnel and had to be evacuated.

Between 1300 and 1400 hours, from a position on a ridge at Frireulle, around 1,200 German troops were observed to be moving to the south-west side of Franleu. An hour later, the order was given for the Brigade to withdraw to Bouvaincourt-sur-Bresle and later in the afternoon, Lt-Col Buchanan decided that the defence of Franleu could not be maintained further. He gave his permission for any man who wished to make the attempt to try to get away to safety and leave in any vehicles that they could find. Lt-Col Buchanan had been magnificent all day, displaying incredible coolness when under enemy fire, and he and the padre, Captain MacInnes, refused to leave in order to stay with the wounded who had been placed in the cellar of the building that was being used as the Battalion headquarters. According to the 7th Argylls War Diary, nothing further was heard from B Company, all of whom were posted as missing, or from C Company, who faced the brunt of the German attack. In just this one day, the 7th Argylls lost 23 officers and nearly 500 other ranks killed, wounded or missing in action.[28] The diary concluded its entry for the day by stating that:

> June 5th must have been the blackest day in the history of the battalion but the great traditions had been upheld and much glory added to the battalion's history. Many brave deeds and acts of self-sacrifice were performed which unfortunately passed unnoticed and were never recorded. The actions and feats of B and C Companies for the present remain a mystery.[29]

The 8th Argylls were also under attack from the German forces that had advanced towards them from the direction of St Valery-sur-Somme. Brigadier Stanley-Clarke had requested that the 51st Division release some of the reserves and in response was advised that French tanks were being sent, as were the 4th Black Watch, which had been in the 153rd Brigade reserve, and had previously been ordered forward in an attempt to relieve the 7th Argylls at Franleu. The

27 S. Longden, *Dunkirk: The Men They Left Behind* (London: Constable & Robinson, 2008), p. 113.
28 J. Marshall-Cornwall, 'Normandy 1940', *War Monthly*, Vol. 45, 1977, p.4.
29 TNA WO 167/704: 7th Argyll & Sutherland Highlanders War Diary.

intention of this was that the 4th Black Watch would also occupy the villages of Feuquières, Fressenneville and Valines and hence begin to form a new line connected to the 1st Gordons on the right and the 8th Argylls on the left. They were prevented from doing this by an enemy attack at Feuquières, however.

The French tanks had attempted to relieve Franleu but could not reach their objective, no further information was available and no advance was made by the 4th Black Watch. Consequently, bad blood would exist thereafter between the 7th Argylls and the 4th Black Watch, with the former accusing the latter of leaving them to their fate.[30] In mitigation, the commanding officer of the 4th Black Watch, Lieutenant Colonel Rory Macpherson, later explained that this advance was not attempted by his battalion due to the late arrival of the French tanks and the lack of clear orders, which meant that his battalion would have been proceeding for over a mile across rough arable land without any support and whilst under enemy fire.

An attack by German AFVs was made against A Company of the 8th Argylls, during which several were killed or wounded before the Battalion withdrew to Sallenelle in an attempt to find a strengthened position. Sallenelle itself was attacked by enemy infantry which had assembled in the woods to the south-west of St Valery-sur-Somme. The Argylls were hampered by not having any machine guns to repel this assault and, as a consequence, a 25 mm anti-tank gun was overpowered and lost. The German forces also began to attack from the north-east and the 8th Argyll's defences had to be re-organised to protect their flank.

At Tilloy, the C and D Companies of the 8th Argylls were in prepared positions and at 0430 hours they opened fire on a squadron of German cavalry. They were then attacked by enemy infantry who were supported by units of cavalry, motor-cycle troops and horse-drawn mortars. The assault came from the direction of Catigny and their troops were able to advance rapidly and in great numbers towards Arrest, Nibas and Ochancourt, which threatened communications with Escarbotin. According to the Battalion's War Diary, the enemy infantry advanced in close formation, which made them, in turn, extremely vulnerable to German artillery fire.[31]

Examples of 154th Infantry Brigade's courageous conduct are provided in a report produced by the Brigade headquarters for the 5 June 1940.[32] The Distinguished Service Order (DSO) was awarded to Captain Thomas Fotheringham for his actions at Valines, when this village was partly occupied and almost surrounded by the enemy. After reporting the situation to the Battalion headquarters, he returned to the village to extricate his men, and, furthermore, on 6 June he set a personal example by the coolness of his behaviour when under machine gun fire.

The Military Cross (MC) was awarded to Lieutenant Donald Mirrieless for entering the village of Chepy whilst unaccompanied, to try to find out whether any enemy troops were present there, even though the information at his disposal was that the village was now held by the Germans. Second Lieutenant, The Lord Glenorchy was also awarded the MC for his actions when, upon seeing 150 German troops approaching his position at Valines, he moved his section to take up a better position, and following which his men were able to inflict over 50 casualties upon the enemy force.

Sergeant P. Bow received the Distinguished Conduct Medal (DCM) for his devotion to duty whilst in charge of a section of stretcher bearers and for his assistance during a difficult and

30 S. David, *Churchill's Sacrifice of the Highland Division, France 1940*, p.132.
31 TNA WO 167/705: 8th Argyll & Sutherland Highlanders War Diary.
32 TNA WO 167/711: 4th Black Watch War Diary.

dangerous night withdrawal in the presence of the enemy. Also awarded the DCM was Private C. Clarence who, as the company runner, demonstrated considerable bravery in carrying the messages to and from the Battalion headquarters when it was being subjected to heavy enemy artillery and machine gun fire.

Captain R.S. Walker of C Company of the 4th Black Watch reported that the night of 5 June was quiet and that it not until the following day that enemy troops were observed to be advancing towards his position from the direction of Friville, which led to Walker's Company withdrawing to higher ground near to Incheville.

In four hours of fighting, the 152nd Brigade received 563 casualties. Captain Derek Lang (later to become Lieutenant General Sir Derek Lang, the General Officer Commanding-in-Chief at Scottish Command and the Governor of Edinburgh Castle) was the adjutant of the 4th Queen's Own Cameron Highlanders, who recorded that the Battalion started the day with a complement of 600 but after three hours they were down to 250 of all ranks, as they were attacked by a full strength German infantry battalion. The 1st Gordon Highlanders inflicted some losses on the enemy in the Grand Bois wood but because the infantry of the French 31st Division failed to take the Rouvray side to their right, the 1st Gordons had to be withdrawn.

The 1st Armoured Division's War Diary recorded that there were indications that the enemy's panzers were now to the south of the River Somme and that there were 16 pontoon bridges under construction between Amiens and Hangest-sur-Somme. Accordingly, all units in the Division were instructed to take whatever local defence measures they could to prevent penetration by isolated enemy AFVs.[33]

According to the War Diary of the Beauman Division Tank Company, which was now located in Bouvray and commanded by Acting Captain P.W.C. Colan of the Royal Tank Regiment, at 0400 hours there had been the order to 'stand to' as it was believed that landings were being made by German parachutists.[34] However, two hours later there was an air raid that lasted for 50 minutes during which a large number of the small incendiary and high explosive bombs were dropped but no casualties resulted from this. Further German air raids took place throughout the day, creating fires in the nearby woods, but again there were no casualties.

The composite armoured regiment, which was now commanded by Lieutenant Colonel C.H.M. Peto, received orders during the morning of 5 June that it was to advance across the River Bresle to give support to the 153rd Brigade at Tours and the 154th Brigade at Belloy, where the enemy had brought up armoured cars and tanks.[35] The purpose of this move was to prevent any further penetration by these enemy forces. The composite regiment was involved in several engagements of this type and it lost a number of its tanks before it was able to regroup at Beauchamps on the Bresle.

Later that day, having received news of enemy activity around Eu and Le Tréport, the composite regiment was joined by a reserve squadron and ordered to reconnoitre these locations, where they surprised two enemy armoured cars that were near to Ponts-et-Marais and were able to put them out of action. Following this, German anti-tank guns were encountered and some of the regiment's vehicles were disabled and several casualties incurred. At 2130 hours, the composite regiment was withdrawn and retired to the west of the River Bresle but it left

33 TNA WO 167/334: 1st Armoured Division War Diary.
34 TNA WO 167/1417: Beauman Division, Tank Company War Diary.
35 TNA WO 167/419: 2nd Armoured Brigade War Diary.

two troops of AFVs to the east of the river, where they remained through the night to guard the approaches to Beauchamps.[36]

A Territorial cavalry unit, the 1st Lothians and Border Yeomanry, was positioned at Bray and needed support if it was to prevent enemy penetration into the Haute Forêt d'Eu but there was no prospect of reinforcements. The Lothians were attacked by German patrols that advanced onto its position near to an abandoned French tank. Realising that British troops were lying in wait, one of the German soldiers put his hands up to indicate that he was surrendering only to be shot and killed by one of his own comrades. In turn, that German was shot by the British troops but eventually the Lothians had to fall back to the village of Oisemont.[37]

By the close of 5 June, the OKH claimed that the *Weygand line* had been broken at several points, as the River Somme and the Oise-Aisne canal had been forced.[38] Whilst the Allies were now less intimidated by German tactics than they had been at Sedan at the outset of *Fall Gelb*, and despite many valiant attempts to stand and fight, by the end of the day, the whole of *Général d'armée* Altmayer's line had been compelled to retreat by five miles from the River Somme.

In a report to the CIGS also dated 5 June, Lieutenant General Marshall-Cornwall stated that the situation of 51st Division was now very serious.[39] It had been fighting continuously for three days and had suffered heavy casualties, being forced to retreat to a line of the River Bresle from Gamaches to Treport. Furthermore, it was attempting to hold a 40-mile front that was too wide for it to be able to mount an effective resistance, with there being no defence in depth or reserves. This made it a relatively easy matter for enemy units to use their infiltration tactics.

The 51st Division was then forced back to a line: Oisemont – Aigneville –Woincourt – Eu, with its withdrawal being covered by the 9th Royal Lancers. In terms of the individual Brigades, the 152nd Brigade was relieved on the Bresle by a brigade of the Beauman Division and was withdrawn to the reserve. As darkness fell, the remnants of the 154th Brigade, which held a series of villages that were too far apart to offer mutual defence, had been pushed back to a line from Woincourt to Eu.[40] On its right, the 153rd Brigade was receiving attention from German artillery and mortars before being attacked by swarms of Junkers Ju 87 Stuka dive bombers, causing it to retreat to Toeufles, through Zoteux and Frières, where the intensive fire returned by the British machine guns and artillery halted the German advance.

Turning to the combat being waged in the air, when the *Wehrmacht's* offensive over the Somme and Aisne rivers had commenced, with attacks from three bridgeheads on the Somme, part of the British response was to call upon the RAF's bomber squadrons. Bombing by the AASF and Bomber Command had taken place during previous the night, with 103 British aircraft being used to carry out attacks on the German communications in France, together with oil and transport targets inside Germany.

On 5 June, there were four strategic reconnaissance flights by the AASF, one of which was intended to provide information on the activities of the panzer divisions in the Amiens, Montdidier, Péronne and Roye areas. After this, there were some 19 sorties by the Fairey Battle bomber squadrons. These were tasked with carrying out assaults on the roads, rail

36 B. Karslake, *1940, The Last Act*, p.154.
37 S. Longden, *Dunkirk: The Men They Left Behind*, p.115.
38 *Manchester Guardian*, 6 June 1940.
39 TNA WO 32/9388: Overseas: Europe (Code O (V)), Despatches from BEF 12-19 June 1940.
40 L.F. Ellis, *The War in France and Flanders 1939-40*, pp.271-272.

communications and woods, even though visibility was poor.[41] At Montdidier, it was reported that seven enemy tanks were hit by the bombs dropped by one aeroplane and, between Vrely and Roye, two Fairey Battles had dropped their bombs on a column of German motor transport.

Fairey Battles of 12 Squadron had been moved from Échemines to Sougé but they were continuing to use Échemines as their advanced base, and from which they had bombed the railway lines near to Trier on the previous day. At 1930 hours on 5 June, eleven aircraft from 12 and 150 squadrons flew from Échemines and they attacked the German Army's columns that were using the Péronne – Roye and Amiens – Mondidier roads, albeit many of the bombs that were dropped failed to hit their targets whilst others hit some French tanks that were near to Tricot. Hence, the Germans were able to enlarge their bridgeheads on the River Somme. Further missions were carried out by other Battles, which attacked targets in the Ardennes, but this did not prove to be of much assistance to the situation in hand.

The 51st Division had made a request to the RAF for some air support but, as there were only 18 Hawker Hurricanes that were operational at this time, and as these were being used to protect Rouen where large *Luftwaffe* air raids were anticipated, Air Marshal Barratt was left with little choice but to send the Fairey Battle squadrons out on bombing missions without any support from the fighter squadrons. The AASF's operational strength on this day was reported as consisting of 28 Fairey Battles with 23 crews and eight Hawker Hurricanes with ten pilots.

Despite the limited numbers of fully functioning RAF aircraft, a total of 41 sorties were carried out by the AASF's fighter squadrons. At 0600 hours, 11 Hurricanes from 1 Squadron were able to intercept an early morning *Luftwaffe* air raid on Rouen that involved a force comprised of at least 50 Dornier Do 17 and Heinkel He 111 bombers that were escorted by approximately 24 Messerschmitt Bf 110 twin-engine fighters. A dog fight then ensued but the remainder of the German aircraft were able to break off and proceed to their target, where they bombed the AASF's headquarters at Boos as well as a nearby army camp.

A further air raid of the same area was attempted at 1855 hours by a combined force of 12 Heinkel He 111 bombers and four Junkers Ju 88 bombers, with an escort of 12 Messerschmitt Bf 110 fighters. Although these bombers were intercepted by nine Hurricanes from 501 Squadron, which shot down five of these enemy aircraft for only one British loss, the airfield and the army camp were bombed again, as were the bridge, power station, railway station at Rouen, and some of the neighbouring factories.[42] By the end of the day, four of the Hurricanes had received substantial battle damage and one of the RAF pilots, Flying Officer Shepherd, had been killed in action whilst he was intercepting the German force that was then over Rouen. It was recorded that of the six *Luftwaffe*'s aircraft that were confirmed as having been shot down and of the four that were unconfirmed as being so, two of them were Heinkel He 111 bombers and three were Dornier Do 17 bombers.

6 June 1940

As a result of the German Army's attacks along the whole of the Rivers Aisne and Somme, on 6 June many units of the French Army were forced to retreat. Consequently, German troops

41 TNA AIR 35/192: Summaries of Operations, 10 May – 16 June 1940.
42 TNA AIR 35/253: AASF Combat Reports.

reached the Bresle and, further east, were observed at Conty, to the south of Amiens. A substantial number of enemy troops succeeded in crossing the River Bresle near to Ponts-et-Marais and were able to establish themselves in the woods there, which they used to provide cover whilst harassing Allied vehicles. Enemy infiltration taking place around Eu and at Ponts-et-Marais was only just averted by the 1st Armoured Division's composite regiment, which then counter-attacked. The German assault at Oisemont was carried out with the support of both the artillery and the *Luftwaffe* but these attacks were beaten back by the tanks of the 1st Lothians and of the French 2nd *Divisions Légère de Cavalerie* (DLC).[43]

Throughout the day, reports were received of breakthroughs by the enemy AFVs but this was not the case, although the 5th and 7th Panzer Divisions had now commenced their drive towards Rouen and the leading elements had extended beyond the Poix-Rouen Road, with the 2nd Motorised Division following after them. Advancing on its left was the German 6th Infantry Division and the 32nd Division was on the right.

This was in accordance with the crucial documents and maps that were recovered by Allied troops from a German Army staff officer who was found dead in his car. This intelligence, which threw considerable light on the enemy's intended plan of operations for 7 and 8 June, included the objectives and centre lines of the German armoured and mechanised divisions, with the axis of movement of the advance to be south-west through Poix and Forges-les-Eaux. In fact, the German objective for 7 June was the approximate position occupied by the Beauman Division in Forges-les-Eaux; whereas on the 8 June, it was to be Rouen itself, with the 7th Panzer Division on the left, which would be heading towards Rouen via Argueil. To support the Beauman Division in trying to hold a front that was 16 miles long, Brigadier Morgan deployed the Royal Artillery's 101st Composite Regiment, which was equipped with 2-pounder anti-tank guns and Lewis machine guns and supported by infantry from the 2/6th East Surrey Regiment. The anti-tank guns were spread out and each of them was guarded by a platoon from the East Surreys.[44] Although the tanks of the 1st Armoured Division were now in a somewhat poor state, Major General Evans also promised that he would arrange for as many of them as possible to be available to render assistance.

The 51st Division also had to withdraw behind the River Bresle and, according to the Division's War Diary, orders were issued for the occupation of defensive positions on the line of the Bresle, which was divided into five sectors. However, difficulties in administration and command meant the French 31st Division would have to sideslip to the right and the extent of the 51st Division's frontage was reduced to extend from Blangy-sur-Bresle to the sea. The 152nd Brigade held the line from Oisemont to the Route Nationale, with the 31st Division holding the next sector. At Hocquélus was the 153rd Brigade, with the 154th Brigade next in the line, to Fressenneville. The French 40th Division was to be moved beyond the Bresle, from Senarpont to Aumale, to reinforce the Royal Engineers and an anti-tank battery there.

B Company of the 7th Argylls arrived at the Haute Forêt d'Co during the early hours before moving to St Remy, where they found out that German tanks had broken through the line, and so they returned to Haute Forêt d'Co. As the Battalion, which now consisted of only five officers and 130 men, was just about to withdraw to the Forêt d'Auberville the *Luftwaffe* conducted an

43 L.F. Ellis, *The War in France and Flanders 1939-40*, p.275.
44 M. Glover, *The Fight for the Channel Ports: Calais to Brest 1940*, pp.158-59.

air raid, dropping 20 to 30 bombs, two of which landed amidst the unit transport but doing no damage.[45] Later still, and having arrived at Woincourt, the 7th Argylls encountered German troops who attacked the Highlanders with hand grenades before their tanks appeared. Having retreated to Dargnies, the remnants of D Company held this position until 1300 hours despite heavy mortar fire. Captain Richie withdrew his men to Incheville on the River Bresle and, in conjunction with the Headquarters Company of the 8th Argylls, held the bridge there until 2230 hours when orders were received for a further retreat to Monchy, which was where the Argylls remained until the following morning.

The 9th Royal Lancers, which was now reduced in strength to a mere 30 vehicles, moved to a position near to Touffreville-sur-Eu to prevent the enemy forces from crossing the River Yères from the direction of Eu. One squadron was sent out on a reconnaissance and dealt with a small enemy force that had penetrated to the south of the river, in the woods. The men of the 4th Border Regiment were also taken from the defensive line of the 1st Support Group for use in close support in this area.

The 8th Argylls were defending a position in the village of Yzengremer, when at 0400 hours a squadron of tanks commanded by Captain J. Scott of the 9th Royal Lancers arrived. Colonel Grant of the Argylls requested that an armoured reconnaissance be made to the north side of this village, as there were suspicions of enemy incursions, with there being three houses which appeared to have been driven down or into, on or around midnight. After fifteen minutes, Captain Scott returned to confirm that he had located a number of enemy machine gun positions, which he proposed to attack from the south. At 0600 hours, German trench mortars and machine gun fire opened up on the positions held by the 8th Argylls. This intensified over the next hour leading to a number of casualties, and Colonel Grant decided that it was necessary to withdraw to Dargnies to save the vehicles and guns that were now in danger of destruction from the enemy's artillery barrage. The War Diary reports that when leaving, a squadron of the 9th Royal Lancers was in position 'hull-down' behind the hedge at the top of the railway cutting on the south side of the village.[46]

The 4th Black Watch's contact with the enemy began at 0600 hours. Due to a breakthrough on the left, at 1100 hours the Battalion withdrew from Meuquieres. Fighting took place for the remainder of the day, due to enemy pressure and constant artillery fire. Therefore, at 2115 hours, the 4th Black Watch pulled back over the River Bresle.[47] The 8th Argyll's headquarters company held their position at Beauchamp until the completion of the withdrawal of the 4th Black Watch and the Royal Engineers' 26th Field Company. When this had been accomplished, at 2330 hours, the bridge over the River Bresle at Beauchamp was demolished.

The 2/6th Queen's Royal Regiment left Gamaches and proceeded to Blanges, where they formed a bridgehead until relieved by the various Highland Regiments. Number 8 platoon took up guard of a bridge at Foucaucourt, but this was destroyed by the Royal Engineers. Other sections of this platoon were further along the river at Senarpont, where they were ordered to remain until the 1st Lothians had withdrawn, after which they would provide covering fire to

45 TNA WO 167/704: 7th Argyll & Sutherland Highlanders War Diary.
46 TNA WO 167/705: 8th Argyll & Sutherland Highlanders War Diary.
47 TNA WO 167/711: 4th Black Watch War Diary.

the Royal Engineers who detonated this and other bridges there. At 8.30 pm, it was recorded that approximately 50 German bomber aircraft flew over and dropped bombs on the bridges.[48]

At 0930 hours, to the south of Woincourt a force of two cruiser tanks and two Daimler Dingo scout cars fought a successful action against enemy infantry, which were in trenches approximately 400 yards ahead of them. Consequently, around 40 German troops (including two officers) were taken prisoner. Unfortunately, during this action Lieutenant Colonel Peto received a severe wound to the hand and was evacuated to hospital, being replaced as the composite regiment commander by Major MacDonnell of the 1st Lothians.[49]

At 1400 hours, Captain Scott of the 9th Royal Lancers returned with his tank and reported to Colonel Grant of the Argylls that regrettably his own Colonel had ordered him to return at once. He had protested that he was supporting the Highlanders but was overruled by his superior. Evaluating this situation, Colonel Grant decided that the best option was to return to the bridgehead at Beauchamp and co-operate with the 4th Black Watch, which had been ordered to hold the south ridge of the Grand Vallee, eastwards from Beauchamp. Five Bren/Universal Carriers and two trucks were used for this journey to Beauchamp, during which some of the officers and soldiers from D Company of the 7th Argylls were picked up along the way.

Upon arrival at the Beauchamp bridgehead, the Argylls found the 26th Field Company of the Royal Engineers to be in position there. On the other side of the river, the village of Incheville was being held by a company of the 6th Royal Scots under the command of Captain Crawford. Liaison being made, it was decided that the Argylls should hold the positions on either side of the road connecting Beauchamp and Incheville on the south side of the River Bresle. Signs of enemy activity being noted at 1830 hours by a sighting of mounted cavalry, by 1900 hours trench mortar shells fell on the outskirts of Beauchamp and then across to Incheville.

Within the 6 June edition of *The Times* and the 8 June *Manchester Guardian*, an Air Ministry communique was reproduced. This concerned the attacks being carried out by the RAF's bombers on the German lines of communication during the day and its troop concentrations and roads, bridges and the Ruhr's railway marshalling yards at night. It was also reported that successful reconnaissance missions had been conducted by Army Co-operation aircraft.

> Two of the RAF bombers were attacked by three Messerschmitt 109s from line astern. Fighting back with their rear guns, the bombers spiralled down almost to ground level, and, in a stunning fight which lasted for twenty minutes, one Messerschmitt was caught by a burst of fire at close range and was seen to be badly damaged.[50]

The role of the RAF's fighter aircraft in providing patrols throughout the day was also stressed in these press reports. At 0520 hours on 6 June, five Hawker Hurricanes of 501 Squadron intercepted three Dornier Do 215 bombers that were flying at 5,000 feet over Forges-les-Eaux and accounted for two of these German aircraft.[51]

The three AASF squadrons were reinforced during the day and a deputation from the 51st Division went to the BAFF headquarters to seek further protection for the troops on the ground.

48 TNA WO 167/810: 2/6th Queen's Royal Regiment War Diary.
49 TNA WO 167/419: 2nd Armoured Brigade War Diary.
50 *The Times*, 6 June 1940; *Manchester Guardian*, 8 June 1940.
51 TNA AIR 35/253: AASF Combat Reports.

The AASF's fighter aircraft were detailed to patrol the area around Rouen during the day and in the evening, and they flew missions to the area in which the French IX Corps was located. In the afternoon, two fighter squadrons had flown from Britain to the Boos airfield, where they had refuelled and then conducted patrols in order to arrive shortly after the *Luftwaffe's* raids on Oisemont and Millebosc.

Twelve Bristol Blenheim bombers flew from their bases in Britain to attack those German Army columns which were moving towards the River Somme crossings. Five of these machines were lost, but later in the day a further raid was undertaken by a larger force of 24 Blenheim bombers, which attacked the bridges and the roads from Abbeville to St Valery-sur-Somme without any loses being incurred.[52]

At 1630 hours, nine Fairey Battles flew from Échemines to bomb the German Army's columns on the Ham-Péronne road, whilst other British bombers targeted the tanks and other vehicles that were to be found between Péronne and Roye. Although in the company of an escort of Hawker Hurricanes from 73 Squadron, the Battles were confronted by a flight of Messerschmitt Bf 109 fighters but the enemy aircraft were not able to press their attack home. It was also notable that an almost continuous stream of Junkers Ju 87 Stukas was now carrying out dive-bombing missions in the Roye area.

During the night, and despite the poor visibility at the target locations, 14 Battles were despatched to attack the enemy convoys in the Guise, Royroi and Givet areas.[53] These raids were to be launched against the German front line at night to enable the Battle pilots from Harbourville and Échemines to fly at a lower altitude and increase the chances of them successfully finding and hitting their targets. The take-off was attempted at 2345 and then at 0115 hours but was initially interrupted by a German air raid. Nevertheless, the Battles attacked the Somme Bridge to the north of Abbeville, roads at Abbeville and Amiens, and other targets that were near to Laon, Guise and St Quentin.

7 June 1940

According to *The Times*, in a piece entitled *Highlanders on the Somme*, 'Highland regiments of a famous division to-day have been fiercely resisting the Germans attacking along the Somme front'.[54] Furthermore, the same edition of this newspaper reported on the enemy assaults that were being carried out on various points between the coast and the Chemin des Danes, with some German units believed to have been successful in infiltrating the Allied positions as far as the River Bresle, and that bomber aircraft of the *Luftwaffe* had attacked Rouen but were opposed there by French fighter aircraft.

By the close of 6 June, the rapid advance of *Panzergruppe Hoth's* divisions was threatening to cut off the 51st Division if it withdrew to the south of the River Seine. The tanks of the 7th Panzer Division, which were leading the advance from Abbeville to Amiens, had crossed the Amiens – Rouen road and were at Thieulloy-la-Ville. The 5th Panzer Division was advancing slightly to the north of the 7th Division, and the 2nd Motorised Infantry Division was in support and following behind the German tanks. The nearest Allied troops were at Aumale

52 L.F. Ellis, *The War in France and Flanders 1939-40*, p.274.
53 TNA AIR 35/192: Summaries of Operations, 10 May - 16 June 1940.
54 *The Times*, 7 June 1940.

and, by dawn on 7 June, two French infantry divisions had been brought into action. Entering the line on the right, the French 40th Infantry Division was holding positions from Aumale to Senarpont, whilst the 31st Division had been moved further to the right, thereby allowing the British 51st Division to take up a shorter position from Gamaches to the coast.

By this time, the 51st Division, which was now behind the Bresle, had seen its constituent 152nd, 153rd and 154th Brigades sustain casualties of 80, 60 and 25 per cent respectively. The remaining companies of the 152nd Brigade then went into the reserve. Some 900 reinforcements from various units and commanded by Major J.R. Mackintosh-Walker of the Seaforth Highlanders arrived from Rouen. They were added to the 51st Division but it continued to be subject to intense enemy pressure.[55] By 7 June, the 7th Argylls was comprised of only five officers and 130 other ranks.

A counter attack against the German troops in the Incheville Forêt was carried out by the Beauman Division's A Brigade and the 154th Brigade although, due to the nature of the wood and the surrounding terrain, it was impossible to clear the enemy from there and the British units were subsequently subjected to heavy artillery fire.[56] During the early hours of 7 June, the 4th Black Watch was withdrawing towards the Beauchamps crossing, where it found that enemy troops were ahead but, with the assistance of the Battalion's anti-tank unit, the German units were driven off completely.

During the early morning hours, men of D Company of the 7th Argylls had moved forward to the southern slopes of Incheville and taken up position there at Breuilly, in reserve to the 4th Black Watch, where they were heavily mortared and shelled throughout the day, with two men being killed and eleven wounded. Captain Ritchie and Lieutenant Clark were among the casualties[57] The Royal Artillery had set up an observation post which was overlooking Incheville and this was now active and able to direct the fire from their 25-pounder field guns onto the enemy concentrations.

At 0845 hours, information was received from the French 10th Army that German forces had launched an attack on the gap formed as a result of the previous day's operations from Poix to Lignières-Châtelain. The 5th Panzer Division had broken through the French lines between Grandvilliers and Formerie, and it was feared that it would now overrun the British troops that were positioned to the south of the Aumale.[58]

Driving west of Amiens on Rouen and the lower Seine, the enemy intention was to split the 10th Army and hence detach it from IX Corps, between the Seine estuary and Dieppe. The German tanks achieved the separation and the 7th Panzer Division advanced 30 miles during the day. By the dawn of the following morning, the German tanks were close to Rouen whilst, on the River Bresle, the French IX Corps was in danger of being cut off. Reports from the 154th Brigade confirmed that considerable enemy forces had pushed forward down the roads towards the coast, and large numbers of German troops had crossed the River Bresle at Beauchamps.[59]

The Beauman Division's A Brigade, which was comprised of the 4th Buffs, the 1/5th Sherwood Foresters and the 4th Border Regiment, was despatched to reinforce the 51st Division's left flank

55 TNA WO 197/124: Movements of 51st Highland Division, April to June 1940.
56 TNA WO 167/314: 51st Division War Diary.
57 TNA WO 167/704: 7th Argyll & Sutherland Highlanders War Diary.
58 TNA WO 167/421: 3rd Armoured Brigade War Diary.
59 TNA WO 167/314: 51st Division War Diary.

as it tried to hold the line along the River Bresle from Eu to Senarpont. The 2/6th East Surreys, 1st Lothians and 1st Armoured Division's composite regiment were at this time defending the flank along the River Andelle.

The East Surreys was a TA battalion and had been a part of 12th Division before it was incorporated first into the Beauforce and then into the Beauman Division, becoming the infantry battalion that was attached to the Support Group. On 7 June, with the terrifying prospect of attempting to defend a 24-mile front against a German armoured division, the unit's 700 men had only the most basic equipment and very little of it at that. Although there were a few anti-tank guns, they lacked not only mortars or other artillery support but even grenades. There were no radio sets, making communication between companies virtually impossible. Each Bren Gun team had only 500 rounds of ammunition and each man was issued a mere 50 rounds for his rifle. At 0900 hours, the tanks of the 5th Panzer Division attacked and promptly knocked out all of the anti-tank guns and overran the infantry's positions and the location of its headquarters. Despite their desperate situation, the East Surreys fought on until they were entirely overwhelmed by the enemy infantry that followed up on the devasting assault that had been made by the German tanks.[60]

D Company of the 4th Border Regiment and A Company of the 1/5th Sherwood Foresters were holding positions at Incheville and had been told to maintain possession of the village and the bridge over the river at all costs. The commanding officer of D Company, Major John Hopkinson, was ordered by the battalion commander of the 4th Borders, Lieutenant Colonel Thomas Tomlinson, 'For God's sake see that no one comes over that bridge'.[61] In an attempt to eliminate the enemy's crossing points, they attacked a pocket of German troops which had congregated on the southern bank of the river. Unfortunately, some of the Foresters were hit and killed by 'friendly fire' from an artillery barrage and the combined units could only push the Germans back to the north-western end of the Haute Forêt d'Eu.

German infantry and tanks, having taken the road from Serqueux, arrived and whilst they were delayed for over three hours, the enemy's attacks were able to force the British troops back. The 4th Border Regiment and the 1/5th Sherwood Foresters managed to hold on for six days, courageously and steadfastly frustrating all German attempts to cross the river, and the only enemy troops that did so were taken prisoner. Orders to withdraw had been issued but failed to reach them and so they stood fast. However, by 13 June, the Germans brought up their artillery and mortars, and it had become evident that the fighting to the north of the River Somme had now ended with the surrender of the 51st Division. Only then, once a captured British officer who was sent into the village by the Germans had communicated this news, did these British troops finally surrender.[62] As Major L. Ellis would record in the Official History, 'It was a soldierly performance in the best tradition'.[63]

The 2/7th Duke of Wellington's Regiment, which from 20 May had been posted to the garrison at Dieppe, received intelligence reports that the River Somme was still held by the Allies and it sent out reconnaissance patrols, which encountered a German machine gun post near to Eu. Road blocks in Dieppe were still being maintained by the Battalion's forward

60 S. David, *Churchill's Sacrifice of the Highland Division, France 1940*, pp.186-88.
61 H. Sebag-Montefiore, *Dunkirk: Fight to the Last Man*, p.459.
62 TNA WO 167/714: 4th Borders War Diary.
63 L.F. Ellis, *The War in France and Flanders 1939-40*, p.283.

companies to provide anti-tank obstacles, but it was argued by Lieutenant Colonel Taylor that whilst these were adequate against small forces, they were too far forward to withstand greater opposition and the companies were withdrawn to a position behind the anti-tank obstacles. Closer liaison was then made with the engineers for the demolition of the river crossings.[64]

As the Panzers had already outflanked the Bresle line, in accordance with orders from Major General Evans, the 1st Armoured Division was ordered up to Gournay-en-Bray to attempt an attack on the flank of the enemy's advance. A composite regiment of the 1st Armoured Division was now placed under the 3rd Armoured Brigade's command. In this Brigade there were 41 cruiser tanks and 31 light tanks, and from the 2nd Armoured Brigade, six light tanks of the Queen's Bays and troops of the 10th Royal Hussars who were mounted in lorries of the 2nd Armoured Brigade, which had been refitted following the May offensive. The composite formation contained two squadrons from 2 RTR, one squadron from 5 RTR, and one squadron loaned from the Queen's Bays. The remainder of the 3rd Armoured Brigade was instructed to remain under the orders of the Brigade's second-in-command, and to move as and when ordered to do so by the 1st Armoured Division's headquarters.

It was now apparent that for the French IX Corps to be able to fall back in anything like good order to the line of the Lower Seine, a position would have to be secured and maintained along the River Andelle, 12 miles to the east of Rouen. Accordingly, the 3rd Armoured Brigade, which by now had been reduced to four rather depleted squadrons that could only muster 30 tanks in total, was ordered to attempt to stiffen up what was going to be the right flank of the Beauman Division's defensive line.

Following a conference of the 3rd Armoured Brigade's officers, 2 RTR was ordered to move from Catenay to the area of Beauvoir, where it was joined by a composite squadron from 5 RTR commanded by Major Winship. Orders were then given to send out five patrols under Captain P.R.C. Hobart, to cover the line between St Fiacre and Saumont-la-Poterie. Until this point, the light tanks and cruiser tanks of the 1st Armoured Division had been able to hold up some of the German motorised units that were penetrating towards Rouen and the Seine Valley. However, the *Heer* now deployed its 5th and 7th Panzer Divisions to attack the point of the junction between the two Corps of French 10th Army.

At 2015 hours, six German AFVs (believed to be the Czech-made Panzer 38(T) tanks from the 7th Panzer Division) were encountered by a patrol from No. 7 (Light) troop comprised of two Vickers Mark VI B light tanks commanded by Second Lieutenant D. Barker and Troop Sergeant Blades.[65] As the only armament fitted to these British tanks was their machine guns, they were no match for the enemy AFVs. In an exchange of fire, Barker's tank was hit, with damage to the turret traversing gear and radio set. Barker, who was later to die from his wounds, was still able to report what had happened and the position. The tank commanded by Sergeant Blades, which had taken up a position in an attempt to shield Barker's tank, received six direct hits and burst into flames but he and Trooper James escaped without injury. In his report, Blades recorded that the tank's driver, Trooper Maggs, continued to drive the burning

64 TNA WO 167/737: 2/7th Duke of Wellington's Regiment War Diary.
65 Bovington Tank Museum Archives: 2nd Royal Tank Regiment.

tank away from the action until the engine gave out.[66] Sergeant Blades and Troopers Jones and Maggs, were unharmed, and were eventually picked up by French forces.[67]

At 1730 hours, a report was received from the Beauman Division concerning a breakthrough of German AFVs in the area Abancourt – Grandvilliers – Formerie –Aumale. At 2000 hours, orders were issued by Major General Evans for all the available tanks of the 3rd Armoured Brigade to take up a position on the line of the River Andelle, from Nolleval to Serqueux; the 2nd Armoured Brigade was ordered to remain in its present position but was put on 15 minutes notice. The 1st Armoured Divisional Headquarters was also relocated to the Forêt de Lyons.[68] At 1945 hours, it was reported that two of the German armoured divisions had broken through between the French 17th and 31st Divisions, on a line south-west towards Formerie and Grandvilliers.[69] According to Brigadier Crocker of the 3rd Armoured Brigade, the 17th French Division never deployed or even attempted to assist in the defence of the River Andelle railway line. As the Germans had crossed the Somme along the whole front, and the French forces were now falling back to the River Seine, it fell solely to the 1st Armoured Division to take what steps it could to cover the withdrawal.

Elsewhere during the day, with the German troops attempting to cross the River Bresle at Eu and Ponts-et-Marais, Sergeant-Major O'Neill of the 6th Royal Scots demonstrated great bravery by manning his post whilst under continuous enemy fire from both machine guns and mortars. He did so in order that he could provide covering fire to a party of Royal Engineers who were struggling to carry out a last-minute demolition of the bridge. In this spirit, he was subsequently able to knock-out a German tank by using an anti-tank rifle, and for these courageous actions he was awarded the Military Medal.

On 7 June, it became necessary to remove the units of the RAF's South Component from north of the River Aisne, some units already having been withdrawn from the advanced landing grounds of the AASF and following negotiation two new aerodromes were then made available to British squadrons by the French authorities.

As the French Army's defence of the Abbeville bridgehead had weakened, a force of 22 Fairey Battles was ordered to fly there to carry out a daylight assault on the German forces lying between Abbeville, the Blangy-sur-Bresle Road and Poix. Although escorted by a flight of Hurricanes from 73 Squadron, and to avoid anti-aircraft fire, the Battles flew into the target area individually and at a height of between 2 and 3,000 feet to drop their bombs and then return to their base. Several of them survived encounters with German fighters but three of the Battles were shot down by the enemy and at least one Messerschmitt Bf 109 was accounted for during the action.

Five Battle bomber sorties were also to have performed operations in the Abbeville, Amiens and St Valery areas, but the eight aircraft detailed for these missions were prevented from doing so due to the *Luftwaffe* having bombed the aerodromes.[70] During the day, other Battle squadrons attacked the enemy's motorised traffic then using the roads from Laon and St Quentin.

66 TNA WO 167/448: 2nd Royal Tank Regiment War Diary.
67 Ibid.
68 TNA WO 167/334: 1st Armoured Division War Diary.
69 TNA WO 167/421: 3rd Armoured Brigade War Diary.
70 TNA AIR 35/192: Summaries of Operations, 10 May -16 June 1940.

A combat report submitted by Flying Officer Hall of the RAF's 73 Squadron recorded that at 1335 hours cover was to be provided by the Squadron's A Flight for French reconnaissance aircraft which were operating between Neufchâtel and Rethel.[71] Hall's report further stated that upon approaching Eperney, and at a height of 15,000 feet, the A Flight encountered a mass of the enemy's aircraft, including bombers and a large number of both Messerschmitt Bf 109 and Bf 110 fighters, and that these were being engaged by Curtis fighters of the French Air Force. A group of five Bf 110s turned towards the RAF Flight, which had dived out of the sun with the leading Hurricane firing a long burst from its machine guns at the enemy. The German aeroplanes then sought refuge in cloud cover. Flight Lieutenant Nicholls, the commander of A Flight, followed a Bf 110 that had attempted to use the evasive tactics of turning sharply but was damaged by the gunfire from Nicholls' Hurricane, with white smoke emerging from the German aircraft as it went into a steep dive.

8 June 1940

On 8 June, the German forces continued their intended advance on the Amiens to Rouen axis, with *Generalleutnant* Hoth's 5th and 7th Panzer Divisions making a strong thrust towards Rouen by attacking Sigy-en-Bray and Forges-Les-Eaux on the upper Andelle. The 7th Panzer Division was advancing towards Sigy-en-Bray, where it would meet opposition from the Beauman Division, but the discovery by some of the advanced German reconnaissance units of two unguarded bridges to the south of this position led to the panzers being disengaged and re-directed to this new bridgehead.

Meantime, the German infantry divisions were waiting for their armoured divisions to envelop the southern flank of the French IX Corps' defensive line. Consequently, IX Corps would be forced into the space between Rouen, Dieppe and Le Havre, and the enemy would be able to succeed in penetrating the British defences positioned between the Rivers Andelle and Béthune, to the west of Forges-Les-Eaux.

The IX Corps, which was comprised of the French 31st and 40th Divisions, was placed under the command of *Général de corps d'armée* Ihler, and it had been ordered to withdraw to a line on the River Béthune. The British 152nd Brigade having been withdrawn into the reserve at Le Havre, units from the 153rd and 154th Brigades of the 51st Division, which was also now under the orders of the French IX Corps, were still holding the line of the River Béthune between Neufchâtel and Dieppe.

The Beauman Division, which was comprised of improvised and poorly equipped infantry brigades and had little in the way of useful artillery support, saw action when its A Brigade held the line of the River Bresle from Gamaches to Eu; its B and C Brigades were in occupation of a secondary line to defend the Béthune – Andelle line along the Rivers Andelle and Béthune between the River Seine and Dieppe.

The Beauman Tank Company was positioned in Les Andelys, which was reported to be in flames following the *Luftwaffe's* air raids there. The latter formation was in the process of being withdrawn through Courcelles-sur-Somme, but its progress was seriously impaired by the large numbers of refugees that were now filling up the roads. A further defensive line had been

71 TNA AIR 50/31/6: Combat report.

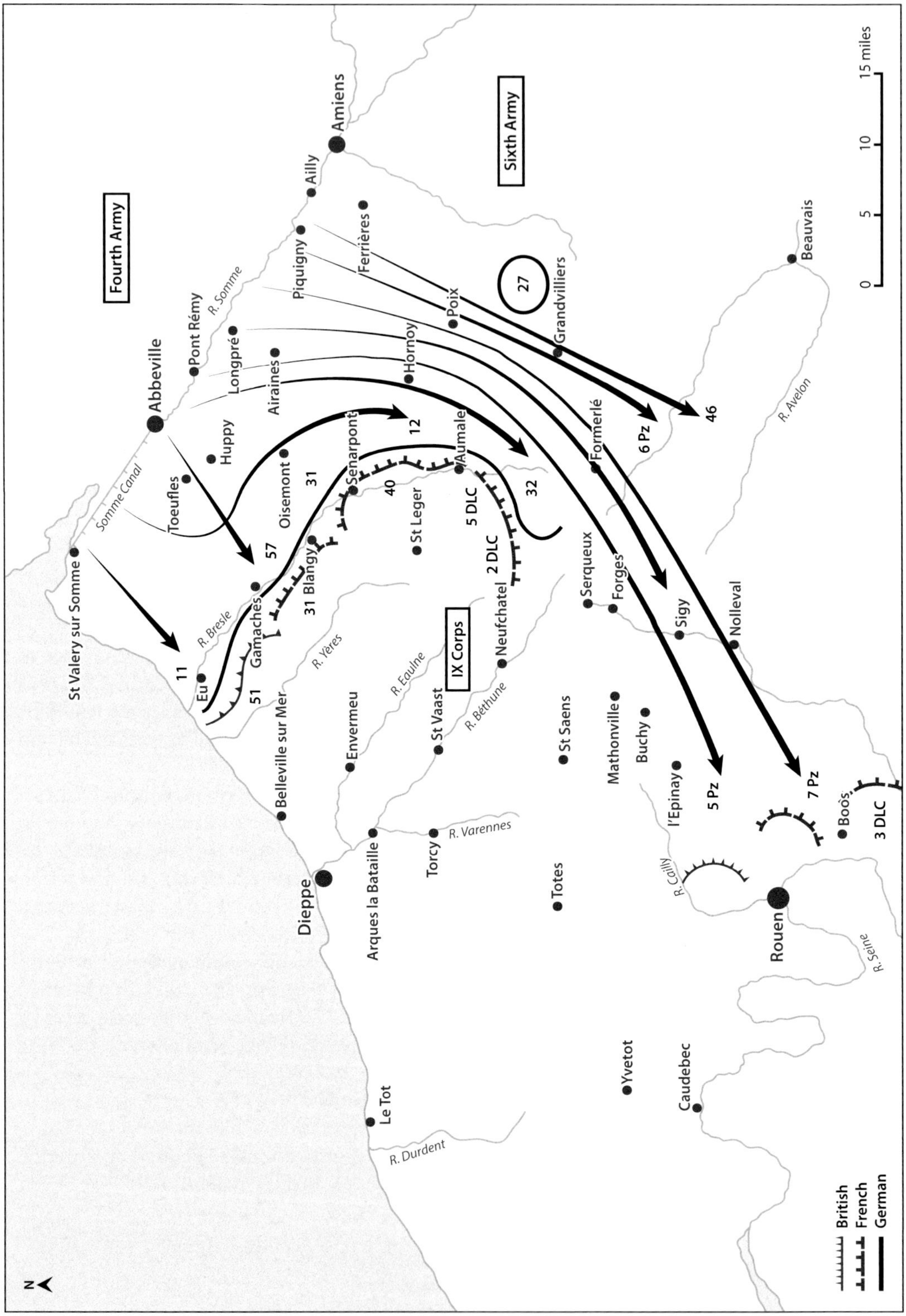
Fourth Army
Sixth Army
IX Corps
Amiens
Abbeville
Dieppe
Rouen
Ailly
Ferrières
Piquigny
Pont Rémy
R. Somme
Longpré
Airaines
Hornoy
Poix
Grandvilliers
27
Beauvais
R. Avelon
Huppy
Toeufles
Somme Canal
St Valery sur Somme
Oisemont
Senarpont
Aumale
Formerlé
12
6 Pz
46
31
40
32
57
St Leger
5 DLC
2 DLC
Blangy
31 Blangy
Gamaches
R. Bresle
11
Eu
51
R. Yères
Serqueux
Forges
Sigy
Nolleval
Neufchatel
R. Eaulne
R. Béthune
Belleville sur Mer
Envermeu
St Vaast
St Saens
Mathonville
Buchy
l'Epinay
5 Pz
7 Pz
Boos
3 DLC
Arques la Bataille
Torcy
R. Varennes
Totes
R. Cailly
R. Seine
Yvetot
Caudebec
Le Tot
R. Durdent
British
French
German
0
5
10
15 miles
N

Rouen

created around Rouen, with the improvised Syme's Battalion defending Isneauville, the 2/4th King's Own Yorkshire Light Infantry (KOYLI) holding the River Seine's Bridges and the 2/6th Duke of Wellington's Regiment defending Boos, to the east of Rouen.[72]

At 0115 hours, 2 RTR was notified that the line of the River Andelle was now being held by a composite infantry battalion together with a composite squadron of the Queen's Bays, and that all of the bridges over the river were to be demolished. Accordingly, 2 RTR was ordered to establish patrols between Sigy-en-Bray and the road and the railway crossing there.[73] This was to counter the German infantry patrols that were being carried out along the river and to impose upon the enemy the maximum conceivable delay. It was subsequently reported that some 30 German tanks, together with units of motorised infantry, had been observed on the eastern side of the Andelle, where heavy bombing and an artillery barrage was in progress. Patrols from the squadron of the Queen's Bays were to report that the enemy tanks had been able to cross the Andelle to the south of 2 RTR's position.[74]

At 0300 hours, Second Lieutenant A. McDonald of the 4th Black Watch had taken out a patrol to mop up any units of German infantry. According to the report made by Captain W.K.N. Guild of the A Company, they opened fire on enemy patrols that had been using the cover of darkness to work their way up the southern side of the Grand Vallee. The actual position of the German troops could not be seen since the exchange of gunfire took place well below the field of view. Second Lieutenant McDonald was wounded and did not return.[75] The enemy broke through on the Battalion's left flank and numbers 7 and 9 platoons were sent there to help with the defence. While taking up these positions, Second Lieutenants D. Innes and Eavy of the Battalion were killed during the action, along with several of the other ranks. After a day of continuous pressure from the enemy, the 4th Black Watch was withdrawn to Arques before being ordered to arrange for a move to Fécamp.

During the afternoon, the 7th Argylls withstood a heavy artillery bombardment before they were shelled out of their positions, with Captain Richie being evacuated after being wounded in the leg. Subsequently, Second Lieutenant Spears, who was sent up by Brigade, collected the 30 men of D Company together with some strays who had reported to Brigade, and returned to assist the remainder of the Battalion, which had now been ordered to move during the hours of darkness to Arques.[76]

Major General Evans's 1st Armoured Division had been split up when it first arrived in France in May and its separate elements had subsequently participated in the offensives against the German bridgeheads to the south of the River Somme. The losses had reduced the remainder of the 2nd and 3rd Armoured Brigades to essentially improvised units that were then used to hold the Andelle line from Nolleval to Serqueux. The armoured composite regiment had remained with the 51st Division, where it was deployed to guard the left flank of the Andelle line. At 0500 hours on 8 June, in a message from 51st Division, the command of the 9th Royal Lancers and the 1st Support Group was reverted to the 1st Armoured Division. The 9th Lancers were then to be diverted to the reserve behind the 3rd Armoured Brigade whilst the 1st

72 P. Takle, *The British Army in France after Dunkirk* (Barnsley: Pen & Sword, 2009), p.95.
73 Bovington Tank Museum Archives: Report on the operations of the 1st Armoured Division in France.
74 TNA WO 167/448: 2nd Royal Tank Regiment War Diary.
75 TNA WO 167/711: 4th Black Watch War Diary.
76 TNA WO 167/704: 7th Argyll & Sutherland Highlanders War Diary.

Support Group was to take up a line to the left of this Brigade, from Serqueux to Neufchâtel. Unfortunately, this message was never received by these units.

Though heavily outnumbered and outgunned by the enemy, a determined rear-guard action against the panzers was still being fought by the 2nd and 3rd Armoured Brigades. With the contraction of this front, the 2nd Armoured Brigade had to retire to a position behind the River Seine so that efforts could be made to repair its damaged tanks. This left the 3rd Armoured Brigade (then consisting of 41 cruiser and 31 light tanks) to fight on and at 1030 hours the enemy had broken through to the north of Serqueux, with forward patrols reporting the sighting of approximately 30 German tanks supported by lorried infantry on the eastern side of the river.[77]

By noon on the following day, British infantry units would have no choice but to retire as their position was untenable because of the advance of the panzer divisions. When engaging the enemy's heavy tanks, it was found that the 2-pounder shells being fired at them by the British cruiser tanks and anti-tank guns had little effect, with one British tank commander reported to have fired 50 shells during the engagement without causing any damage to the enemy vehicles. Possibly this was because the shells were 'plugged' rather than being 'solid shot'.[78] The 3rd Armoured Brigade was ordered to retreat to the line from Vascoeuil to Morgny. Nevertheless, by 1730 hours it was retiring over the River Seine at the Les Andelys Bridge. This was completed by 0100 hours, with the bridges there being demolished later that day.

The 5th Panzer Division had launched an attack in the direction of Rouen, at Isneauville, with intense artillery and air support provided by the *Luftwaffe's* Stuka dive bombers. This force was able to advance from Buchy and initially made its presence felt at around 1300 hours during an engagement with the 4th Provisional (Syme's) Battalion, which had taken up a defensive position behind road blocks, mines and barbed wire on the previous day.[79] Commanded by Lieutenant Colonel A.G. Syme of the Royal Scots, this unit had been hastily improvised during the previous week from the various drafts of reinforcements found at the base reinforcement depot, together with the 2/4th of the KOYLI and the 2/6th Duke of Wellington's Regiment. It was equipped with four 2-pounder anti-tank guns and a machine gun platoon. The 2/4th KOYLI were deployed on a bridge over the River Seine and the 2/6th Dukes were positioned along the railway, south of Boos.

A determined rear-guard action was fought, with 12 German tanks, an aeroplane and a field gun being put out of action, and a considerable number of casualties were inflicted on the enemy's infantry. This continued until 1900 hours when the Syme's Battalion was forced to withdraw and crossed the Seine via one of the main Rouen bridges. Before doing so, however, Syme's men had laid the type of barbed wire known as concertina or dannert wire, and planted land mines in an attempt to prevent the German armoured divisions from reaching Rouen.[80] In this endeavour, the Syme's Battalion effectively delayed the city's capture by twelve hours, thereby allowing thousands of other Allied troops to reach the south bank of the River Seine.

At 1400 hours, the 2/6th Duke of Wellington's Regiment reached Louviers and sought to secure positions at Les Andelys and St-Pierre-du-Vauvray, despite these being 12 miles apart. It was found that the bridges over the Seine were heavily guarded by French troops, with

77 TNA WO 167/448: 2nd Royal Tank Regiment War Diary.
78 TNA WO 167/419: 2nd Armoured Brigade War Diary.
79 TNA WO 167/1412: Beauman Division, Headquarters.
80 TNA WO 167/334: 1st Armoured Division War Diary.

anti-tank guns sited on the north and south banks. A reconnaissance party was despatched to Les Andelys, which it was found had been bombed by the *Luftwaffe*, and due to the bridge there now being blocked, it was necessary for the Battalion to proceed another nine miles further to the Gaillon bridge, and this was duly crossed. The A and B companies of the Battalion were deployed, whilst C and D companies were sent to Hedebrauville. Progress was unavoidably slow due to the large area covered by the troops, and it was soon realised that this made it difficult to guard against enemy infiltrations and, accordingly, patrols were sent out and sentries posted.[81] This problem was exacerbated during the day as contradictory orders were received from the various French commanders.

Nevertheless, the Battalion held firm on this broad front until it was eventually forced to retire, just as all the French troops in the vicinity had done previously. At 2100 hours, the French commander of the Les Andelys to Gaillon area requested help from 2 RTR. Accordingly, Captain Carey-Thomas set out for the bridge at Gaillon with two A13 Cruiser tanks and a Daimler Dingo scout car, whilst a troop from 5 RTR made for the bridge at Les Andelys. On the following morning, Captain Carey-Thomas reported that four enemy tanks, two mortar positions and an unknown number of men had been killed or wounded during the action at Gaillon. Due to depleted ammunition and fuel, 2 RTR had rallied at Canappeville.[82]

During the day, Forges and Neufchâtel were both captured by German troops. At the latter place, a number of French AFVs had approached the British position, which had been told to expect them. As the vehicles had their turret hatches open and were flying the Allied recognition signal, they were allowed to pass. However, it transpired that these vehicles had been captured and commandeered by the Germans because as soon as they had passed through the defensive perimeter, their crews traversed the turrets of the tanks and opened fire on the British troops. These vehicles had preceded some German tanks, which then made their way through the British defences by following the path established for them by these captured French tanks.[83]

Similarly, at Serqueux, a column of what had appeared to be French tanks was allowed through the British road blocks only for the defenders to find to their immediate cost that these vehicles had also been captured by the enemy and were being crewed by German troops.[84] As the main force from the 5th Panzer Division made a frontal assault on the village, these captured tanks then continued to attack the defences from the rear. Initially they were driven back but then counter-attacked, and this deception led to the capture of Serqueux by the enemy.

By now 51st Division was cut off from what should have been its proper line of retirement. This failure can be attributed in the main to the inability of the French Army's High Command to carry out the orderly withdrawal of the left wing of its forces whilst there was still sufficient time for this to be achieved. *Général d'armée* Weygand had ordered the French IX Corps to retreat to Les Andelys and to Rouen, but by now parts of this Corps were beginning to fall into German captivity. The IX Corps Commander, *Général de corps d'armée* Ihler, received the orders due to problems communicating with *Général d'armée* Altmayer's 10th Army headquarters. According to Lieutenant General Marshall-Cornwall, who that day had been forced to follow the 10th Army on account of its headquarters having been evacuated without the courtesy of

81 TNA WO 167/736: 2/6th Duke of Wellington's Regiment War Diary.
82 TNA WO 167/448: 2nd Royal Tank Regiment War Diary.
83 M. Glover, *The fight for the Channel ports: Calais to Brest 1940*, p.161.
84 TNA WO 167/1412: Beauman Division, Headquarters.

telling him, Altmayer had broken down and was incapable of commanding his forces with confidence.[85] Whilst there was a proposed programme for retirement, in which Rouen was to be reached within four days; unfortunately, this was superfluous given that the forces of the *Heer* were now a mere four hours away from capturing the city.

That night, the German armoured divisions had penetrated as far as Rouen whilst the French 10th Army could not communicate with the French IX Corps in the Rouen-Dieppe cul-de-sac. As Lieutenant General Marshall-Cornwall later commented in his contribution to Lieutenant General Brooke's post-war account of the campaign, 'it was becoming clear that the French High Command was issuing "die in the last ditch" orders, which their troops had no intention of carrying out'. He added that from this time onwards, and until the BEF's final evacuation, it became increasingly obvious that the spirit of the French armed forces was crushed and that its troops had very little intention of offering any serious resistance to the enemy's forces.[86]

According to the RAF's Summaries of Operations report, a number of reconnaissance sorties were carried out on 8 June, either by Bristol Blenheims or Hawker Hurricanes.[87] With evidence from this aerial reconnaissance of an imminent German attack over the River Aisne to the east of Paris, on the night of 7 to 8 June, in view of the number of tanks and trucks being reported there, a force of eight Fairey Battles was despatched to attack the Laon to Soissons Road. This mission was supported by Hurricane fighters from 17 and 242 Squadrons, which had arrived from Britain that day, and were now becoming heavily involved in operations.

At 1330 hours, the German Army's motorised columns at Abbeville, Longpré, Poix and Aumale were attacked by twelve Fairey Battles that were escorted by seven Hurricanes. Three of the Battles were reported to have been shot down. Later, at 1530 hours, eleven unescorted Battles attacked more columns of German AFVs and mechanised transport, which was estimated to be five miles long. One of the Battles was lost in action during this mission. Returning from this mission, another of the Battles encountered a flight of Junkers Ju 87 Stuka dive bombers and was able to attack and damage one of them with a burst from the aircraft's wing-mounted forward machine gun before the German fighter escorts could intervene. Another of the Battles engaged a Junkers Ju 88 twin engine medium bomber on the same day.

Twelve sorties of British Hurricane fighters flew over the River Seine and later 19 sorties were in evidence over the area that was now being held by the 51st Division, although they encountered no enemy aircraft there. However, at 1335 hours, seven Hawker Hurricanes from 501 Squadron were involved in a large dog fight with up to 80 Messerschmitt Bf 109 fighters, when they were flying approximately 10 miles to the south-east of Abbeville. In the subsequent combat report, it is noted that five of the enemy's aircraft were claimed to have been shot down and two of the RAF machines were recorded as being missing in action.[88]

85 S. David, *Churchill's Sacrifice of the Highland Division, France 1940*, p.191.
86 *The London Gazette*, 22 May 1946, p.2438.
87 TNA AIR 35/192: Summaries of Operations 10 May - 16 June 1940.
88 TNA AIR 35/253: AASF Combat Reports.

9 June 1940

The Paris Correspondent of the *Manchester Guardian* wrote on 9 June that 'France is living through hours of bitter anguish. That the situation is now of extreme gravity is not denied'.[89] It was felt that until 7 June, the outlook had seemed fairly promising. Since then, the Allied left flank had fallen back from the lower Somme at Abbeville and the right flank was being pushed back hard to the Aisne, and a mechanised force of 300-400 German tanks followed up by infantry had pierced the new French line.

During the morning of 9 June, the German armour finally reached Rouen, where its entry was now unopposed, as the British and French troops had departed, but not before demolishing the bridges over the River Seine.[90] The 7th Panzer Division journeyed through the night to seize the bridge at Elbeuf, which was weakly held by the French Army, and the German tanks were met with no opposition there.

At several locations the enemy established more bridgeheads, which were crossed at midday via the pontoon bridges that were set up at Pont de l'Arche and at St Pierre-du-Vauvray. As the forces of the *Heer* undertook this crossing, they effectively cut off from the main body of the Allied forces the French IX Corps and the 51st Division, both of which were north of the river, forcing them into what would be a fierce rear-guard action as they fell back to St Valery-en-Caux. The 153rd Brigade was now holding the ridge on the other side of the Béthune to the south-east, whilst the 154th Brigade was ordered to hold the line from Fécamp to Bolbec in conjunction with French troops already in position there in order to cover the withdrawal of the remainder of the 51st Division. At the same time, the German armoured and mechanised divisions raced north in an attempt to intercept them.

The French IX Corps began to retire when the German AFVs turned towards the north but were cut off from the X Corps to the east and from the River Seine to the south. In the afternoon, enemy tanks were reported to be 6 miles from 51st Divisional headquarters, the 7th Panzer Division having advanced from Rouen, via Yvetot to Cany-Barville and Veulettes-sur-Mer on the River Durdent. The French 10th Army headquarters had lost contact with the IX Corps and the 51st Division had lost contact with everyone else until a despatch rider from Le Havre arrived with a message, which was that the Port Admiral there reported that the enemy had reached Rouen.

Having arrived at Les Andelys during the previous evening, and then being ordered to take up defensive positions at Pont de l'Arche on both sides of the River Seine, at 0300 hours, the C and D Companies of the 2/4th KOYLI were attacked by panzers and mechanised infantry, and at 0600 hours the bridge was destroyed and those British troops that had been in the forward positions were required to withdraw by swimming back across the River Seine. Shortly after this, both Companies were ordered to withdraw to Bernay. They did so in small parties, collecting any stragglers they could, and whilst under heavy fire from the enemy before they could concentrate in the woods at St Quentin des Iles. Of the casualties and fatalities that were inflicted on the Battalion that day, Captain the Viscount Gormanston and Second Lieutenant P.M. Lambeth were both reported missing, believed to have been killed in action.[91]

89 *Manchester Guardian*, 10 June 1940.
90 L.F. Ellis, *The War in France and Flanders 1939-40*, p.283.
91 TNA WO 167/777: 2/4th KOYLI War Diary.

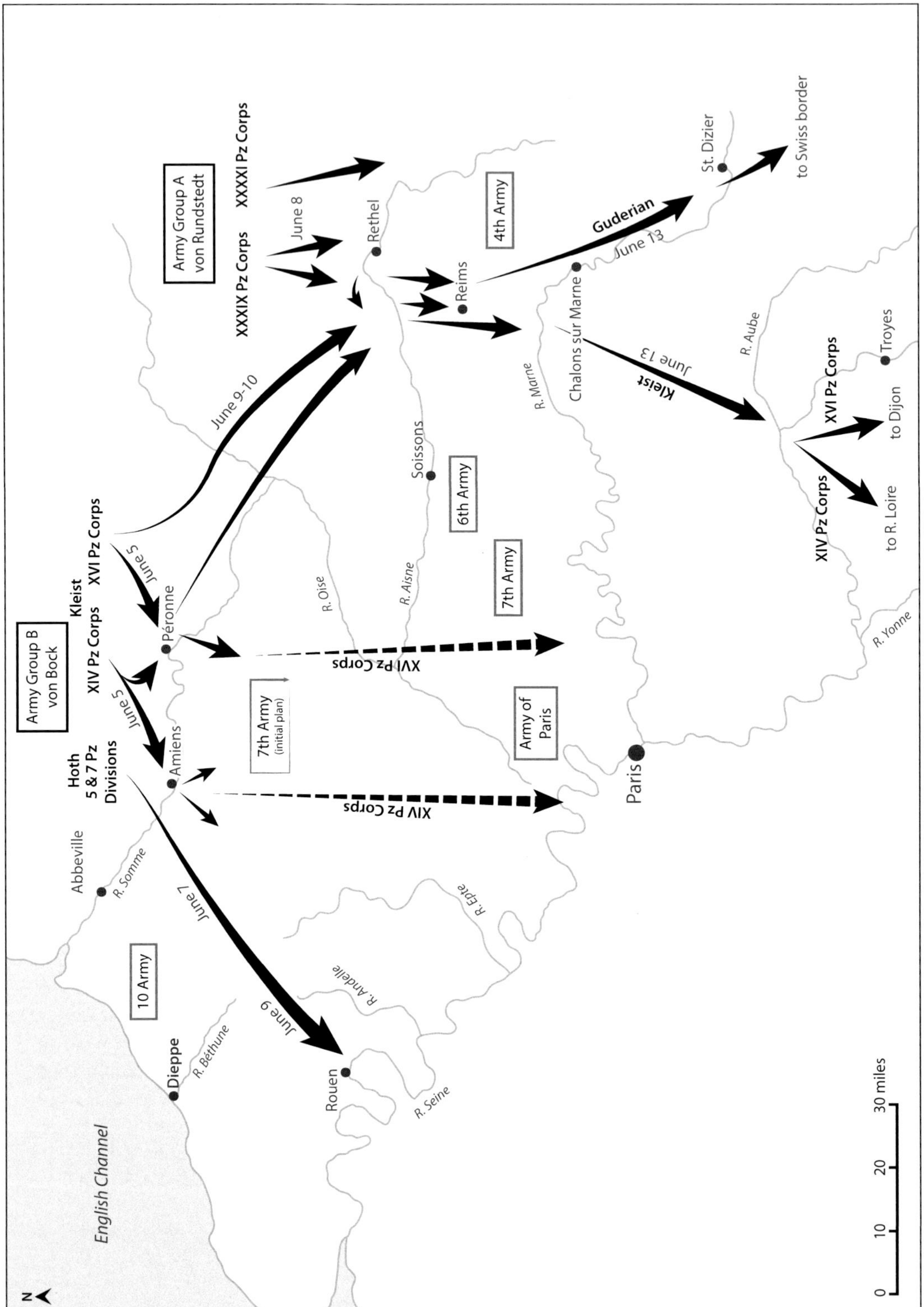
Army Group A
von Rundstedt
XXXXI Pz Corps
XXXIX Pz Corps
June 8
Rethel
4th Army
Reims
Guderian
June 13
St. Dizier
to Swiss border
Chalons sur Marne
Kleist
R. Marne
R. Aube
Troyes
XVI Pz Corps
to Dijon
XIV Pz Corps
to R. Loire
June 9-10
Soissons
6th Army
7th Army
R. Aisne
R. Oise
R. Yonne
Army Group B
von Bock
Kleist
XIV Pz Corps
XVI Pz Corps
June 5
Péronne
XVI Pz Corps
7th Army
(initial plan)
Army of
Paris
Paris
Amiens
Hoth
5 & 7 Pz
Divisions
XIV Pz Corps
Abbeville
R. Somme
June 7
R. Epte
10 Army
R. Andelle
June 9
Dieppe
R. Béthune
Rouen
R. Seine
English Channel
N
0
10
20
30 miles

Drive south

At 0530 hours, the Information Officer of the 2/6th Duke of Wellington's Regiment, Lieutenant P.S. Cooper, contacted the 51st Divisional headquarters, which was now at La Valler, to inform them of the Battalion's dispositions. He also made an urgent request for additional transport and maps of the vicinity to be provided but was informed that none were available. When asking which troops were on the Battalion's left and right flanks, Cooper was shown a message confirming that it was the 2/4th KOYLI, which was heavily engaged by enemy's tanks at Pont de l'Arche.

It was reported later that German tanks had reached the Les Andelys Bridge and had opened fire on the British and French positions there, with action against them taking place at various locations on the River Seine. At 1100 hours, a message was despatched, which was that the 2/6th Duke of Wellington's Regiment should remain in position and operate under French orders. The bridge at Les Andelys was blown up, after which the Allied positions received a barrage of enemy mortar and machine gun fire originating from the high positions on the other side of the river bank. The B Company of the 2/6th Dukes and other French units were forced from their positions and had to relocate to Bernières-sur-Seine, astride the main road to cover the withdrawal of the other companies as they retired from their positions.[92]

In the early afternoon, with the enemy now crossing over the river at several points by making use of the readily available small boats, it was reported that the French troops had retreated, with the exception of one officer and six other ranks who had dug in and continued to fight on. The 2/6th Duke of Wellington's Regiment were ordered to take up new positions on the neck of the peninsula of the river, on the high ground forward of the village of Venables, with B Company to the right and A Company to the left, on a three-and-a-half-kilometre front. C Company was by now at St-Pierre-du-Vauvray, where it had come under heavy artillery and machine gun fire, but it was still holding its position there.[93] The bridge at St Pierre was kept open but, at around 1130 hours, three German light tanks had appeared in its vicinity. They were vulnerable to small arms fire because their hatches had not been fully closed down and a number of casualties were inflicted upon the panzer crews, including on their commanding officer who had dismounted from his vehicle.[94]

The 2/6th Dukes Battalion war diary reported that a conference was held at the Chateau du Hazey. During this, *Général de brigade* Marie-Michel-Gustave-Louis Maillard explained that he was only concerned with his own (the Les Andelys) sector, although this actually cut right through the centre of the front that was held by the 2/6th Dukes, and that a new line would be taken up on the railway that crossed the neck of the peninsula in front of Venables and Grandvilliers. It was agreed that the right of this position would be defended by D Company of the 2/6th Dukes, the centre by units of the French Army, and the left side by A and B Companies of the 2/6th Dukes. The officer commanding D Company sought to reconnoitre by taking his company forward to occupy the position at Grandvilliers.[95] These orders were never carried out, however, because the enemy had by this time appeared in considerable strength in front of Venables and the men of D Company were either wounded, as was their officer Captain R.S. Stell, or they had been killed in action. The A and B companies were by this time pinned

92 TNA WO 167/736: 2/6th Duke of Wellington's Regiment War Diary.
93 Ibid.
94 TNA WO 167/419: 2nd Armoured Brigade War Diary.
95 TNA WO 167/736: 2/6th Duke of Wellington's Regiment War Diary.

down in a battle with the German infantry whose attack was being supported by light artillery and trench mortar units. In the meantime, the French were attempting to reinforce the front with a composite force of infantry and dismounted cavalry that they had been holding in reserve.

The battle for Venables lasted until nightfall, with the British troops doing all that they could to prevent the German infantry from breaking through. C Company of the 2/6th Dukes was heavily engaged with the enemy at Pont St-Pierre-du-Vauvray and held its ground despite the attempted infiltration of its northern flank. During the night, the river front was patrolled along its extent from St-Pierre-du-Vauvray to Venables but it was impossible for it to be covered comprehensively and it transpired that the river was crossed by numerous German machine gun detachments at many points during the night.[96] French artillery came into action and bombarded the enemy, and the river crossings that were still being made, with an intense fire but which was responded to in kind by the German artillery. Even though they had been considered to be merely a labour battalion, on 9 June the 2/6th Dukes fought with tenacity, courage and in a manner that was deserving of the utmost credit.

The 3rd Armoured Brigade and Beauman Division units had been withdrawn in an attempt to re-organise, with the latter moving to take up a tactical position on high ground on the road west of Gaillon, and from which they would be able to withdraw in the direction of Évreux. As they crossed the River Seine at Courcelles-sur-Seine, they found the road leading to the bridge to be badly blocked with refugees and their carts, cars and other transport. The French troops on the bridge refused to give any help but, with the assistance of a French liaison officer, progress was completed after an hour and a half.[97] Later, a column of enemy AFVs was observed to be approaching the bridge from the north and a German armoured car attempted to cross the bridge. This prompted the French troops to fire at it and to blow up the bridge. In a report from Captain Carey-Thomas of 2 RTR, it was pointed out that his patrol had engaged with and destroyed two enemy light tanks and four medium tanks and had silenced the mortar detachments of the accompanying German infantry.[98]

Meantime, the 2nd Armoured Brigade (which was in the course of re-fitting at Louviers) received orders to provide support to the French III Corps commanded by *Général de corps d'armée* Benoît-Léon de la Laurencie, and which was still trying to hold the Seine to the south of Rouen. At 1000 hours, this French commander had arrived at the Divisional headquarters of Major General Evans and asked him to place himself under the orders of III Corps, to assist in the defence of the River Seine. Evans agreed to this, with the 3rd Armoured Brigade being allocated to the defence of a number of the bridges, including Pont de l'Arche, where they would be at the disposal of *Général de division* Robert Petiet, the commander of the 3rd DLC, who was to take charge of the sector from Les Andelys to Elbeuf. Evans reported that the maximum forces that could be disposed were three or four troops from the 2nd and 3rd Armoured Brigades and two quickly improvised lorried squadrons, which would comprise the dismounted crews of damaged tanks and who would be armed with rifles so that they could function as infantry and carry out patrols of the river bank. Hence, it was agreed that the 2nd Armoured Brigade would assist with whatever resources it had, which included the two motorised transport squadrons of the Queen's Bays and the 10th Royal Hussars, and these units remained on the Seine until they

96 Ibid.
97 TNA WO 167/421: 3rd Armoured Brigade War Diary.
98 Bovington Tank Museum Archives: 2nd Royal Tank Regiment.

were relieved by French infantry. During the day, it was responsible for knocking out four of the enemy tanks at the bridge at Gaillon.[99] At 1800 hours, the Beauman Division's Tank Company investigated a report that four German AFVs had been seen in the vicinity of Venables and Villers-sur-le-Roule.[100] Following a later discussion with Lieutenant Generals Karslake and Marshall-Cornwall;, Major General Evans took the decision that those non-effective elements of the 1st Armoured Division should be withdrawn to Le Mans.

According to the *Manchester Guardian*, 'One battalion famous in every corner of the Empire was ordered to retire in a few hours. It decided to spend those hours in launching violent attacks on the Germans. So bitter was the fighting that both sides had an informal truce to bring in the dead and wounded'. It added that this was 'typical of the magnificent courage of this British force who have carried out a feat which, when it can be fully told, will becomes as historic as the withdrawal from Flanders'.[101] The exploits of two battalions received further attention. One had counter-attacked and retaken a village that had been occupied by panzers and infantry; the other battalion, which was equipped with anti-tank guns, had been attacked by *Luftwaffe* dive bombers but delayed the German advance by knocking out three German tanks and had held up their infantry by intense rifle and machine gun fire. By these actions, the withdrawal of other units was permitted.

On 9 June, two officers of the Royal Navy had come ashore and sought out Major General Fortune to advise him that arrangements could be made to support his Division from the sea. More importantly, they informed him that it would no longer be possible to embark British troops from Dieppe as the entrance to the port had been mined and block ships placed there as an impediment. In view of this news, Fortune made the proposal that the IX Corps should retire to Le Havre and *Général de corps d'armée* Ihler agreed with this. It was decided that two brigades of the 51st Division, namely the 154th Brigade and the A Brigade of the Beauman Division, should be deployed as an advance party to secure the route for the remainder of the Division's troops before occupying a defensive position for the Le Havre peninsula.

On the night of 9/10 June, the 51st Division made arrangements for the bridges across the Arques and the Eaulne, which the Germans had been attacking, to be demolished. The 4th Seaforths and the 1st Black Watch had held on, despite attacks at Arques la Bataille and Martigny, using artillery to defeat several of the attempted German incursions. The remainder of the 51st Division and the French IX Corps made preparations to retreat after darkness had fallen but a reconnaissance by the 1st Lothians discovered that there were German troops on the river crossings at Veulettes-sur-Mer.

By the close of the day, at the River Bresle the 51st Division, with the French IX Corps on its right, had now been cut off from the remainder of the French 10th Army. The 2/4th KOYLI was at Pont de l'Arche, the 2/6th Duke of Wellington's Regiment was further east and the Beauman Division was on the Risle. The 7th Panzer Division was heading at speed for the Coast with the aim of cutting off the British and French from Le Havre, and the 5th Panzer Division was consolidating its position at Rouen. At 2204 hours, the 51st Division transmitted a signal affirming that should the enemy break through the French lines, Major General Fortune would

99 TNA WO 167/334: 1st Armoured Division War Diary; TNA WO 32/9388: Overseas, Europe (Code O (V)), Despatches from BEF 12-19 June 1940.
100 TNA WO 167/1417: Beauman Division, Tank Company War Diary.
101 *Manchester Guardian*, 11 June 1940.

have to order his brigades to pivot on the northern part and attempt to evacuate his troops from behind a bridgehead. This was the first indication that an evacuation on a large scale might now be necessary, taking place from a north coast port other than Le Havre.

In terms of aerial combat, on the night of 8 to 9 June, several sorties were flown by the Fairey Battle squadrons, with bombs being dropped on the crossings of the River Somme at Amiens and Abbeville, and the forests at Laon, north of the River Aisne, as the German forces were believed to be using these areas for cover. On 9 June, the RAF's planned aerial attack on the German columns reported to be near to Argueil had to be cancelled. This was due to the Hurricanes, which were to provide a fighter escort for the mission, being required in the attempt to give what protection they could to the 51st Division.

It was reported by the British Air Ministry's news service that during the night of 9 to 10 June, British bombers had ranged from the mouth of the River Somme to Flushing in the north, Mezieres in the south and throughout the industrial areas of the Ruhr. Flying over the woodlands, they had dropped in excess of 6,000 incendiary bombs. One aircraft had to be abandoned as a consequence of engine trouble, but its crew had descended by parachute. Ten of the Battles attacked the bridges and roads at Abbeville and Amiens, whilst nine aircraft dropped incendiary bombs on the Forêt de St Gobain to the north-west to flush out the German forces at Laon that were believed to be using the wood for cover. Despite the rather hazy weather conditions, the industrial areas and key railway centres of the Ruhr were also attacked.[102]

Due to the speed of the enemy's advance, the AASF squadrons had very little choice but to relocate to bases in the Loire basin, with operational control still being directed from Troyes. From mid-May to approximately 10 June, the conduct of bomber missions against the well-armed ground forces of the *Heer* and a *Luftwaffe* that had easily achieved air superiority proved to be very costly when carried out during daytime and at low or medium altitude. In order to continue operations whilst minimising aircraft losses and casualties, a change to night-time operations was necessitated. Fighters continued to escort bombers on their missions, and the number of individual combats reduced when compared to the earlier weeks in May.[103]

In relation to the consequences of the first days of the *Fall Rot*, the German offensive launched on 5 June was in stark contrast to the Allied assault of the 4 June that had failed to make any discernible impact on the Abbeville bridgehead. With the troops and resources at his disposal, namely overstretched battalions and a limited number of tanks and artillery and negligible air support, Fortune was unable to defend all of the gaps in a line that was too long. In a request for air support, he stated 'Forgive me for being vindictive but I do not want to see the 51st destroyed and useless for the future, which it will be at the present rate. I am quite willing to ask them for a good deal, but I do not think they have been asked for too much'.[104] Not only the men of the 51st Division but of all the other BEF formations were now increasingly short of ammunition, food and sleep, and were daily subjected to sheer physical and mental exhaustion during what was a traumatic time of confusion and growing desperation.

102 *The Times*, 11 June 1940.
103 TNA AIR 35/255: Report on the AASF in France, September 1939 - June 1940.
104 TNA PREM 3/188/5: Despatches on operations of British Expeditionary Force, September 1939-June 1940.

Part II

Operation Cycle: 10 to 13 June 1940

4

An Increasingly Desperate Situation

10 June 1940

Summarising the previous day's communiques, the *Manchester Guardian* reported that from the sea to the River Oise, the enemy had heightened the pressure between the road from Amiens to Rouen and from Amiens to Vernon, reaching the lower Seine at certain points. To the east of the Oise, German columns had resumed the fighting that had occurred there during the previous day, just as they had done in Champagne with new divisions that were being supported by tank units and air support.[1]

At dawn, C Company of the 2/6th Duke of Wellington's Regiment was being outflanked on both sides by German infantry units that were equipped with light machine guns and trench mortars, and which had support from artillery. With no assistance from the French Army, C Company was forced to fight a rear-guard action and return to a position on the main St-Pierre-du-Vauvray to Gaillon Road, where its attempts to join with its Battalion headquarters were met with more enemy machine gun fire. The A, B and D Companies were holding their front against mounting pressure and the situation was becoming increasingly serious with the Battalion also being outflanked. The Battalion Commander had applied to *Général de brigade* Maillard for reinforcements but was informed that none were available and that he should apply to Colonel Watteau (north of Louviers) for assistance or permission to withdraw. The Battalion's War Diary remarks that this was a strange tactic given that the French were also being outflanked.[2] However, by good fortune a British tank commander was also contacted and promised to do all that he could to assist them, with a detachment of tanks being placed on the 2/6th Headquarters Company's northern flank. This was to have a delaying effect on the enemy.

Fighting continued throughout the morning, with the northern flank receiving an attack from detachments of German infantry. These were beaten back by the heavy rifle and machine gun fire from the Bren guns of D Company of the 2/6th Dukes, aided by two of the light tanks. Nevertheless, D Company was outflanked by the enemy's AFVs, two of which had broken through the French position and then appeared at the rear of the British troops and, in

1 *Manchester Guardian*, 11 June 1940.
2 TNA WO 167/736: 2/6th Duke of Wellington's Regiment War Diary.

conjunction with the strafing being carried out by low flying *Luftwaffe* aircraft, this inflicted many casualties. At 1400 hours, the British and French forces were compelled to fall back to Heudebouville, on the left flank of the Heudebouville to Gaillon Road. The A, B and D Companies were withdrawn, with D Company then moving to Ailly. A message was forwarded to the 10th Royal Hussars at Louviers seeking assistance for the Heudebouville position, and the nine tanks that were sent remained in action there until the last.[3] Due to the continued German advance, the British troops were ordered to proceed and to join their comrades to the west of the River Eure, via Acquigny. The remnants of the Beauman Division were also required to withdraw via Neuberg to Bernay, where it was intended that they should join up with the 2/6th Dukes men at 1640 hours.

According to the 2/7th Duke of Wellington's Regiment's War Diary, during the early hours of 10 June the bridges on the front being held by the 152nd Brigade were demolished. A platoon 25 men from the Kensington Rifles also came under the Battalion's command now. Later, enemy patrols were observed at 1400 hours and refugees passing through the lines informed the British units that some of the German AFVs were in Neuville. An attack commenced at around 1800 hours, to the right of the 2/7th Dukes position, where the enemy was using mortars and its infantry came into view through the wood. This lasted until nightfall, when the British troops were withdrawn to a position in Petit Appeville, which was to the southwest of Dieppe.[4]

At 0530 hours, there were reports that the enemy's tanks and motorised infantry had turned north from Totes and towards Dieppe. This part of the line was presumed to be held by the French IX Corps. Further reports also confirmed that the panzers were now only six miles away from the 51st Division's headquarters situated at La Chaussée and, therefore, orders were given for the available 2-pounder anti-tank guns to be placed at key points on the roads.[5] It was later established that the enemy had crossed the River Seine by means of the bridges to the north of St Pierre, at Les Andelys and Vernon, and subsequently they were already forming new bridgeheads at Louviers and Venables.

Early that morning, the 1st Armoured Division received further requests for assistance from *Général de division* Petiet, the commanding officer of the 3rd DLC. As a result, all of the battle-worthy tanks of the 2nd Armoured Brigade were placed under his command, together with the parties of lorried troops, although those located in Louviers were to remain there until they were relieved by the French infantry.[6] By 0700 hours, German forces appeared to be established on the high ground just to the east of Louviers and they were attempting to enlarge the bridgehead to the south, thereby threatening a battalion of the Beauman Division that was located at Heudebouville. Brigadier McCreery ordered that the 10th Royal Hussars should hold the bridges on the north-eastern and eastern outskirts of Louviers, to provide cover for the withdrawal of the 2/6th Dukes, and that the tanks of the 9th Royal Lancers should be moved up to hold a position on the River Eure.[7]

The mechanical condition of the 3rd Armoured Brigade had by this time become very serious indeed. This was due to the tanks that participated in the operations which had taken place to

3 Ibid.
4 TNA WO 167/737: 2/7th Duke of Wellington's Regiment War Diary.
5 TNA WO 167/314: 51st Division War Diary.
6 TNA WO 167/334: 1st Armoured Division War Diary.
7 TNA WO 167/419: 2nd Armoured Brigade War Diary.

the north of the River Seine over the past three days being in pressing need of maintenance. This left 19 light tanks and 16 cruiser tanks that were fit for duty. A report in its War Diary stated that 2 RTR had, including tanks that were not battle worthy, only 11 cruiser tanks (two A9 models fitted with mortars, one A10 and eight A13), eight light tanks and ten Dingo scout cars; whilst 5 RTR had seven cruiser tanks (two A9 models, one with a gun and the other a mortar, five A13), seven light tanks and nine Dingo scout cars; and the Headquarters Battalion had three A10 cruiser tanks, three light tanks and eight Dingo scout cars.[8]

At 1300 hours, a column of three AFVs from the Beauman Division's tank company moved off towards Venables, but upon their approach they came under fire from what were well-concealed German anti-tank guns and machine guns that were located in the woods to the left- and right-hand sides of this village. The War Diary records that Captain Colan's tank received a direct hit on its turret from the left flank but no damage was done to the vehicle or to its crew. Accordingly, his tank engaged the enemy position on the left flank and swung round to get under cover when the road ran through a shallow cutting, but the vehicle received a further hit that damaged the tracks and prompted the crew to abandon it. Intensive fire from Sergeant Locke's tank resulted in a cessation of fire by the enemy. Captain Colan's abandoned vehicle was further immobilised, so as not to be used by the enemy, by being blown up by the 2-pounder shell fired at it by the tank of CSM Hair. The two remaining tanks withdrew and came under machine gunfire again after travelling for half a mile.

At 1900 hours, Brigadier McCreery, the commander of 2nd Armoured Brigade, met with *Général de division* Petiet and made representations that it was quite clear that unless fresh French units were to be made available on a large scale to counter-attack the enemy, it would be impossible for the Allies to regain the line of the River Seine. McCreery confirmed that he did not wish to commit the motorised troops from the Queen's Bays and the 10th Royal Hussars as infantry because, with such small numbers, they could in no way influence the general situation. Furthermore, as several of these men were tank drivers, they could undoubtedly be deployed more effectively elsewhere. Therefore, at 2200 hours he ordered the squadrons to be withdrawn from Louviers and the woods south of Pont de l'Arche to the rear echelon area near to Romilly.[9] Furthermore, the Brigade's War Diary recounted that whilst this order was carried out, Petiet had only agreed to it with considerable reluctance, and because a measure of support remained for the French from the five A13 Cruiser IV tanks, two light tanks and a Daimler Dingo scout car of the Queen's Bays and one A13 Cruiser IV tank, seven light tanks and three Dingo scout cars of the 9th Royal Lancers.

At 2000 hours, a liaison officer from the 2nd Armoured Brigade arrived at the headquarters of the 1st Armoured Division with a message intended for Major General Evans from Brigadier McCreery. This reported that the enemy had strengthened the bridgeheads in the St-Pierre-du-Vauvray and Les Andelys areas and, furthermore, that the promised support of French troops had not materialised. Therefore, under the circumstances, he was withdrawing those of his men who were performing the role of infantry, whilst leaving the 15 tanks (from the Queen's Bays and the 9th Royal Lancers) until the next morning, when he intended to withdraw them unless he received orders to the contrary. Major General Evans responded that he realised the military

8 TNA WO 167/421: 3rd Armoured Brigade War Diary.
9 TNA WO 167/419: 2nd Armoured Brigade War Diary.

ineffectiveness of remaining but the situation demanded the presence in the forward area of some British troops, and this had been impressed upon him by Lieutenant General Marshall-Cornwall. Hence, whilst endorsing the withdrawal of the lorried troops, Evans ordered that the Armoured Division's tanks should remain where they were and continue to be in support of the forces of *Général de division* Petiet, and that they should only withdraw when forced to do so.[10]

However, by the close of 10 June, so utterly depleted was the 1st Armoured Division that it had almost ceased to exist as a recognisable fighting force and it had to withdraw to a position near to Neubourg. The 10th Royal Hussars, which by now had only two serviceable tanks and four troops of dismounted men acting as improvised infantry and who were transported in lorries, moved to the area around Louviers. Although in reality it was now scarcely more than a composite squadron, 2 RTR reached Alençon with the remainder of the 3rd Armoured Brigade.

On the night of 9 to 10 June, the BAFF's advanced operational headquarters was moved from Coulommiere to Orléans. This was because an urgent new requirement had arisen, which was for air bases to be clear of the enemy's rapid advances, and two aerodromes in the neighbourhood of Caen were made available to the RAF by the French authorities. It became possible, therefore, for the AASF's headquarters to also move to a new location at Muidee, near Blois on the Lore, so the fighter and the bomber squadrons could be operated from the Loire basin. Simultaneous to this was the need for yet more fighter cover to be provided to support both the evacuation being carried out at Le Havre and the 51st Division's situation at St Valery-en-Caux. However, it was the advance of the enemy into the region of Soissons that made it necessary to evacuate the advanced refuelling facilities at Champagne on 12 June.[11]

That morning, four of the RAF's Bristol Blenheims had performed reconnaissance flights to take photographs of the bridges crossing the River Seine. This was in advance of a mission in which twelve Fairey Battles were to be despatched to attack the large concentrations of enemy columns approaching the bridge at Vernon.[12] The attack involved these aircraft both machine gunning and dive-bombing the German columns, and also the bombing of the bridge itself. Due to the concentrated anti-aircraft fire originating from the enemy's positions on the north bank of the Seine, one of the Battles was shot down. Another plane sustained damage during the operation, although this was believed to have been accidentally caused by one of Hawker Hurricanes that was flying as an escort. A further attack on the German motorised columns at Vernon and, further to the south, on the bridge over the Seine at Pont-Saint-Pierre, was carried out later in the day by a flight of twelve of the Battles. During the hours of darkness, fifteen of the Battles returned to these targets, while seven carried out attacks on the enemy's crossing points over the River Meuse.

According to the RAF's Summaries of Operations, there were seven fighter aircraft patrols during the day but with few of the enemy's aircraft being encountered. All of the Fairey Battles involved in the missions carried out on 10 June survived in spite of the Hurricanes that were to have been on escort duty having been directed to Le Havre in order to cover the naval evacuation that was being carried out there.

10 TNA WO 167/334: 1st Armoured Division War Diary.
11 TNA AIR 35/255: Report on the AASF in France, September 1939 - June 1940.
12 TNA AIR 35/192: Summaries of Operations, 10 May - 16 June 1940.

11 June 1940

On 11 June 1940, units of the *Heer* occupied Reims and the French Government fled from Paris and headed further southwards, towards the Loire. The German forces had succeeded in holding and enlarging their bridgeheads and continued to cross the River Somme having now built a third bridge in this sector. *The Times* described some of the detail of the kind of fighting that was being carried out in France, namely the type of fiercely fought rear-guard actions that were being made against the advancing German panzer and infantry divisions.

> At some places the Germans have launched infantry in such masses that our men have become physically fatigued with the effort of continually firing – their rifles and machines guns have become almost red hot.[13]

As reported in the following day's edition of *The Times*, to the west of the River Oise, the enemy's efforts were now being concentrated in order to facilitate a crossing of the River Seine between Rouen and Vernon. Smoke screens were being employed by the enemy's engineers, to disguise the positioning of pontoon bridges, and provide cover when some of their tanks were conveyed across the river using floats of boats. To the east of the Oise, German troops supported by tanks were reported to be on the Oureq from La Ferté to Fère-en-Tardenois, where they had engaged with the rear guard of Allied troops whose divisions had already retreated in order to establish a new line of resistance to the south of the River Marne.[14]

With the roads already being packed with British and French military transport that continued to move from Dieppe towards St Valery-en-Caux, orders were issued by the 152nd Brigade for the 2/7th Duke of Wellington's Regiment to take up new defensive positions. These were to be from the coast at Veules-les-Roses to the road from Blosseville to Le Bourg-Dun. By this stage, a bridgehead was being held from Veules to St Valery with enemy tanks observed to be in operation, and there was intense fighting, but with no artillery or machine gun support on the Veules front. The only communication with the Brigade's headquarters was via the liaison officers, who reported at noon that the Brigade had been ordered away, and that battalions should now fall under the orders of the Commander of 153rd Brigade.

There were air raids on Veules at noon, with high explosive and incendiary bombs being dropped by the *Luftwaffe*. The fighting continued into the evening, with small arms fire and mortars now used against the positions of the 2/7th Dukes by the German infantry until an assault was made by 40 of their light and medium tanks, which attacked down the main road from Dieppe. A lull was then experienced, after which there was an artillery bombardment followed by a further massed attack of German AFVs at 2100 hours, reported to be of the order of 200 vehicles that pierced the British lines and drove towards the Battalion's headquarters before swinging towards St Valery on the main road running south west of the bridgehead.

There was no indication of whether the Royal Navy would be able to evacuate the troops at Veules that night, so the British units there had to hold off the enemy forces until the darkness provided at least some cover. At 2145 hours, when the action appeared to be decreasing, the

13 *The Times*, 11 June 1940.
14 Ibid., 12 June 1940.

2/7th Dukes were ordered to withdraw in small parties and to make for the beaches near to St Valery. However, before the Battalion headquarters had fully prepared to move, enemy AFVs began to advance again, leading to an urgent departure. Some German artillery had been placed on the high wooded ground to the south-west of Veules and was able to use the illumination created by the burning buildings in Veules so that it could zero-in on targets there. It was at dawn on the next morning before any British boats were able to reach the coast and the evacuation of British troops commence. Nevertheless, this was harassed by the *Luftwaffe's* fighter aircraft and, when the mist slowly began to clear, by the guns of the German artillery that had taken up positions near to St Valery.[15]

On the evening of 11 June, the Allied situation continued to deteriorate further and a gap was opened up in the French III Corp's front between Caillonet and Ecquetot (a distance of 16 miles). To rectify this condition, the British 157th Brigade commanded by Brigadier Laurie was instructed to take up a position there on the following day. At 1145 hours, the 3rd Armoured Division, which was now situated in the Forêt de Perseigne, received a message from Lieutenant General Karslake. This ordered it to proceed at once to Conches with any tanks that were available and battleworthy, and then to report to the advanced headquarters, even if some drop out. The order emphasised that 'There must be no delay, SITUATION CRITICAL'.[16]

Earlier in the day, at 1000 hours, the 156th Brigade of the 52nd Division had left Plymouth and was conveyed to France by two French destroyers, arriving in Brest early on the following morning. This Brigade was comprised of the 4/5th Royal Scots Fusiliers, the 6th and 7th Cameronians, 156th Field Ambulance, 202nd Field Company and 70th Forward Regiment.[17] The 7th Cameronians were aboard the *Ville d'Algier*.

The speed with which German forces had advanced made the use of such forward airfields as Échemines increasingly problematic for the British squadrons, and the aerodromes at Beaumont and Évreux had already been abandoned during the previous day, as the advanced operational headquarters of the AASF was withdrawn from South Champagne. Throughout the day and the evening, a series of air raids were carried out by the RAF on various enemy positions, with squadrons of medium bombers concentrating on the German offensive's right wing and harassing the enemy's armoured and mechanised columns that were to the east of Rouen.

During the previous night, 16 Fairey Battle sorties had been flown and attacks made on every road and rail communication point to the north of the River Seine, together with the places where troop concentrations were believed to be situated on both sides of the river. This included the forests near to Vernon and Les Andelys, Seury and Pont de l'Arche.[18] At dawn on 11 June, twelve Battles had bombed the River Seine crossing that was to the south of Les Andelys. At noon, six of the Battles returned with the support of a fighter escort to attack the other bridges in this area, and later in the afternoon 16 Battles, also with fighter escort, made further forays. Attacks near to Rouen were also carried out. During some 38 sorties carried out by these light bombers during this day, only three of the RAF's aircraft were lost.

A total of 59 sorties by the RAF fighter aircraft had given cover to the day's bombing operations. At 1520 hours, Flying Officer Anthony Eyre of 615 (County of Surrey) Squadron

15 TNA WO 167/737: 2/7th Duke of Wellington's Regiment War Diary.
16 TNA WO 167/448: 2nd Royal Tank Regiment War Diary.
17 TNA WO 167/412: 156th Brigade Headquarters.
18 TNA AIR 35/192: Summaries of Operations 10 May - 16 June 1940.

was taking part in a patrol along the French coast, ranging from Dieppe to Le Havre.[19] Flying their Hurricanes at 16,000 to 18,000 feet, Eyre's patrol spotted a number of aircraft that were not easily identifiable. He had already caused damage to a Messerschmitt Bf 110 but then became cut off from the other RAF aircraft in his patrol. Following this, he sighted a Messerschmitt Bf 109 flying one mile to his east and around 200 feet below him. Diving from 20,000 feet, Eyre opened fire on the German aircraft and gave it four long bursts from his machine guns that exhausted his ammunition. This caused a large quantity of white smoke to erupt from the German aeroplane's engine, and he was able to claim this as being destroyed.[20] Later in the day, at 1910 hours, whilst near to Louviers, it was reported that a Hawker Hurricane from 73 Squadron had shot down a single Dornier Do 17 bomber.[21]

12 June 1940

On 12 June, Acting Major General Beauman issued a special order of the day, which was to be communicated to all the troops in his improvised Division. This stated:

> I wish to make clear to all ranks the importance of the task that the division has performed and is still performing. The mere fact that the line in front of Rouen was held by British troops undoubtedly had a delaying effect on the German advance and a steadying effect on our allies. When the attack was made by two German mechanised divisions on a narrow front, it was in such strength that our thinly held line had no chance to withstand it. I realise that the subsequent retirement entailed very great physical and mental strain on all concerned, and that it will be some days before troops can be expected to fully recover from it.
>
> I similarly hope that a few days' comparative rest will be possible before the division is again called upon to occupy the very strong defensive position that has been selected. Fresh British troops, fully equipped, are being landed rapidly, and some are already in position on the right flank. But I wish all ranks to realised that our allies are being desperately hard pressed by enormous German as well as Italian forces on a very long front, and we must be prepared to play our part if necessary, however tired we may be. I know I can rely on all ranks to do any duty that may be necessary without grumbling and with that determination that has always been shown by the British Army in a crisis.[22]

The 157th Brigade had been disembarked at Cherbourg during the previous day. It now moved into the front line at Conches, on the right of the French 10th Army, and taking over the right-hand sector of the French III Corps on the River Risle, which was moved to the south of

19 Joining 615 Squadron in 1938, Anthony Eyre began full-time service in 1939. During the Battle of Britain, he was credited with seven enemy aircraft destroyed and several damaged and was awarded the Distinguished Flying Cross (DFC). Shot down in 1942, he and spent three years as a prisoner of war then resumed his RAF service as a Wing Commander but died in an air accident in 1946.

20 TNA AIR 50/175/6: Combat Reports.

21 TNA AIR 35/253: AASF Combat Reports.

22 TNA WO 167/736: 2/6th Duke of Wellington's Regiment War Diary.

Beaumont. The French 237th Division filled a gap to the left, but there remained an opening of eight miles to the right, and German troops were advancing through this at Évreux.[23] The 157th Brigade was sent into immediate action on the line from Faverelles to La Bonneville-sur-Iton, and was able to force the enemy's divisions to swing in a south-easterly direction.

The 1st Armoured Division's situation report for 12 June stated that German formations had now crossed the River Seine. Their 6th Infantry Division was near St Pierre and occupied Louviers and the woods to the west; the 32nd Infantry Division was near Gaillon; and the 40th and 64th Infantry Divisions were near Vernon. Unconfirmed reports at 1000 hours were that two enemy infantry divisions and one panzer division were advancing in a south-westerly direction between Évreux and Dreux. Reconnaissance could not confirm this, but the French III Corps withdrew from Quittebeuf to St Cyr, with the 2nd Armoured Brigade in support.[24]

According to the 2nd Armoured Brigade's War Diary, at 0700 hours Lieutenant de Boislambert arrived from the headquarters of *Général de division* Petiet with the news that the enemy were not pressing the French withdrawal, which had been to the general line from Vernon to Elbeuf. To the south of Vernon, however, there was a gap of twenty miles with no French troops, and it was believed that German light armoured units were already in Évreux. This situation was confirmed by a liaison officer from the 1st Armoured Division's advanced headquarters, with the verbal instructions that the 2nd Armoured Brigade was to continue to support Petiet's Division, including if the French were forced to withdraw to the north-west. At 1030 hours, the Brigade moved to Rouge-Perriers to protect the right flank of Petiet's units, which were now at Le Neubourg and to counter-attack any advanced enemy AFVs that might attempt to push into the open country to the south of Le Neubourg.

At 2130 hours, whilst positioned in Bernay Wood, the men of the 2/6th Duke of Wellington's Regiment and of the Beauman Division received a visit from the Divisional Staff and the Assistant Director Medical Services. As these men had been in continuous engagement with the enemy over a number of days, the ADMS concluded that the majority of them were now not fit for battle and needed rest for at least three days. The Battalion Commander was ordered to take a period of rest and was sent to Le Mans. Hence, it fell to his second-in-command to execute the order subsequently received from Brigade headquarters to supply a force of five officers and 150 other ranks to take up a position in the area reconnoitred earlier that day; the remainder of the men were to proceed to a locality one kilometre north of Sees.[25]

By 12 June, it was necessary for the RAF to recall the advanced landing ground parties from Troyes, as it became clear that the German advance south of the River Seine would soon become a threat to those aerodromes located around Chateaudun.

Between 1315 and 1345 hours, twelve Bristol Blenheim bombers escorted by sorties of RAF fighters were tasked to carry out a low dive-bombing attack on the enemy targets at St Valery-en-Caux. Later that afternoon, another target was the Pont de l'Arche railway bridge to the south of Le Manoir, and south of Les Andelys. Furthermore, an aerial attack was to be made on the pontoon bridge that had been constructed by the Germans at Vezillian but this did not prove successful, with one Fairey Battle bomber being lost and another damaged in combat. In contrast, a raid on a similar structure at Courcelles-sur-Seine resulted in two direct hits

23 TNA WO 167/326: 52nd Division War Diary.
24 TNA WO 167/334: 1st Armoured Division War Diary.
25 TNA WO 167/736: 2/6th Duke of Wellington's Regiment War Diary.

being made on the bridge. Later that evening, the roads around Les Andelys were again the target but only seven of a force of 15 Battles were able to reach this location as a consequence of the inclement weather, and those that did approach the target area were met with heavy anti-aircraft fire from enemy positions situated there.

On this day, RAF fighter aircraft began patrolling the area of the port of Le Havre, with there being six patrols totally 49 sorties. This was effective in deterring more enemy air raids from being carried out, as four Heinkel He 111 bombers were shot down by the Hurricane fighters of 17 Squadron during just one engagement.[26]

Interestingly, in the Summaries of Operations, the report of this combat states that a Heinkel He 113 fighter aircraft was also destroyed during this action. This was almost certainly a case of misidentification by the pilots concerned. It was probably a Messerschmitt Bf 109 because the Heinkel He 113 was fictitious and wholly a propaganda exercise describing the introduction of a new high specification German fighter aeroplane. In reality, some of the small number of pre-war Heinkel He 100 D 1 fighters were photographed at various German airfields, each bearing a different paint scheme and markings, and the pictures then published in the press with them being described as the Heinkel He 113 recently supplied to the *Luftwaffe*. During the early years of the war, when this disinformation exercise was at its height, there were various accounts of the Heinkel He 113 being encountered and shot down.

13 June 1940

On 13 June, *The Times* made some reference to the German use of motor-cycle troops and it provided an account of an unnamed Scottish soldier who, having shot and killed the rider of one of these machines by use of an anti-tank rifle, had gained possession of his motor-cycle and its machine gun. He noted, 'Why it was just like an arsenal, full of ammunition, even cameras. The same piece in *The Times* also stated that when examined, some of these motor-cycle sidecar combinations had British battle dresses packed away in them so that they could be used as disguises. Furthermore, German infantry had been reported to have also been seen wearing khaki uniforms.[27]

The 10th Army, which now included 157th Brigade, the 1st Armoured Division (less one Brigade) and the Beauman Division, was holding a line from the sea to the west of the River Seine to Neubourg, and then to the east of Conches. This was a particularly exposed position because there was an eight-mile gap from the southern flank of the 157th Brigade's position to Damville, and this was supposed to be held by the armoured units of the light mechanised French 3rd DLM. To the south of this area, the Allied line was supposed to being held by the French Army of Paris.

The 4/5th Royal Scots Fusiliers arrived at Fresnay-sur-Sarthe at 0530 hours and once they had disembarked from their train, marched for approximately seven miles towards the outskirts of Sougé, 125 miles south-west of Paris. Due to the possibility of enemy air raids, the Fusiliers kept clear of buildings and the Battalion headquarters was established in a nearby field under the cover of trees.[28] By 1600 hours, each of the Battalion's rifle companies had erected road blocks

26 TNA AIR 35/192: Summaries of Operations 10 May - 16 June 1940.
27 *The Times*, 13 June 1940.
28 TNA WO 167/817: 4/5th Royal Scots Fusiliers War Diary.

on all of the main roads within the area to the north. The men bivouacked and throughout the day manned the various check points that had been set up, but the information which they had regarding the enemy's position was at best vague and conflicting. The 6th and 7th Cameronians also arrived at Fresnay-sur-Sarthe later during the day and then marched to their respective positions, with the 6th Battalion marching to St Aubin and then on to St Christophe, whilst the 7th Battalion settled in around St Victeur, and established the Battalion headquarters in a farm two miles north of the village.[29]

At 0700 hours three ships appeared off St Malo, and an hour later the disembarkation commenced from the *Princesse Astrid*, *Prince Baudouin* and *Manxman*. From there, these troops from the 7/9th Royal Scots, 4th and 5th KOSB, the Brigade headquarters and the anti-tank company, marched to a rest camp at Cancale, eight miles to the south, with the lead elements arriving at midday and the last of the troops at around 1500 hours.[30] By 1000 hours, the 5th KOSB had landed at St Malo and marched the six miles to their billet near to Cancale. The Battalion's War Diary records that the inhabitants showered flowers and cider on the troops.[31]

The 3rd Armoured Division now being placed under the orders of *Général de division* Petiet, commander of the 3rd DLC, a part of the III French Corps, and was sent to fill the gap in the defences from Barquet to Barc. The Divisional War Diary records that: 'it is relevant to say that whereas the French right was about Neubourg, there were no other troops disposed on the ground in the south, except for the 157th Brigade of the 52nd Division, which held the line Conches to Ferrières-Haut-Clocher'.[32]

The continued advance of German forces was an immediate and daily threat to the airfields of the AASF and, consequently, a retreat towards Nantes and Bordeaux was ordered. At the same time, impressed on the RAF crews was the importance of providing support to the Allied troops for as long as they were able to keep fighting.

On 13 June, the RAF made strenuous efforts to provide what assistance it could to the French armies. In the east, the line on the River Marne had been broken through by the German divisions, who were now threatening the Maginot Line; whereas, in the west, the River Seine had been crossed and Paris was under threat as the French Army fell back.[33] During the night of 12 to 13 June, 15 Fairey Battles had been sent to attack Les Andelys again, this time concentrating their efforts on the approaches to the town. It was noted that as a counter-measure, the German ground troops employed the tactic of firing parachute flares that dazzled the Battle crews and hampered their attempts to aim and release their bombs accurately.[34]

The AASF flew reconnaissance missions over the River Seine from dawn onwards. Unfortunately, poor weather hampered this, making it difficult for the crews to locate their targets with any degree of precision and, whilst it was not possible for these bombers to have a fighter escort, the weather also prevented the *Luftwaffe's* fighter aircraft from being sent up to intercept them. The poor weather persisted and, later in the day, a mission carried out by the 142 and 150 Squadrons was affected with a number of the aircraft having to return to their base

29 TNA WO 167/722: 6th Cameronians War Diary; WO 167/723: 7th Cameronians War Diary.
30 TNA WO 167/411: 155th Brigade Headquarters.
31 TNA WO 167/775: 5th King's Own Scottish Borderers War Diary.
32 TNA WO 167/334: 1st Armoured Division War Diary.
33 L.F. Ellis, *The War in France and Flanders 1939–40*, p.295.
34 TNA AIR 35/192: Summaries of Operations, 10 May - 16 June 1940.

and, with there being no fighter support, as this was also affected by bad weather and limited to coastal patrols, four of the Fairey Battles were shot down by the enemy fighters.

During the day, 40 Fairey Battles took part in aerial attacks on the enemy columns on the roads from Pacy to Évreux, Pacy to Vernon and Gravigny to Louviers. At 1500 hours, 12 Fairey Battles were sent without a fighter escort to attack the German columns that were south of Montmirail, and which had exploited a gap between the two French Armies that were to the east of Paris, and which had diverged as they tried to retreat from the River Aisne to the River Marne. It was recorded that so concentrated were the panzers and the motorised transport that there was an abundance of targets and 26 Battles were despatched to carry out a second raid on this target. The German anti-aircraft fire that came from the ground troops and the numerous fighter aircraft nevertheless took a heavy toll on these British aircraft and six of the Battles were shot down, four of them being accounted for by the German fighters. A third raid was made by 15 of the twin-engine Bristol Blenheims from Bomber Command, with four of these aircraft also being shot down by the enemy.

The RAF continued to launch attacks on the German positions throughout the night of 13 to 14 June, and 164 of Bomber Command's medium and heavy bombers were used, with there being 44 sorties over the Seine, 20 to the north of Paris, 41 on the Marne, and 50 against road and rail communication centres and against wooded areas that were reported to be providing cover for concentrations of German troops. These were heavily defended by ground-based anti-aircraft guns and the *Luftwaffe's* fighter squadrons. As a consequence, the AASF received a high number of casualties.

The diminishing capacity for resistance that was increasingly being exhibited by the troops of the French Army also reduced the overall effectiveness of the raids by the AASF's bombers on enemy columns and positions, so that they took on the appearance of, to all intents and purposes, independent air operations, and were usually carried out at night. Fighter squadrons were employed on providing escort cover to the bombers and to protecting the forces which were being evacuated from Le Havre. Aerial combat against enemy aircraft was becoming more frequent as the *Luftwaffe* increasingly took advantage of its ability to concentrate its efforts following the Dunkirk evacuation.

5

Le Havre and St Valery-en-Caux

Planning and Implementation

The Allied Higher Command's original plan that 51st Division should break to the south and then conform to the southward movement of the main Allied line had proven impossible. Staging an evacuation from Dieppe was discounted as it was known that the harbour was now unsuitable for the embarkation of ships due to bomb damage caused by the *Luftwaffe's* air raids and mines had been laid at the harbour's entrance. It was also thought that block ships had been sunk in the harbour, which made it impossible to carry out the type of operation required.[1] Moreover, no orders, either from the French IX Corps or the British Government, had been supplied to Major General Fortune to instruct him to evacuate 51st Division from Dieppe.

Once the order for the 51st Division to withdraw was given, Fortune was convinced that Le Havre would be the best place for an evacuation to be carried out from as he was aware that ships were still able to access the port. Moreover, Fortune had decided that his Division should withdraw in conjunction with the French IX Corps. This decision, although made in the best spirit of good comradeship, would ultimately constrain the 51st Division's progress. This was because, whilst the British troops had the use of lorries, the French were mostly still reliant on horse-drawn transport and would therefore take far longer to reach their destination, especially given the sheer volume of traffic on roads already congested with refugees.

With the enemy forces doing everything they possibly could to prevent another evacuation and, having learnt from the experience of Dunkirk, it was assumed that they would be advancing towards Le Havre without delay. If the Germans arrived at the port before the Allies, the extraction of 51st Division would be thwarted and its fate sealed. Fortune reasoned, therefore, that the roads between Fécamp and Bolbec should be defended and, accordingly, an improvised formation was created with orders to take up a position from Fécamp to Lillebonne, and to set

1 On 10 June, HMS *Vega*, commanded by Captain G.A. Garnon-Williams, escorted three block ships that were to be used to block the harbour at Dieppe. Two of these block ships were sunk in the approach channel but the third was damaged when it hit a mine that prevented it from being placed at the entrance to the inner harbour.

up a defensive line that was 19 miles to the east of Le Havre. This would enable it to provide cover for the withdrawal of the remainder of the 51st Division and the French IX Corps.

This force was placed under the command of Brigadier Arthur Stanley-Clarke of the 154th Brigade and was named Arkforce after the village of Arques-la-Bataille, where it was formed.[2] It was comprised of the 154th Infantry Brigade (4th Black Watch and the remaining elements of the 7th and 8th Argylls), together with the Beauman Division's A Brigade, the 6th Royal Scots Fusiliers and the support from two artillery regiments and various engineer units. Effectively, by dividing his forces into these two components, Fortune had envisaged that the Arkforce and the other Brigades would operate in such a manner as to leap-frog over each other, thereby providing themselves with protection along the route. Fortune gave the order that:

> Should it be apparent that an enemy attack from the north or east on the IX Corps has made any organised evacuation from Havre impossible you will withdraw and evacuate at Havre as many of your force as you can, destroying all material and taking off such material as can be carried.[3]

The men of the Arkforce travelled at night. This was to minimise the risk of unwanted attention from the *Luftwaffe*, although the dense smoke emanating from Rouen, which covered the whole area from St Valery to Le Havre, also provided an effective screen to obstruct observation from the air.[4] Unfortunately, because the roads were so congested, Arkforce's progress was unavoidably impeded, and only some of the units reached Fécamp by midday. Two companies from the 1/5th Sherwood Foresters and the 4th Buffs (a part of A Brigade of the Beauman Division) did not arrive at their destination and would stay under the orders of 152nd Brigade.[5]

Regrettably, Arkforce was unable to keep the intended escape route clear for the 51st Division because it was unable to hold off the enemy's forces. These had swung northwards from Rouen, reaching the coast at Fécamp and decisively severing the proposed evacuation route planned for the British troops. Arkforce Operation Order No. 2 confirmed that the German armour and mechanised troops had reached Fécamp during the course of the previous day. It also stated that the positions now being held were to be maintained until definite orders were received to the contrary. In the event of an attack by the enemy, it was the responsibility of each and every officer and man to hold out at all costs, and for them to inflict the maximum losses possible on the enemy. It concluded by stating that this order was to be impressed on all ranks.[6]

Arkforce was then ordered to withdraw and head for Le Havre. From there it was to be rescued as part of Operation Cycle, which was the codename for the mission to evacuate Allied troops from that port. This was planned to take place from 10 to 13 June 1940 and it was not originally intended for the 51st Division to be evacuated, as the IX Corps was to have retired to the Somme but when the Germans reached Rouen on 9 June, the only line of retreat had been cut and it was debatable whether it would reach Le Havre before 13 June.

2 There has also been some speculation that the choice of this name possibly owed more to an ironic reference to Noah's Ark.
3 L.F. Ellis, *The War in France and Flanders 1939-40*, p.285.
4 TNA WO 167/314: 51st Division War Diary.
5 S. David, *Churchill's Sacrifice of the Highland Division, France 1940*, p.208.
6 TNA WO 167/711: 4th Black Watch War Diary.

As the 51st Division was about to commence its retirement towards Le Havre with the French units of the IX Corps, information was received of a further advance by the German divisions. In order to stand any chance of reaching this destination before being intercepted by the enemy, progress would have to be stepped up considerably. In addition to the 51st Division, there were also some 1,200 men who had been part of the Le Havre garrison and those L of C troops who had been cut off in the peninsula. Consequently, it was determined that a move should be made by part of the Division during the evening of 10 to 11 June to the River Durdent and from there, by means of the railway line, to Doudeville and on to Yvetot. At the same time, the remainder of the Allied troops would make an attempt to join up with the Arkforce.

Major General Fortune had by now started to realise that the success of the enemy's advance, through an area previously held by the French Army, would entail the cutting off of those elements of the 51st Division still holding a position on the River Béthune from Dieppe to Martigny, to the south of Arques-la-Bataille. These battalions were the 2/7th Duke of Wellington's Regiment, 4th Seaforths, 5th Gordons and 1st Black Watch. And further back were also the 2nd Seaforths, 1st Gordons and 4th Camerons, with the tanks of the 1st Lothians held in reserve but being tasked with reconnaissance towards Fécamp. This was to attempt to estimate the strength of the enemy's forces and secure a route to a possible point of evacuation between the Durdent and St Valery-en-Caux. The latter infantry units were ordered to assist the 1st Lothians and, to maximise the use of the limited number of vehicles available, were told to jettison all of their non-fighting equipment and kit such as blankets, retaining only their weapons, ammunition and food. Unfortunately, by this time the German forces had already taken control of the crossing points on the River Durdent.

The *Luftwaffe's* air superiority made the prospect of a successful evacuation uncertain. Contrary to the views of many ground troops at the time, it was the use of suitable RAF aircraft, operating in relays as a fighter umbrella, that helped to prevent the evacuation from Dunkirk turning into an unmitigated disaster. However, the numbers of RAF aeroplanes available to support the 51st Division was miniscule by comparison, and their patrols were rare, with the fighters being disadvantaged by being at the end of their operational range. Hence, cut off from Rouen and prevented from reaching Le Havre, and with its back to the sea, the only hope for rescue would be from St Valery-en-Caux. A small fishing port surrounded by high steep cliffs; it was soon evident that its harbour could not accommodate many of the larger types of ship that had been able to successfully evacuate the British troops at Dunkirk.

On the evening of 8 June, Captain Frank Pegram joined the staff of the Royal Navy's Commander-in-Chief, Portsmouth, Admiral William James.[7] Pegram was to provide him with a general outline for the proposed operation and, as Admiral James noted later in his report to the Secretary of the Admiralty dated 18 June 1940, at the time it was still considered possible that an evacuation from Le Havre might be able to take place but no date could be given. Available transports were at once taken up and their captains and crews brought to short notice. The Dutch coasters, which were known as schoots or schuyts, were commissioned and the

7 Sir William Milbourne James (1881-1973) was appointed to the rank of full Admiral in 1938 and from 1939 he served as the Commander-in-Chief, Portsmouth. During the First World War, he had served with the Naval Intelligence Division.

smaller vessels organised at Newhaven and the Hamble River into a number of flotillas of about ten craft, each of which was now placed under the overall command of a Royal Navy officer.[8]

On 9 June, the Admiralty reports commented on the position in France and stated that the 51st Division was holding the line from Dieppe to Neufchâtel, thence south west to westward of the Rouen docks. The local French garrison was positioned on the line from Lillebonne to Fécamp, and the enemy's advanced forces were nearing Rouen. The numbers estimated for evacuation from Le Havre were considered to be 23,000 of the 51st Division, 5,000 of the British local garrison, 5,000 French troops and 20,000 military labour corps (plus an unknown number of other French troops).[9] Having regard to Dieppe, it had been noted that whilst this appeared clear, a barge had been sunk near to the entrance of the port and it was possible that magnetic mines had also been placed there as well. However, it was deemed feasible for all supplies to be landed, although Le Havre was considered to be preferable for this purpose. The Admiralty had been advised that the evacuation of French troops from Le Havre was to proceed during the night of 9 to 10 June and that the British evacuation must be delayed because of this, as the French evacuation was to take precedence. In view of this, troop carrying vessels were ordered to return to their harbours and the Royal Navy's destroyers remained ready to turn back any merchant ships if the order was given.

Admiral James stated in his report that the situation was obscure at this point, and because he did not know how far the evacuation of the French troops had progressed and what the true position was regarding the French IX Corps, he decided to take the initiative and went to Le Havre on Motor Boat MTB 29 to find out this out for himself.[10] Admiral James had appointed Captain G.L. Warren to be the Senior Naval Officer afloat, and for him to transfer to HMS *Codrington*, and for Captain Armstrong to be the Senior Officer Flotillas in HMS *Saladin*. This decision was taken so that these senior Royal Navy officers would have a better opportunity for overseeing and controlling the various ships to come under their command.

At 1320 hours on 9 June, the Admiralty issued orders for an evacuation to be instigated, with all available ships to be sent to Le Havre in the first instance and HMS *Laird's Isle* was to convey beach parties there as soon as possible. Available schoots and boats, together with a number of Royal Navy ships were to rendezvous five miles north-west of Cap de la Heve between 2200 hours on 9 June and 0100 hours on 10 June. These included HMS *Ambuscade,* HMS *Boadicea,* HMS *Broke,* HMS *Bulldog,* HMS *Codrington,* HMS *Fernie,* HMS *Gardenia.* HMS *Hampton*, HMS *Harvester,* HMS *Saladin, and* HMS *Wellington,* and they were accompanied by two Canadian destroyers, HMCS *Restigouche* and HMCS *St Laurent.* Embarkation would commence on 10 June and those troops rescued were to be taken and disembarked at another French port, such as Cherbourg, and not return to Britain.[11]

In addition to the obvious political implications of an evacuation of British forces, and the message it was felt this would send to the French, there was also the potential for the ships of the Royal Navy to be placed in considerable jeopardy. Indeed, at 0530 hours on 10 June, *HMS Ambuscade*, which was part of the destroyer force that had been providing the 51st Division with fire support over several days, was damaged by shellfire from the guns of the 7th Panzer

8 TNA ADM 1/10481: Operations Cycle and Aerial.
9 TNA ADM 199/2206: Operation Cycle, Report.
10 TNA ADM 1/10481: Operations Cycle and Aerial.
11 TNA ADM 199/2206: Operation Cycle, Report.

Division's artillery and tanks that had now been established on the high cliffs overlooking St Valery-en-Caux. HMS *Boadicea* was also hit by enemy fire whilst it was embarking troops from the beach near to Veulettes-sur-Mer and HMS *Bulldog* was hit during an air raid by the *Luftwaffe's* Stuka dive bombers. Angered by the success of the Dunkirk evacuation, the German forces were determined that there would not be a repeat performance.

On 10 June, Admiral James arrived at Le Havre, where he learnt of the damage to HMS *Ambuscade* and HMS *Boadicea* and he ordered the destroyers to reconnoitre the smaller ports to the east. In a signal sent to the Admiralty, James stated that he planned to extract a large number of men from the port and that this would have to be done at night. At 1225 hours on 10 June, the 51st Division's naval liaison officer sent a telegram to Admiral James, which was repeated to the senior naval officer at Le Havre, that 'anticipate 5,000 to 10,000 will be ready to embark night of 12 to 13 June'.[12] In fact, by 13 June some 2,222 British troops had been taken back to Britain and 8,837 were conveyed to Cherbourg, where the intention was that they should return to action alongside the French troops holding positions on the Loire. In the meantime, James had also concluded that the 51st Division would not be able to reach Le Havre, and so he had sent a message to the Admiralty and the War Office to begin to plan the Division's evacuation from St Valery-en-Caux.

Le Havre

On 9 June, the French Port Admiral for Le Havre had informed the General Officers commanding the 51st Division and the IX Corps that the enemy's forces had captured Rouen, turned north and were now heading for the coast. Major General Fortune and *Général de corps d'armée* Ihler had concluded from this information that the only hope for their respective formations was to attempt to make an escape through Le Havre, even if this did mean the abandonment of their existing plans for a retirement via Rouen.

The Port Admiral requested that the Royal Navy send a sufficient number of ships to take off 85,000 men, even though this was contrary to the orders that had been issued for IX Corps by *Général d'armée* Weygand, who was still adamant that under no circumstances should any Allied troops be evacuated from Le Havre. In the confusion, due to the partial information that then prevailed, and despite being called upon several times to accelerate this retirement by Lieutenant General Karslake, the CIGS, General Sir John Dill, hesitated to issue the requisite orders and by doing so effectively made the plan to retreat impossible. In fact, it was only after he had contacted the British Military Mission to the French High Command, which was based at Weygand's headquarters and headed by Major General Richard Howard-Vyse, that the CIGS received the message from Fortune and discovered the true position. This was that the 51st Division was a part of the retreat of IX Corps.[13]

On the night of 9/10 June, the improvised Arkforce moved towards Fécamp and most of its troops managed to pass through before the arrival of the 7th Panzer Division. However, any expectation of the Arkforce holding the line from Fécamp to Lillebonne was really very limited, and in pursuance of the instructions given to him by Major General Fortune, Brigadier

12 TNA WO 167/314: 51st Division War Diary.
13 B. Karslake, *1940, The Last Act*, pp.180-181.

Stanley-Clarke had ordered the Arkforce units to drive towards Le Havre. They reached the port and were taken off by the Royal Navy by 13 June. Arkforce was transported to Cherbourg, where it was intended that the British Army would send further resources to continue to fight.

The Royal Navy estimated that the total number of personnel to be evacuated from Le Havre was 65,000, of which 23,000 were British. By 1600 hours, the arrival of the German forces to the south of Fécamp increased the imperativeness of evacuating the 12,000 troops from St Valery, as a matter of the utmost urgency. By 2139 hours, two brigades from the 51st Division were co-operating with the Le Havre local defences but these troops were exhausted and reliance could not be placed on the French forces from this point.

On 10 June, Royal Navy beach parties landed at Le Havre to co-ordinate the planned evacuation. A report from Commander G.F.N. Bradford, the Royal Navy's principal beach master, indicated that after their arrival at 1030 hours, the beach parties were divided into four separate parties covering the most likely places of embarkation, namely the Quai d'Escalde, the Quai Nord and the beach to the north-west of the docks.[14] The quays and approaches were heavily bombed by the *Luftwaffe* on 10 and 11 June. Despite being hindered by air raids that caused damage and cut off electrical power, the beach parties received only four casualties. *The Times*, referring to the material contribution made by the *Luftwaffe* to the success of the German Army, indicated that in bombing the harbour at Le Havre, this resulted in it being responsible for the sinking of or damaging of seven transport vessels.[15]

At 1400 hours, HMS *Ambuscade* was ordered to investigate that stretch of the coast between Fécamp and Durdent with a view to evacuating the troops from there. At 1525 hours, it came under an artillery barrage and at 1530 damage was sustained to the ship's structure, namely three holes at the water line with flooding to the fore shell room, engine room and ward room, and injuries were suffered by 10 men. As a result, the *Ambuscade* proceeded out to sea, where it could carry out the necessary repairs. The beach at Veulettes-sur-Mer was considered suitable for the evacuation of troops by use of the smaller craft that were available, and it was reported that approximately 60 men had been taken off before being transferred to HMS *Boadicea*.

All available fast passenger ships had sailed for Le Havre to be ready for the evacuation after dark during the night of 10 to 11 June. This was in accordance with the request of the Senior Naval Officer at Le Havre. The final Admiralty report of the day stated that eleven fast ships would arrive off Le Havre during the evening, although owing to their low endurance they would need to be refuelled before commencing the return trip, or should they be delayed at Le Havre.[16] However, during the night of 10 June the ships lying off Fécamp, Le Havre and St Valery-en-Caux were subjected to heavy artillery bombardment by the enemy and HMS *Bulldog* and HMS *Boadicea* were both hit. Consequently, and further to communication with the Admiralty, these warships were ordered not to make any approaches that were deemed too close to the evacuation areas in daylight, except for urgent reasons.[17]

RAF Fighter Command was to send sorties from two British-based squadrons at a time to offer air protection over the Le Havre area. Heavy bombing by the *Luftwaffe* had occurred on the morning of 12 June but the British fighter patrols had reduced this to negligible proportions.

14 TNA ADM 179/158: Operation Cycle, Information on British and French troops in Havre district.
15 *The Times*, 13 June 1940.
16 TNA ADM 199/2206: Operation Cycle, Report.
17 TNA ADM 267/126: Operation Cycle, Report.

However, no fighter protection was to be available until around three hours before dark. Evacuation without fighter protection was not to be attempted during weather in which the enemy bombers were able to operate. Following a postponement for 24 hours, with the issuing of the code name 'Whoopee', orders were transmitted for the commencement on 11 June of the evacuation. With the exception of those troops who were holding the port's inner defences, and which were to be evacuated at 0600 hours on 13 June, the remainder of the units of Arkforce and the Le Havre garrison were evacuated from the port between 2100 hours on 12 June and 0400 hours on 13 June without opposition.

In total, 11,059 British troops, including those from the Arkforce and the other British formations were evacuated from the port of Le Havre. Of this number, 2,222 military personnel were taken off and conveyed back to England and 8,837 were transported along the French coast to the port of Cherbourg. The decision to divert these men was so that they might then be allowed to participate in the counter-offensive that it was envisaged by the British and French military would be launched from there by the second BEF, with the 52nd Division and the 1st Canadian Division having already been sent there. In fact, as the German Army's advance pressed on fervently and relentlessly, the troops from all of these British units and Divisions would in due course have to be re-embarked on to Royal Navy ships and between 15-18 June 1940 during Operation Aerial they were evacuated back to Britain.

St Valery-en-Caux

On 10 June, the French Government fled from Paris and it was declared an open (that is to say, entirely undefended) city to spare it from destruction. This was also the day when Admiral James received a communication from Major General Fortune advising him that he might be forced to evacuate the 51st Division from a position between the mouth of the River Durdent and St Valery-en-Caux. Having assessed the situation during his visit to Le Havre, James ordered the Royal Navy's destroyers to proceed to the smaller ports east of Le Havre, including St Valery, to determine whether they were suitable for troops to be evacuated from if they could reach them.[18] Hence, James was doing all within his power to facilitate the evacuation of the 51st Division and to determine to where the Royal Navy's ships should be sent.

On first reading, these actions might appear to be contrary to the War Office's telegram to the 51st Division issued at 12.30 am on 11 June. In fact, rather than reinforcing the message that the French orders must be obeyed, regardless of how unreasonable or unrealistic they were, this telegram obliquely allowed Fortune to progress, provided that this action was sanctioned by the French commander of IX Corps. This assisted Fortune to disregard the protestations of *Général d'armée* Weygand that the IX Corps was advancing towards the Somme which, if respected for fear of being accused of contributing to the French defeat, would place the British troops in a hopeless position. By withdrawing towards St Valery, they might have a slim chance rather than no chance at all. James also concluded from his visit to France that another evacuation was required and that it would need to be imminent:

18 TNA ADM 199/2206: Operation Cycle, report.

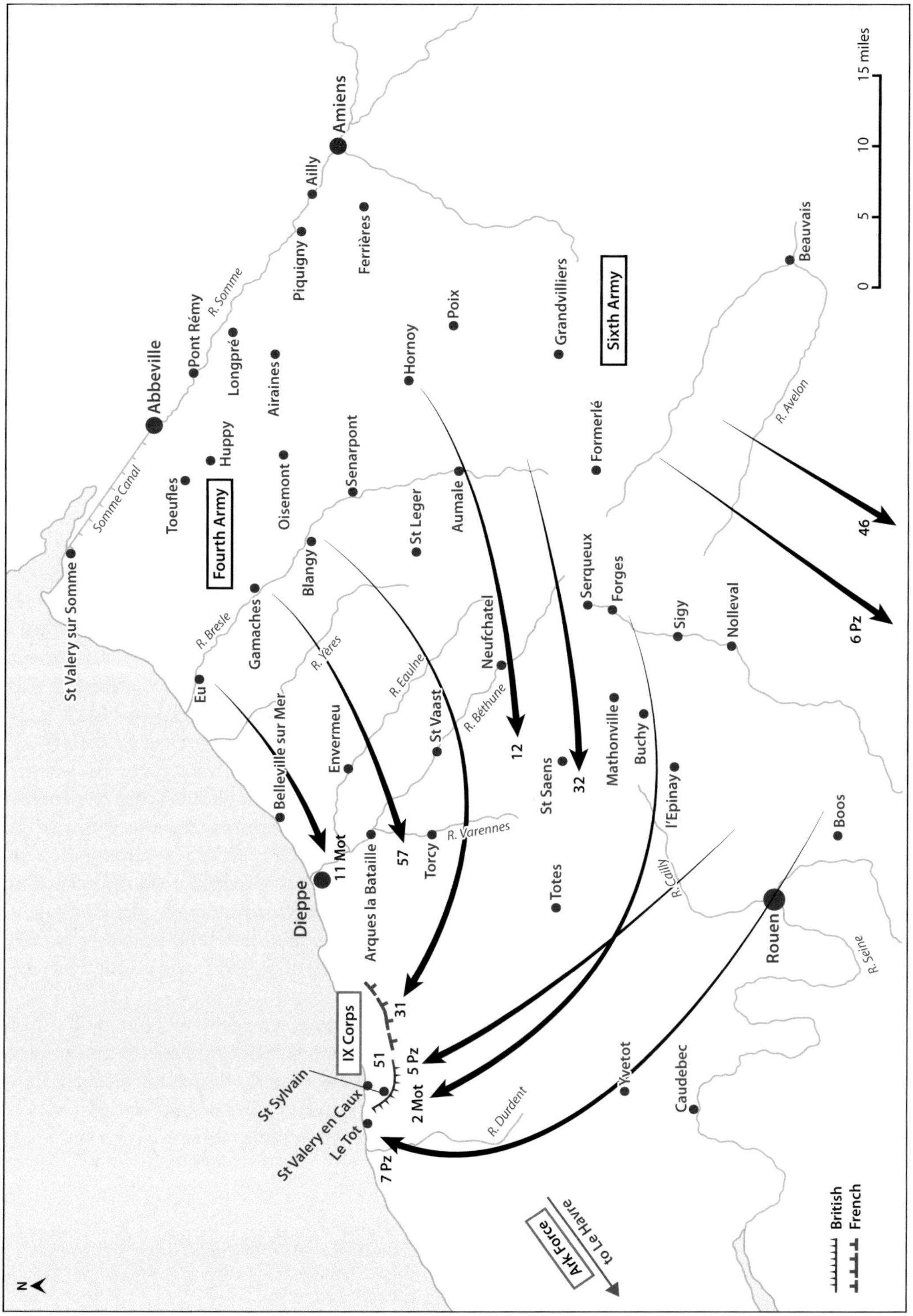
Amiens
Ailly
Ferrières
Piquigny
R. Somme
Pont Rémy
Abbeville
Longpré
Airaines
Hornoy
Poix
Grandvilliers
Sixth Army
Beauvais
Somme Canal
Toeufles
Huppy
Fourth Army
Oisemont
Senarpont
St Leger
Aumale
Formerlé
R. Avelon
St Valery sur Somme
Gamaches
Blangy
R. Bresle
Eu
R. Yères
Belleville sur Mer
Envermeu
R. Eaulne
St Vaast
Neufchatel
R. Béthune
Serqueux
Forges
Sigy
Nolleval
46
6 Pz
12
32
St Saens
Mathonville
Buchy
l'Epinay
Boos
Dieppe
11 Mot
Arques la Bataille
57
Torcy
R. Varennes
Totes
R. Cailly
Rouen
R. Seine
IX Corps
31
51
5 Pz
2 Mot
St Sylvain
St Valery en Caux
Le Tot
7 Pz
R. Durdent
Yvetot
Caudebec
Ark Force
to Le Havre
British
French
N
0
5
10
15 miles

St Valery

> Telegram to 51 Div from the War Office reference General Weygand's orders to move south to bridge the Somme. War Office explained importance of acting strictly in conformity with any orders issued by the IX Corps Commander.[19]

At 1100 hours on 10 June, a radio truck, which had been making its way to join the Arkforce to assist with that force's communications with the 51st Division, encountered German troops outside of the town of Cany-Barville, on the River Durdent. Before being captured, the radio operator was able to transmit his predicament, which was that he was surrounded by units from the 7th Panzer Division, and that the enemy was driving towards the sea at Veulettes-sur-Mer.[20] A detachment of the 1st Lothians was sent to find out more, and it was discovered that the stretch of the Durdent from Cany-Barville to the coast was under enemy control. Consequently, the 51st Division's options for carrying out an evacuation were reduced even further to waiting to be rescued by the Royal Navy from the small port of St Valery-en-Caux. A conference was convened on 10 June at the 51st Division's headquarters, when it was agreed that with its withdrawal to Le Havre now being cut off, the Division should be directed to the positions covering St Valery-en-Caux, from where the Royal Navy would seek to evacuate the Division and the IX Corps.[21]

Regrettably, the retreat to the coast was not conducted in an orderly manner, beginning as it did after dark with the last of the troops departed from Béthune at 2300 hours, and this contributed to jeopardising the proposed evacuation. It was found that the German forces had bombed, shelled and mortared the road from Dieppe to St Valery. Major General Fortune despatched a signal to the War Office stating that each of his men now had rations for only two days and an evacuation from a position between St Valery and the mouth of the Durdent was necessary. In view of this, all of the Division's non-essential equipment was dumped and ammunition for the guns reduced to 100 rounds each to make room on the transports.

The 2nd Seaforths had been despatched to Ouville-la-Rivière, mid-way between Dieppe and St Valery, where they were to provide an advanced guard and to secure the area to the south-west of St Valery up to the River Durdent. Upon arrival, however, they found that the enemy already had control of the Durdent. Instead, they established a perimeter line to the west of St Valery, passing through Le Tôt and St Sylvain.[22] Eventually, they would be surrounded by the enemy's troops, but it is a testament to the bitter fighting that took place there that seven German tanks were destroyed before the 2nd Seaforths eventually surrendered. An equivalent perimeter line was set up on the eastern side of St Valery, from Houdetot and passing through St-Pierre-le-Viger to Veules-les-Roses on the coast. To the south of St Valery, positions covering the approaches to the town were held by the French Army.

By 9 June, the 2/6th Queen's Royal Regiment were three miles outside of Dieppe, and on 10 June were ordered to 'Stand To', and then to destroy all surplus kit and relocate to an orchard situated inland from St Valery, which was being used as a base for the Battalion's HQ. They arrived in St Valery amid bombing, shelling and machine gun fire. According to Sergeant L. Harding, attempts were made to reach the outskirts of St Valery but this proved impossible

19 TNA WO 167/314: 51st Division, General Staff War Diary.
20 J. Thompson, *Dunkirk: Retreat to Victory* (London: Sidgwick & Jackson, 2008), p.287.
21 TNA WO 167/314: 51st Division War Diary.
22 H. Sebag-Montefiore, *Dunkirk: Fight to the Last Man*, pp.470-71.

and so he and his men set off along the cliff tops in the direction of Veules-les-Roses. They hoped to be reunited with their Brigade, but upon their arrival, they found themselves virtually surrounded by enemy troops. With there being no British officers remaining in Veules, Sergeant Harding placed himself and the 20 men with him at the disposal of a French officer there, and it was decided to defend the town until night fell, when it was hoped that ships would approach the beach to pick up those present. Taking a position ahead of the French artillery, the 2/6th Queen's fought through the day, with there being one casualty, namely Corporal Jarvis, who was left with the French troops. Sergeant Harding's men withdrew to the beach at 2315 hours and they were picked up by various boats at 0230 hours.[23]

The 7th Argylls had moved to Fécamp and had only been there for a few hours when further orders came through to them that their Battalion was to withdraw immediately to Montivilliers. When they reached this location, they were to take up a defensive position due to the enemy tanks that were breaking through to the north of Fécamp, it being doubtful whether the remainder of the Division could get back.[24]

The position at Le Havre had been critically examined by the Admiralty and the decision taken to send a flotilla of vessels to St Valery. This was due to enemy action forcing the 51st Division to move along the coast towards that location. In the Admiralty reports is a message from Major General Fortune sent at 2245 hours on 10 June to the Admiralty stating, 'I too think possible that in this rapidly changing situation that I might ask you to embark as much personnel as possible of my Division between St Valery and the mouth of the River Durdent'.[25] On 10 June, the Royal Navy destroyer HMS *Broke*, which included amongst its crew Lieutenant-Commander Peter Scott, the son of the Arctic explorer Captain Robert Falcon Scott, was brought to St Valery to take off as many of the 51st Division's men as possible. In the event, only 120 troops, 95 of whom were wounded, could be embarked.

Upon arrival at St Valery, it had been Fortune's intention that the 51st Division and the other British forces with it would hold the entire three-sided perimeter, but at Ihler's insistence this was changed with the British units holding two flanks, and the tanks of the 1st Lothians and the French cavalry units holding the southern edge.

From 10 to 11 June, and until the 7th Panzer Division took up control of the key positions on the cliffs overlooking St Valery, and from which the fire of its artillery units and machine gun teams could dominate the harbour and its surrounding area, the Royal Navy had been able to evacuate 2,137 British and 1,184 French troops. However, even as Fortune attempted to arrange for the taking off of the remainder of his troops, German artillery began to bombard the town. By 0300 hours, Fortune realised that any men on the beaches would be exposed to enemy fire, and he gave orders for a rendezvous in the Station Square to form a defensive position to hold the town until the next night. He issued a Directive, the last paragraph of which stated:

> Finally, if the enemy should attack before the whole force is evacuated all ranks must realise that it is up to them to defeat him. He may attack with tanks and we have quite

23 TNA WO 167/810: 2/6th Queen's Royal Regiment War Diary.
24 TNA WO 167/704: 7th Argyll & Sutherland Highlanders War Diary.
25 TNA ADM 199/2206: Operation Cycle, Report.

> a number of anti-tank guns. If the infantry can stop the enemy's infantry that is all that is required, whilst anti-tank guns and rifles inflict casualties on AFVs.[26]

At 1400 hours on 11 June, the German formations that surrounded St Valery were units of the 5th and 7th Panzer Divisions, 2nd Motorised Division, 11th Motorised Brigade, 31st and 57th Infantry Divisions. They closed in on the western perimeter and, whilst met with valiant opposition from the 1st Gordons and 2nd Seaforths, including intense close quarters house-to-house fighting to prevent infiltration, the Highlanders lacked anti-tank weapons and those that they were to have received from the French Army had not arrived. To settle matters, the Germans used artillery, mortar fire and 90 tanks of the 7th Panzer Division to break through at Le Tôt. After this, they took possession of the high chalk cliffs overlooking St Valery from the west, which dominated the town, the beaches accessible only at low tide. and the narrow approach to the harbour and located their artillery to thwart any evacuation.[27]

On the southern perimeter, companies of the 1st Gordons and 4th Camerons were facing west and south, and on the eastern side were the 5th Gordons, 4th Seaforths and the 2/7th Duke of Wellington's Regiment, who were being attacked by the German 31st Infantry Division and the 11th Motorised Brigade. The 4th Black Watch was cut off whilst attempting to hold Saint-Pierre-le-Viger against the 5th Panzer Division. The 51st Divisional Headquarters had now withdrawn into the town itself and was trying desperately to communicate with the Royal Navy and those ships that were lying off-shore to arrange an evacuation for the evening of 11 June. As was the case at Dunkirk, the troops followed the orders to destroy their vehicles by slashing tyres, smashing up batteries and draining the oil and water from tanks and radiators (only the Bren/Universal carriers were retained by the rear-guard) and so the town was by now surrounded with a tangled mass of wrecked cars, trucks and other transport.

The German artillery's continuous bombardment of St Valery began to reduce it to a labyrinth of demolished and burning buildings. Its narrow streets were crowded by many of the British units, including the 4th Camerons, 5th Gordons, 4th Seaforths and a small contingent from the Black Watch, which had moved into the town during the hours of darkness to seek out the intended embarkation points. Others, such as the 2nd Seaforths, 1st Gordons, the 4th Black Watch, the Duke of Wellington's Regiment and the 7th Norfolk Regiment, the latter being a pioneer unit of whom not much was expected in terms of fighting ability, had continued with grim determination to do their utmost to hold up the panzers. This was despite some of these men now finding themselves to be cut off from the harbour and as a consequence unable to render any assistance to the defence of St Valery itself. The 2nd Seaforths were sharing their position with units of French cavalry but when the Germans attacked in strength, the French soldiers cut loose their horses and, rather than assisting the Highlanders in their attempt to repel the enemy, they sought cover. Major Murray-Grant eventually found the commander of these French troops and ordered him and his men to either stand and fight or to clear out. Once the fire began to slacken, the Frenchmen choose the latter option and melted away.[28]

As those British troops who were able to approach the harbour had already done, others had obeyed their orders to destroy their heavy guns and disable vehicles to make them useless to the

26 TNA WO 167/314: 51st Division War Diary.
27 P. Takle, *The British Army in France after Dunkirk*, p.96.
28 H. Sebag-Montefiore, *Dunkirk: Fight to the Last Man*, p.473.

enemy. These men were only equipped with light arms and, should any attempted evacuation by the naval flotilla stand any chance whatsoever, they would have to dislodge the German troops and artillery from firmly held positions on the high cliffs.

Troops from the 1st Black Watch and the 5th Gordons were told to secure the high ground to the east, whilst those of the 4th Camerons were to try to take the west cliffs, which were held by the 7th Panzer Division. These British troops were certainly in no mood to give up without a fight, and that they even contemplated let alone attempted such a hopeless enterprise, is a sterling testament to their bravery and fearlessness. Whilst the Royal Artillery's 23rd Field Regiment had begun to disable its guns by stripping them of their breechblocks, to prevent use by the enemy, when called upon to provide supporting fire, they began to try to restore the guns to working order. Unfortunately, being deprived of this artillery cover, the Highlanders were easily outflanked and quickly surrounded by the advancing German forces.[29]

The 1st Black Watch and some units of French cavalry were in action St-Pierre-le-Viger. At the same time, at nearby Veules-les-Roses, the 5th Panzer Division's tanks were attacking the 2/7th Duke of Wellington's Regiment, and they also encountered the 4th Seaforths and the 5th Gordons, but the British troops were unable to stop this advance and they had to abandon their positions and make for the beach at Veules-les-Roses. Sheer desperation eventually led a number of the British and French troops that had reached the cliff tops to try to descend down to the beach below. If available, they used ropes, and even fashioned makeshift ones by tying together the belts and the webbing straps from their personal equipment. Because these were not long enough to reach the ground, many of these men either fell to their deaths on the rocks below, or because they were unable to climb back up again, they were easy prey for the strafing of the German machine gunners. For those of them that did manage to reach the beach, there was bombing by the *Luftwaffe's* Stukas and the withering machine gun and sniper fire from the German infantry to contend with.

During the evening of 11 June, *Generalmajor* Rommel sent a number of captured prisoners bearing white flags into St Valery. Their purpose was to seek out those who were in command there and inform them that if they did not surrender by 2100 hours the German artillery would begin a sustained bombardment of the town. No response being received, at 2100 precisely the German forces unleashed a further torrent of artillery shells on the harbour of the small port to deter an evacuation and to thoroughly demoralise the surviving Allied troops that were sheltering there. The bombardment was initially performed by tanks but was followed by the use of 88mm anti-aircraft guns and machine guns. The chances of the British troops being rescued was diminishing rapidly, their ammunition was running out and the number of dead and wounded increased with the explosion of every artillery shell fired. The end must have seemed imminent for the 51st Division. Unfortunately, the 207 ships that were awaiting the order to sail towards St Valery were driven further away from the port due to relentless German artillery fire. By the evening, the fog would close in to such an extent that an evacuation would be judged to be impossible that day.

However, still in the belief that the Royal Navy's ships were nearby and waiting to carry the 51st Division away to safety and following permission to evacuate being granted earlier that day by *Contre-Amiral* Charles Platon, the French Navy Rear-Admiral in command of Dunkirk,

29 S. Longden, *Dunkirk: The Men They Left Behind*, p.144.

Calais and Boulogne, Fortune planned to evacuate his men that night. He had signalled the War Office to advise that he considered an evacuation that night would be the last possible chance for the Division and he estimated that approximately 24,000 men would need to be embarked. Regrettably, he had not been able to contact the Royal Navy for most of the day and was unaware that the ships were now lying six miles off the coast due to the shellfire from enemy artillery and the aerial attacks being carried out by the *Luftwaffe's* dive bombers.

HMCS *Restigouche* embarked a few stragglers from the beach at Veules-les-Roses at 0530 hours on 11 June. At 0600 hours, a Royal Navy beach party and an officer from HMS *Hampton* had been landed at St Valery. This was during a brief time when there was no firing ashore, although this began from shore batteries established on the cliffs three or four miles down the coast at 0640 hours. It was here that the beach party met 51st Division's RN liaison officer, Commander R.F. Elkins.[30] Instructions were passed for the evacuation to commence at 2330 hours on 11 June, provided that Major General Fortune decide to evacuate then, but by 1100 hours the beaches were being bombarded by shellfire from the German artillery.

At St Valery, it was reported at 0830 hours that the situation ashore was most disorganised, and that the enemy presence was increasing. At 0952 hours, there was a further report to the effect that the 51st Division had formed a hollow square, with its south-west flank extending to the Durdent River and its north-east flank being four miles from St Valery and extending to six miles inland. It was estimated that there were some 60,000 Allied troops in the area, as the French rear-guard troops had started to enter the town, and that the earliest night for an evacuation would now be 12 to 13 June. Hence, arrangements were made for the evacuation to take place at night, and the Divisional headquarters had requested that the ships refrain from retreating so as not to warn the Germans of an impending rescue operation.

Some of the wounded men were embarked during the afternoon on the ships and transports that were waiting, whilst those vessels in the vicinity of St Valery were ordered to retire due to the high risk of being dive-bombed by enemy aircraft, with these being present in considerable numbers. As Admiral James reported, at one time HMS *Hampton* was attacked by 30 German aeroplanes and the naval forces were fortunate not to suffer even more damage and loss due to the absence of British fighter cover, with the only opposition being from those ships that were equipped with the means to provide some anti-aircraft fire.[31] It was also noted that the tactic successfully employed by the German Stukas was to dive, release their bomb load at a height of between 500 and 1,000 feet, and then to machine gun their target both before and after releasing their bombs. The Admiralty reported via a communication from the Commander-in-Chief, Portsmouth to the Senior Naval Officer afloat that there was no objection to its destroyers being used to carry troops away from France but, in view of the importance of conserving the naval forces for other operations, its policy was that it did not wish for them to be unnecessarily exposed to the risks posed by enemy bombers.

Sub-Lieutenant F. Perkins of the trawler *Milford King* reported that during the afternoon of 11 June, his ship together with several others were engaged in mine sweeping when they came under the violent aerial bombing intended for the French battleship *Paris*. Accordingly, these

30 Commander Elkins was captured by German forces whilst on the western pier of the harbour at St Valery-en-Caux, when attempting to communicate by radio with the Royal Navy's ships then off-shore but was subsequently able to escape.

31 TNA ADM 267/126: Operation Cycle, Report.

vessels withdrew to anchor further out. Due to engine damage suffered as a consequence of these air raids, on 12 June the *Milford King* had to be ordered to return to Portsmouth.[32]

At 1750 hours, two German aeroplanes attacked HMS *Lairds Isle*, the first attacking with machine guns and dropping its bombs on the port bow, whilst the bombs of the second aeroplane fell about thirty yards starboard of the ship. Responding with a Lewis machine gun and its 12-pounder gun, the second German aircraft was hit and smoke was seen to be emerging from one of the two engines before it flew away. At 1845 hours, *Lairds Isle* arrived off Veules-les-Roses, where land was within 8,000 yards, but no Allied troops were seen either at St Valery or at Veules, and having received fire from enemy shore batteries, with five shots falling astern, it was decided that the ship should retreat beyond the range of these guns.[33]

On the evening of 11 June, the commander of HMS *Codrington*, Captain George Stevens-Guille, received the order to begin the evacuation, which Major General Fortune had signalled was probably 'now or never'. An armada of 67 merchant ships and 140 other small craft having been assembled and placed under the command of the local Senior Naval Officer was then despatched from British ports. The numbers, time and place were not all known until 1700 hours on 11 June and throughout the operation much of the information that was available or received was either inconsistent or even contradictory. Also, in many cases these ships were less than suitable, as only 16 of them had winches, and the majority were vessels with low speed and low endurance, and few of them even had the means of radio communication. What was even more challenging was that the points of evacuation were over 80 miles from Britain, thereby making it necessary for this flotilla to be assembled at a point some distance away from the French coast and to await developments there.[34]

A thick fog that impeded visibility to the extent that it kept the ships off St Valery and prevented them from moving inshore. According to Captain Warren's report of 15 June, on 11 June this fog was first encountered at 1430 hours, but cleared at 1810 and then there was more fog at 2015.[35] Furthermore, there were too many troops to try to embark during daylight given the likelihood of attack by the *Luftwaffe's* bombers and the shelling by the German artillery, which had set up shore batteries between St Valery and Fécamp that would prohibit the ships and even the smaller craft from being able to take these troops on board. Hence, an evening operation was deemed preferable provided that enough ships could be made available to do so. Should this prove not possible, Admiral James proposed that the evacuation could be attempted on the following morning if air support was made available to neutralise the threat of the *Luftwaffe* and to tackle the German artillery emplacements.

In the absence of radios, communication between the ships and with the British and other forces at St Valery was impaired, and the weather prohibited visual signalling. Therefore, none of the ships were able to reach their place of destination safely. Furthermore, the intention that the ships should seek to shelter at St Valery proved impossible due to the harbour area coming under direct fire from enemy artillery and machine guns. High casualties were to be expected should this be attempted. Much of the higher calibre artillery was positioned with considerable skill to make it be difficult to hit by counter fire from the Royal Navy's larger ships. But at least

32 TNA ADM 179/158: Operation Cycle, Information on British and French troops in Havre district.
33 Ibid.
34 TNA WO 106/1608: Evacuation from St Valery.
35 TNA ADM 179/158: Operation Cycle, Information on British and French troops in Havre district.

the weather conditions also prevented the *Luftwaffe's* bombers from being brought into action against those smaller ships assembled off the French coast.

The transports and boats that had sailed during the previous day arrived north of St Valery had to be ordered to withdraw due to enemy artillery fire. Admiral James stated in his report that there was a considerable number of smaller craft in St Valery harbour and off the coast during the early hours of 11 June, and thus available for evacuation if required. However, no British troops were there then except a few wounded who were taken off. He added that it became known that the 51st Division was much delayed in its withdrawal to St Valery by roads blocked by French horse drawn transport and, in any case, an evacuation had yet to receive approval from the French High Command.

The 51st Division War Diary recorded that whilst it appeared that the British forces resisted the German land and air attacks during the 11 June, its French allies failed to do so and that by the evening St Valery was in the hands of the enemy, so that British and French troops arriving at the outskirts of the town found it to be occupied by German troops and that there were no ships in sight to carry out the planned evacuation.[36]

Believing that the Allied troops were surrounded at St Valery and might now be on the point of surrender, the Germans sent a captured French soldier to deliver a message inviting the British forces to do so. Major General Fortune sent this man back with the message that no such thought had occurred to him.[37] His defiance resulted in another heavy bombardment by the German artillery. *Général de corps d'armée* Ihler of the French IX Corps, had now concluded that further resistance was futile and drafted a message to his superior, *Général d'armée* Weygand, informing him that the French were to surrender. By this stage, he lacked working communications and requested that Fortune transmit the message to Weygand via London on his behalf. Fortune, however, determined that it should not be sent until it was evident that there was no possibility of evacuation and no alternative but to capitulate.

At dawn, the British troops gathered at the harbour were ordered to return to the town and, at 0730 hours, Fortune signalled that it might still be possible for there to be an evacuation on the following night. The original agreement with the French was that the outer defences would be held until 1500 hours. In a message sent to him by Ihler, stating 'Le feu cessera à huit heures' (fire is to cease at 0800 hours) Fortune was ordered to cease fire but he informed Ihler that he could not comply with this until he was sure that there was no possibility of evacuating any of his Division by boat later and the British efforts to clear the enemy cliffs of machine guns continued. Fortune then discovered that the French commander in the town had already negotiated a surrender with the Germans and was infuriated to find out at 0815 hours that a white flag had been raised on the church steeple near to the latest building to be commandeered for use as his headquarters, a villa near the railway station. He demanded that the flag be cut down and the culprit found and arrested, but it transpired that this was the action of a French Army officer acting on Ihler's orders.

Fortune dispatched a message to the War Office advising that the 51st Division would cease fire at 1030 hours. This stated, 'I have informed Corps Commander that my policy is that I cannot, repeat not, comply with his orders until I am satisfied there is no possibility of evacuating

36 TNA WO 167/314: 51st Division War Diary.
37 P. Warner, *Battle of France, 1940*, p.217.

any of my Division later'. In turn, he received a message from Admiral James stating that regrettably the fog had prevented the evacuation on the previous evening, and that the Senior Naval Officer would endeavour to evacuate that night, with additional ships coming to assist.

By the time this message arrived, a ceasefire was ordered and at 1130 hours the 51st Division's headquarters surrendered to the 7th Panzer Division. Some troops, including the 1st Black Watch, the 1st Gordons and the 2nd Seaforths, continued to fight on and did not surrender until 1700 hours. The reality of the situation was that without the French troops of the IX Corps fighting alongside them, the 51st Division men were unable to hold out any longer against such overwhelming opposition and any attempt to do so could only result in further bloodshed. A total of 46,000 Allied troops, including 8,000 men from the 51st Division, and 12 General Officers (including four divisional commanders) surrendered on 12 June. This catastrophe was due mainly to the German forces proactively preventing an evacuation being undertaken, with the result that there was no second Dunkirk at St Valery-en-Caux.

French troops who, regardless of such messages, had already decided to surrender to the enemy now took it upon themselves to disarm, fashion their own white flags from bandages which were then affixed to their rifles, and to march across the front that was held by the 1st Gordons. Seeing this, the German troops used the opportunity to slip in behind the French troops because, naturally, the British unit held their fire so as not to risk killing or injuring their allies, and the Germans were consequently shielded. By the time that the French had passed by, the panzers had arrived and the 1st Gordons had no alternative but to surrender. Similar situations also occurred in those sections of the line that were being held by the 1st Black Watch and the 4th Camerons.[38]

Fortune had sent two of his officers to tell Ihler that his men intended to fight on even if the French surrendered. Whilst he was contemplating disobeying the order from the French general, a German tank arrived outside Fortune's headquarters and trained its main gun on the door. The tank's commander then opened his hatch and called out 'Where is General Fortune?' and, when he emerged, Fortune was immediately taken to Rommel, who had been following his tanks on foot, and was now in the town square. Following the formal acceptance of Fortune's surrender, Rommel extended to him the courtesy of inviting Fortune to share lunch with him. However, this was too much for Fortune's pride as a professional soldier and was no doubt influenced by the belief that if he did so he would be betraying the men of his Division who had endured so much and with many having made the ultimate sacrifice. Fortune therefore politely declined Rommel's offer, saying that he would have something in his own mess, even though he knew that there was nothing left, and like all of his men he was now famished. Rommel also allowed Fortune to retain his personal batman, despite it being customary for captured officers to be separated from the other ranks.

What numbers might have been evacuated, even were it not for the weather, cannot be accurately estimated because of the likely loss of life that would have been incurred by the German artillery and machine guns situated on the cliffs overlooking the harbour. As well as those soldiers waiting at St Valery to be taken off, the ships and their crews could also have been the victims of such a likely carnage. It was only at the eastern end of the perimeter, between St Valery and Dieppe, at the small fishing port of Veules-les-Roses, which was even smaller than

38 J. Thompson, *Dunkirk: Retreat to Victory*, p 289.

St Valery, where despite the heavy bombardment of the German artillery, the damaged HMS *Ambuscade*, HMS *Boadicea* and HMS *Bulldog*, were able to rescue some of the Allied soldiers who had made it to there. The numbers were 2,137 British (mainly from the 2/7th Duke of Wellington's Regiment), 1,184 French troops, and 34 seamen. It might have been possible for more to have followed but the *Luftwaffe* were aware of what was happening and its aircraft attacked the ships there.[39]

Attempts to evacuate the British and French troops from St Valery during the night of the 11 to 12 June had failed due to the heavy fog off the coast. At 0035 hours on 12 June, boats from the flotilla had again approached the harbour but when it was observed that white flares were being fired from the shore, in order to avoid being illuminated by the intense fires raging in some of St Valery's buildings, they made for the western side but nevertheless fire from the German artillery sank two of these vessels. The Tug *Fair Play* had closed in towards the beach to the west of St Valery and disembarked beach parties but the enemy fire resulted in the loss of four other boats. A small coaster, the *Jade*, approached St Valery but also drew heavy fire. To avoid further losses, the other boats retreated from the harbour.[40]

At 0100 hours, HMS *Saladin* reported that the town of St Valery was under heavy shellfire and that it appeared to be in the possession of the enemy, that the beach also appeared to be under sustained fire and that consequently she was proceeding to Veules-les-Roses.[41] At 0215 hours, acting on reports from *Saladin*, Captain Warren closed HMS *Codrington* to Veules and Commander Chatwin landed at 0400 hours as beach master. The evacuation commenced earlier and was carried out with determination regardless of the increased fire from German machine guns and shore batteries. However, despite the continuation of this blaze, between 0200 and 0400 hours, the *Hebe II*, a small Dutch schuyt-type vessel with a British crew, took 80 soldiers away from the beach at Veules-les-roses. Unfortunately, the ship was grounded and was sunk with there being no record of any survivors.[42]

At 0330 hours, Admiral James reached the decision that the last chance of saving the 51st Division would be during the few hours after dawn, and only provided that maximum fighter coverage was made available. Hence, this was arranged from 0515 to 0815 hours. As well as fighters over the area, central command provided protection for the ships lying between St Valery and Cherbourg. The Navy's evacuation flotilla was actually kept in position until late on 12 June in the hope of it being able attempt to evacuate should better weather prevail, but the factor preventing this was the number of enemy guns that had been located on the coast.

From time to time, the destroyers engaged the German artillery but the careful concealment of the enemy's batteries meant that they could only be bombarded effectively from the air, and their existence continued to make any evacuation extremely hazardous. A request was sent from Admiral James and the Senior Naval Officer afloat, to the Air Ministry advising that the situation was critical at St Valery as the evacuation had been delayed and could not continue during daylight as British forces would be dangerously exposed. Maximum support was urgently required to protect the ships against possible enemy air attack or by the German Navy's E-Boats

39 R. Broadhurst, 'The Royal Navy's Role in the Campaign' in Bond, B & M. Taylor (eds), *Battle for France and Flanders Sixty Years On* (London: Cooper, 2001), p.135.
40 TNA ADM 179/158: Operation Cycle, Information on British and French troops in Havre district.
41 TNA ADM 1/10481: Operations Cycle and Aerial.
42 S. Longden, *Dunkirk: The Men They Left Behind*, p.147.

(fast torpedo boats). Between 1315 and 1345 hours, a force of Bristol Blenheim bombers carried out low-level bombing attacks against enemy targets at St Valery. Admiral James noted that strong fighter support was provided for these bombers and that this had undoubtedly prevented there from being an even higher loss of Allied lives.[43]

Nevertheless, it was increasingly evident that there was nothing further that could be done for the 51st Division. Captain Armstrong of HMS *Saladin* had signalled to his superior, Captain Warren of HMS *Codrington*, advising him that St Valery was full of the enemy and its beach was under heavy fire. Therefore, at 1521 hours Admiral James ordered the Senior Naval Officer afloat to withdraw his force from St Valery and arrange to search the beaches in case of stragglers. Many of the men rescued were from the 2/7th Duke of Wellington's Regiment, who had held a position on the eastern perimeter near to Veules-les-Roses. The Royal Navy's ships were finally withdrawn at 1856 hours on 12 June and in a message from Admiral James to the Admiralty on 13 June 1940, it was stated that the: 'Evacuation from Le Havre of 11,000 satisfactorily completed but profoundly regret that the we only succeeded in bringing off about 1,500 British and French from the St Valery area'.[44]

On 13 June, *The Times* reported that the German High Command had issued a special bulletin in which it stated that the force that had been surrounded at St Valery had now capitulated. The number of prisoners of war captured, it was claimed by the Germans, exceeded 20,000 and included one French Corps commander, and one British and four French commanders of divisions.[45] This account was updated on the following day, with the number of prisoners taken being increased to 26,000 and among them from the senior ranks, there were five French generals and one British general.

A War Office announcement was issued on 13 June and also reproduced in *The Times* on the following day. It stated that 'One of our Divisions, which was operating with its left on the north coast of Normandy, had its communications cut by German forces which had penetrated the line farther to the south'.[46] It added that two of its brigades were ordered to assist the French forces in their defence of Le Havre whilst its other units in the north were unable to withdraw south-west towards Rouen because their line of retreat had been severed by German armour and so they had retired towards St Valery-en-Caux. It was here that they were surrounded by four German divisions, one of which was an armoured division. The attempt to evacuate the British troops by sea was only partially successful due to a heavy fog on the night of the evacuation working against the rescuing forces by preventing them from landing, and therefore about 6,000 British prisoners had been captured, with many of them believing that they had been abandoned to their fate by the Royal Navy.

Reporting on the events at St Valery-en-Caux two days later, the *Manchester Guardian* cited the testimony of one of the civilian volunteers who had sailed with the flotilla of ships that were despatched to try to rescue the encircled Allied troops. He commented that 'It was murder. The miracle of Dunkirk was not to be repeated. St Valery has high cliffs, not a beach like Dunkirk; there was a heavy fog, the sea was rough, and the Germans were ready for us this

43 TNA ADM 1/10481: Operations Cycle and Aerial.
44 TNA WO 106/1608: Evacuation from St Valery.
45 *The Times*, 13 June 1940.
46 Ibid., 14 June 1940.

time'.[47] The *Manchester Guardian* also described 'the last stand of a British regiment at the little harbour town of St Valery-en-Caux' as 'a story of courage unequalled by anything in the last war. Completely surrounded, they fought all night at barricades in the midst of the burning town, after driving the enemy back at the point of the bayonet'.[48]

Mistreatment of British Prisoners of War

Within the Treasury Solicitor files are found details of the various war crimes that were alleged to have been committed by soldiers of the German Army on or around 12 June 1940. This was when those British prisoners of war, mainly from the 51st Division, who had been forced to surrender at St Valery-en-Caux, were marched for their humiliation in columns through various French towns and villages, such as St Pol, Doullens, Béthune, Sectin, Sensix, Hinoul, Alost, Forges-les-Eaux, Hazebrouek, Poix and Lille, and thence onwards into four or even five years of German captivity.[49] The crimes were described as being those of murder or manslaughter; and of the ill-treatment of prisoners of war, and which were in clear contravention of Articles 2, 4, 7, 10, 11 and 54 of the Geneva Convention 1929.

In the account provided by Edward Prady, MM, a Lance Corporal serving in the 7th Battalion of the Royal Northumberland Fusiliers, it was stated that he personally witnessed the killing of a British soldier. This man had received wounds to both of his feet during the battle, and consequently he was unable to keep up with the marching column of British prisoners. He had fallen out of the column and, upon doing so, was immediately shot with a rifle by a German NCO and was killed outright. Prady also confirmed that the British prisoners were treated with excessive harshness by their German guards, being over-marched (covering up to 30 km per day). The rations that were supplied to the prisoners were wholly inadequate (one packet of British Army hard biscuits per day had to be shared by three men and, at the end of the day's march, they were given half a pint of an indeterminate warm black liquid, which they were told was coffee) and it was only due to the generosity of some of the French civilians that these British soldiers received anything else to sustain them.

Furthermore, there was no accommodation or protection from the weather when the prisoners were eventually halted for the night. As well as being fired at indiscriminately by their German guards if they fell out of the column without permission, the prisoners were frequently assaulted with rifle butts or even stabbed with bayonets. Prady's testimony described one incident where a German guard had used the bayonet that was fixed to his rifle to stab a British prisoner in the thigh simply because this man had collapsed as a result of his sheer exhaustion.

Prady regretted that he was unable to identify the particular German units that were involved in these matters, or to give the names of the individual guards who had been responsible for the harsh treatment of these British prisoners. In the file's case notes, Prady observed that it was very noticeable that the French prisoners of war were comparatively well provided for with food, and that the virtual starvation of the British prisoners and the inadequate arrangements which were made for them must therefore have been quite deliberate on the part of their German captors, presumably in retaliation for the fight they had put up at St Valery and elsewhere.

47 *Manchester Guardian*, 15 June 1940.
48 Ibid., 17 June 1940.
49 TNA TS 26/207: Brutality to prisoners on the march from St Valery-en-Caux.

Also discovered in the Treasury Solicitor's files are the documents that are concerned with the mistreatment of Colour Sergeant Edwin Fields of the 2nd Seaforth Highlanders by the troops of a German armoured division following his capture at St Valery-en-Caux on 12 June. The relevant allegations were subsequently registered with the United Nations War Crimes Commission on 5 June 1944 and they were related to him being forced to take up a position on the front of a German armoured vehicle that was then driven towards the British lines without a white flag being flown and whilst the fighting was still in progress. Against his will, Colour Sergeant Fields was to have been made to carry a message to the British troops demanding that they surrender and, by this action, it was the case that he would also have been deliberately exposed to gunfire from the weapons of his own comrades.

In his sworn affidavit, to which additional testimony was provided by the officer who was second-in-command of the Battalion, Major James Murray Grant, Colour Sergeant Fields confirmed that following the retirement to a new position by his Company during the previous evening, and along with a number of other British troops, he was captured by a German patrol early on the morning of 12 June.

Upon becoming captives, the British soldiers were then taken to the commanding officer of a German panzer unit who interrogated them to try to ascertain the number of British troops and their positions held in the nearby villages of Saint-Sylvain and Le Tôt, south-west of St Valery-en-Caux. These places were being held by the 2nd Seaforths, who were to have been supported by artillery and anti-tank guns but these were not available, having been held up on roads that had been heavily congested with refugees. Nonetheless, and although surrounded, the Highlanders put up a valiant fight with seven of the enemy AFVs being disabled or destroyed in the process. This was an area that the British forces needed to hold for an evacuation to be viable; once it fell to the German forces, its artillery was able to take up a crucial position on the high western cliffs overlooking the beach and harbour at St Valery. The British troops from the Kensingtons, Norfolks and the Northumberland Fusiliers had attempted to eject the Germans from the location, but without success.

In response to his interrogation, Colour Sergeant Fields informed the German panzer officer that he had no information, because he had no knowledge of what had happened to the rest of his Battalion. Furthermore, in any case, he was not obliged to communicate to the enemy information regarding the disposition of British troops. Fields suggested to the German that the resistance being met by his units might be from French troops, but the German commander instantly dismissed this notion, replying that only the British troops could put up such a force of resistance, including the characteristic use of Bren light machine guns.

As the senior British non-commissioned officer present, Colour Sergeant Fields was then ordered by the German officer to take up a position seated and unprotected on the bonnet of a German tank. He protested that this was contrary to the Geneva Convention, but he was forced to do this at the point of a German NCO's automatic pistol. Whilst being driven towards the British lines, the same German soldier kept his weapon trained on Fields. However, at approximately 1400 hours, and as this tank came towards a crossroads on the road that approached one of the villages, there was burst of small arms fire from the British positions, some of which actually hit the German tank, but which did not harm Fields. The German NCO being distracted by the gunfire, this allowed Fields to jump from the tank and to run across a field to where he could see that some of the British unit's slip trenches were situated.

Fields was taken to the unit's commanding officer, Major Bonar, and related to him the German officer's ultimatum, which was that the British troops in the village should surrender immediately. If they did this, the panzer officer had stated that the men would be treated honourably as prisoners of war, and any wounded would receive medical attention immediately. He also communicated the news that the rest of the 51st Division had already surrendered and the whole of the area was now occupied by the German Army.

If no reply to the ultimatum was received within the hour, mortar fire and artillery fire would be directed on to the village by the German troops. Following some consultation, and it being decided that their position really was hopeless, it was agreed that any small parties that wished to try to escape should do so in the hope that they could get away to the coast and be evacuated. The wounded and any others should stay and surrender. Despite being a part of a group of men who made it to the coast and found a boat, because this was unseaworthy and there was no other possibility of escape, Fields and his comrades were later captured by German forces.

As it was not possible to identify the panzer officer and other enemy troops, or the units with which they were serving, despite the breach of Article 9 of the Geneva Convention 1929 relating to the treatment of prisoners of war, it was not possible for the UN War Crimes Commission to proceed any further with this matter.

Lieutenant General Sir Alan Brooke.

Lieutenant General James Marshall-Cornwall.

Major General Victor Fortune (GOC 51st Division) with *Generalmajor* Erwin Rommel at St Valery-en-Caux. (Imperial War Museum RML 342)

Acting Major General Archibald Beauman.

Admiral Sir William James.

Admiral Sir Martin Dunbar-Nasmith, VC.

Air Marshal A.S. Barratt.

Air Vice Marshal P.H.L. Playfair.

Vickers Light Tank Mk VI B.

A13 Cruiser Mk IV.

Hawker Hurricane Mk I, France 1940.

Bristol Blenheim Mk I.

Vickers Wellington Mk I.

HMT *Lancastria*. (Private Collection)

7th Panzer Division column near Abbeville, June 1940.

Evacuated British Troops on a transport during Operation Aerial.

Part III

Operation Aerial: 14 to 18 June 1940

6

Withdrawal

14 June 1940

On 14 June, Paris fell and German troops entered the city unopposed whilst elsewhere the 7th Panzer Division reached Le Havre. Two days of rest were taken by Rommel's troops before they commenced their advance towards Cherbourg. The German forces renewed their pressure on the French 10th Army, although it was evident that many of their armoured and motorised divisions and the aircraft of the *Luftwaffe* were now being used for the attacks that were being made on the south-easterly axis. There was a pause in the advance of the *Heer* over the River Seine to allow for the bridges to be built or re-built. At this point, the remnants of the British 1st Armoured Division, together with two Brigades of the Beauman Division and thousands of Line of Communication troops, were south of the River Seine.

The 1st Armoured Division War Diary and of the Beauman Division headquarters both record that during the early morning of 14 June attacks were made by enemy troops from two infantry divisions at Neubourg and Bourgtheroulde-Infreville. These were combined with considerable air support by the *Luftwaffe*.[1] Following reports that the German infantry had been able to infiltrate there, 2 RTR was sent to patrol in the area around Combon, Le Tilleul-Lambert and Tournedos-Bois-Hubert. A troop consisting of three light tanks led by Second Lieutenant Bell, with the other vehicles being commanded by Sergeant Cross and Corporal Jasper, was to patrol Emanville – Combon – Sainte-Colombe-la-Commanderie – Le Tilleul-Lambert. At the crossroads near Combon, this patrol encountered heavy rifle and machine gun fire followed by the heavier ordnance from the German anti-tank guns. Bell's tank was the last to pass through and was hit by an anti-tank shell and his driver was wounded. The gunner of his tank, Corporal Draper, was ordered to run and bring up the other tanks, but as they approached the German anti-tank guns opened fire on them but then ceased firing.[2] Later there

1 TNA WO 167/334: 1st Armoured Division War Diary; WO 167/1412: Beauman Division, Headquarters.
2 TNA WO 167/448: 2nd Royal Tank Regiment War Diary.

were reports that heavy fighting had taken place just to the north of Le Tilleul, at Ferme de la Commanderie, with units of German troops gaining a position in this village.[3]

At 1710 hours, a message was received from the 1st Armoured Division putting the 2nd Armoured Brigade once again under the command of *Général de division* Petiet. At this time, two German divisions were known to advancing south-west on the line of Les Planches, Bérengeville-la-Campagne and Ormes, whilst the French 10th Army was withdrawing on its left flank.[4] It was further observed that this was: 'A curious situation, being taken from one general's command to another when half the Brigade's available force is already in active support and might be in action at any moment'. At 2130 hours, an urgent message was sent from the 1st Armoured Division headquarters to Brigadier McCreery of the 2nd Armoured Brigade. There was news that the German forces were now advancing westwards from Évreux and orders were given for the Brigade to proceed to Brest immediately. The Brigade's few remaining vehicles (there were now only 14 of the A13 Cruiser IV and 26 of the light tanks) were to be entrained at Le Mans and the remainder of the Brigade was ordered to proceed to an area near to Brest. These tanks did not reach their intended final destination of Cherbourg, however, owing to the railway line being blocked.[5]

The 4/5th Royal Scots Fusiliers War Diary noted that a bombing attack was made by *Luftwaffe* aircraft about six miles from their position, and that a man wearing the uniform of a French Army officer was arrested on the suspicion that he was an enemy agent before he was handed over to the French authorities.[6]

Only 157th Brigade, which was part of the 52nd Division, had been engaged in operations by occupying defensive positions to the east of Conches-en-Ouche and it was under the command of the French 10th Army.[7] An enemy attack developed on the Brigade's left flank, which led to 50 casualties being inflicted on the British troops there, and also to the French infantry and artillery that were supposed to be providing support but which were retiring, effectively leaving the 157th's position completely exposed. A message was sent from 157th Brigade to the 3rd Armoured Brigade requesting assistance, but in response the Armoured Brigade advised that it had been placed under the command of *Général de division* Petiet and had itself been ordered to withdraw by him.[8] These British forces were then instructed to retreat to a line connecting Verneuil to Argentan and the Dives River, where their position was an eight-mile front on either side of the Mortagne-au-Perche to Verneuil-sur-Avre road. Later that day, and following an order from Lieutenant General Brooke, the 52nd Division was instructed to move to Cherbourg as soon as possible and the 157th Brigade was withdrawn from the front line.[9]

On the previous night, the German controlled railway marshalling yards and certain forested areas were bombed by the RAF, as was the River Rhine which had mines dropped into it and, on 14 June, the attacks against the *Heer's* units operating south of the River Seine were resumed. These missions were hindered by the weather conditions, which continued to limit the number

3 TNA WO 167/421: 3rd Armoured Brigade War Diary.
4 Ibid.
5 TNA WO 167/419: 2nd Armoured Brigade War Diary.
6 TNA WO 167/817: 4/5th Royal Scots Fusiliers War Diary.
7 TNA WO 32/9388: Overseas: Europe (Code O (V)): Despatches from BEF 12-19 June 1940.
8 TNA WO 167/421: 3rd Armoured Brigade War Diary.
9 TNA WO 167/326: 52nd Division War Diary.

of sorties that could be flown by the AASF. Merville airfield was now held by the enemy and hence became the target for a bombing raid carried out by 24 Bristol Blenheims. Despite being provided with a fighter escort, this still resulted in the loss of seven RAF aircraft. Ten Fairey Battles were sent to attack the German columns near to Évreux but were unable to locate their targets due to the bad weather conditions. During the afternoon, nine Battles attacked the woods near to Évreux and the Le Coudray airfield, as *Luftwaffe* aircraft were reported as having been seen there. Three Fairey Battles from 12 Squadron were allocated to this task and two of them were shot down by the enemy.

During 14 June, it was clear that the AASF's aerodromes were now highly vulnerable to the rapid advance of the German mechanised divisions, should they be directed against them. A prompt withdrawal was therefore imperative. Accordingly, the BAFF's headquarters was moved to Nantes and the AASF's headquarters re-located to Angers. Upon arrival there, the AASF received instructions for a general withdrawal of the Fairey Battle squadrons, with a view to evacuation for fear of the impact to be felt should the RAF's bomber forces be kept in France any longer. Air Marshal Barratt directed the Air Officer commanding the AASF to complete one final sortie before flying these aircraft back to bases in Britain. The ground support personnel of the AASF were to proceed to the port of Brest, where embarkation onto boats that would take them back to Britain was being arranged. In spite of the myriad logistical problems that this presented, it was successfully carried out and was fully completed by 17 June. Fighter Command's aircraft flew two sorties either as part of a patrol or as an escort to the above-mentioned bombing missions. This was their most significant display of force since the fighter umbrella had been provided to cover the Dunkirk evacuation, but fewer enemy aircraft were in evidence to confront the RAF on this day.

15 June 1940

The *Heer* was now directing its foremost efforts towards and beyond Paris, and *Generaloberst* von Kluge's 4th Army was moving towards the south with Chartres on its left, and with the XVI Armoured Corps together with *Panzergruppe Kleist* being specifically employed for this purpose. The meant that one Armoured Corps and the greater number of infantry divisions remained active in the area held by the French 10th Army. On 15 June, *Generalmajor* Rommel received orders to take his 7th Panzer Division to Cherbourg, to try to intercept and capture the remaining British forces and prevent them from being evacuated. This required his Division to move to the east, to Vernon, before then turning westwards and towards Cherbourg. At the same time, the 5th Panzer Division and the 2nd Motorised Division were to attack on the left of the Allied line, to try to cut the French formations off from Brittany.

Following orders from *Général d'armée* Altmayer, it was intended that the Beauman Division would be used to hold a gap through which the French formations could retire, if necessary. The Beauman units moved, firstly to Pont-l'Évêque, and then to Caen. After reaching the latter, instructions were received from Lieutenant General Marshall-Cornwall which confirmed that whilst he was now in command of the British forces that had been under the orders of the French 10th Army, they were still to support the French Army. In the likelihood of such support being limited, Acting Major General Beauman ordered the withdrawal of his troops to Cherbourg.

At 0030 hours, the Commander of 155th Brigade, Brigadier T. Grainger-Stewart, also issued verbal orders for his Brigade to start to move towards Cherbourg. All of the Brigade's equipment was to be taken, but if this was not possible then it was to be abandoned, as the men were now deemed to be the first priority. Later, at 1400 hours, more verbal orders were given, this time for the 155th Brigade to occupy defensive positions around Cherbourg, on the line La Rocque to Taflaret to Mont a la Quesne. On the right were the 4th KOSB, with 5th KOSB on the left and the 7/9th Royal Scots were in reserve. At 2100 hours, the 5th KOSB was moved to a defensive position on the line of Lessay to Carentan.[10] The 156th Brigade was on the left of the sector and despite only reaching the Continent three days earlier and having been advised on the previous evening that it was to withdraw to Cherbourg, the Brigade was now ordered to an area one mile to the east of the road from Valognes to Cherbourg to take up a defensive position in order to provide cover for Cherbourg.[11]

At 1700 hours, the 3rd Armoured Brigade was ordered to move from its position at the Forêt de Beaumont once it had received the code word 'SCRAM'; in the meantime, it was to continue to co-operate with and assist the withdrawal of the French 10th Army until such time as it could be released from this obligation. In the Brigade's War Diary, it is succinctly recorded that 'It looks as if the French may be packing in completely. Similar messages received from General Marshall-Cornwall'.[12]

The second-in-command of the 2/6th Duke of Wellington's Regiment was instructed to proceed to Le Mans with 22 wounded men who were to be taken to the No. 9 general hospital there. He was also to arrange the transport for the 300 men and officers still at Sées but, upon reaching Le Mans, he found that the entire town was completely evacuated of all British troops. Therefore, he had to arrange with the French authorities to take the 22 wounded men on a hospital train that was destined for Rennes.[13] Shortly after midnight, the 4/5th Royal Scots Fusiliers were ordered to withdraw to the vicinity of Cherbourg, using their motor transport as far as possible and, if necessary, by discarding any surplus equipment.[14]

Two officers and a unit of men from the Royal Engineers had been issued orders to prepare the bridges in the 157th Brigade's area of operation for urgent demolition. During the day, the Brigade's units strengthened their position and the 5th Highland Light Infantry (HLI) reported that the enemy was gathering its forces in the area of Conches-en-Ouche. German infantry had engaged with the 6th HLI, resulting in a number of casualties in that battalion. The Brigade had started the process of extricating itself from the front line and, as the 52nd Division's War Diary records, 'this was a difficult operation in view of the lack of French co-operation'.[15]

Orders having been received on the previous evening for the AASF's Fairey Battle Squadrons to return to Britain, one final attack was made at dawn on 15 June. Escorted by Hurricane fighters, ten Battles from 150 Squadron attacked targets around Évreux. They then proceeded to Nantes, which was the first stage of the departure for the AASF. Of the 261 RAF fighter aircraft that had been sent to France during the ten days since the commencement of *Fall Rot* (the second phase of the German offensive), 75 aeroplanes had either been shot down during combat or had been destroyed on the ground during air raids by the *Luftwaffe's* bombers. The

10 TNA WO 167/411: 155th Brigade Headquarters.
11 TNA WO 167/412: 156th Brigade Headquarters.
12 TNA WO 167/421: 3rd Armoured Brigade War Diary.
13 TNA WO 167/736: 2/6th Duke of Wellington's Regiment War Diary.
14 TNA WO 167/817: 4/5th Royal Scots Fusiliers War Diary.
15 TNA WO 167/326: 52nd Division War Diary.

120 aircraft that were now unserviceable or were otherwise unable to fly back to their RAF bases in Britain were wrecked by their ground crews to prevent them from being utilised by the enemy. What was especially serious for the RAF was that in these ten days, a quarter of the total strength of its fighter force had been lost.

16 June 1940

In his report on operations conducted from 14 June until the final evacuation, Lieutenant General Marshall-Cornwall reported that the *Heer's* armoured and mechanised columns had already followed up swiftly on the French withdrawal. They were now attacking the southern sector of the French 10th Army, which was held by the Cavalry units of the French III Corps commanded by *Général de corps d'armée* de la Laurencie. Poor visibility had made air reconnaissance difficult but there were some reports that showed that the enemy was attacking seriously only against that part of the front being held by the 157th Brigade, which was under assault throughout the day. The French units on either side of the Brigade's position retreated without offering any serious resistance to the enemy. Moreover, both of the 157th Brigade's flanks were in serious danger of being turned. Further to the south, the enemy's movement was seemingly being directed towards Chartres.

The 157th Brigade, together with the Royal Artillery's 71st Field Regiment, was holding a front-line sector that was eight miles wide, on either side of the road from Mortagne-au-Perche to Verneuil-sur-Avre road, and it was covering the north-eastern outskirts of the Forêt du Perche and the Bois de Cherencey, with the French 237th Infantry Division on the left. The 157th Brigade had two battalions in the front line and one in support. To the right of this was the French Cavalry Corps, consisting of two light armoured divisions, which were by now considerably reduced in strength. Beyond this, to the south-east was a gap of 30 miles, between the French 10th Army and the Army of Paris, the latter force being in retreat from the Loire.

German forces carried out a particularly heavy attack at Marchainville, on the front of the French 3rd DLC, and to the right of the 157th Brigade. Pressure was also directed southwards so that the 157th Brigade was in danger of being outflanked from both sides. As a result, *Général d'armée* Robert Altmayer decided to withdraw the entire French 10th Army into Brittany, so that at 1930 hours orders were given for a retirement on the axis of Alençon – Laval – Rennes, to create a front of nearly 100 miles, from Angers on the River Loire to Avranchine. This being contrary to the instructions he had received, Lieutenant General Marshall-Cornwall issued orders to the 157th Brigade and to the 3rd Armoured Brigade for a withdrawal north-westwards towards Cherbourg. Simultaneously, Acting Major General Beauman's force was also withdrawing in the direction of Cherbourg, through the lines of the French XVI Corps, which had been ordered to hold the line on the River Orne. Whilst this was a relatively straightforward manoeuvre for the Beauman units and the Armoured Brigade, it was problematic for the 157th Brigade and Royal Artillery as they were still fighting, and because of contact with the enemy and the retirement of French troops to the left and to the right of the Brigade. Although attacked by the *Luftwaffe* when near to Domfront, no losses were suffered and it was able to complete the 200 miles to Cherbourg. In its War Diary, the Beauman Division's Headquarters recorded the statement made by Acting Major General Beauman that 'It became obvious that there was an uneasy attitude amongst the French troops and staffs'.[16]

Earlier that day, Lieutenant General Brooke received the authorisation necessary to embark the 155th and 156th Brigades of the 52nd Division. In the meantime, the 157th Brigade was to remain in support of the French 10th Army, which was still of the opinion that the British forces were to play a part in the defence of Brittany. It was apparent that the 157th Brigade, which was positioned near to Mortagne-au-Perche, continued to be in danger of having its flank turned as the French cavalry there were receiving greater pressure from the enemy forces.

At 0045 hours, Second Lieutenant H. Griffiths of the 1st Armoured Division arrived at the headquarters of the 2/6th Duke of Wellington's Regiment at Sées. He had been sent there by Lieutenant General Brooke in order that he might arrange transport for the 2/6th Dukes, either to Brest or to St Malo, for their evacuation. Unfortunately, no such transport could be found and the Battalion had to move by foot to Redon near to Alençon, in the hope that some transport for them might be found there.[17]

From 0230 hours, orders were given for 155th Brigade to occupy a defensive line from La Roque to Mont a la Quesne, with 156th Brigade on the left. The 5th KOSB, was now a part of the 'Normanforce', which had been placed under the command of Lieutenant General Marshall Cornwall. This was to provide the rear-guard to cover the withdrawal of all the British forces from Cherbourg by safeguarding the vital bridges and ensuring roads were kept open, and it was ordered to remain at its current position. To allow this retirement through the rear-guard, the 5th KOSB was to make sure that the French Army did not blow any bridges or block roads, thinking that the units passing through were Germans.[18] In an order to this effect, it was stated that 'Coys will therefore get in touch with the French troops in the areas mentioned, explain they have come to help them. Of course, no mention is to be made that they are there to stop the bridges being blown, but they must prevent it in a tactful way'.[19]

At 0300 hours, 2 RTR received orders to leave all their vehicles in their present position at Landerneau, taking only their Bren guns, anti-tank rifles, rifles and ammunition, and were then to march to the docks at Brest for embarkation.[20]

From 1000 to 1100 hours, companies of the 5th KOSB were to advance forward and to carry out patrols at La Haye du Puits and St Sauvier le Vicomte. They were instructed to contact the French troops in the vicinity and seek to prevent them from demolishing the bridges until the 157th Brigade and 1st Armoured Division had passed through.[21] At 1300 hours, the A Company of the 5th KOSB was occupied a position at Carentan where, later in the evening, it was given orders to establish a defensive line from Lessay to Carentan. This was because the French forces were of the view that Carentan was the vital point in the line and they were anxious that at least one British Company should be positioned at the bridge at Les Veys. It was noted by the 5th KOSB troops that the civilian morale of the French seemed to vary considerably, ranging from despondency to a desire to fight on right until the end.

16 TNA WO 167/1412: Beauman Division, Headquarters.
17 TNA WO 167/736: 2/6th Duke of Wellington's Regiment War Diary.
18 TNA WO 167/775: 5th King's Own Scottish Borderers War Diary.
19 TNA WO 167/326: 52nd Division War Diary.
20 TNA WO 167/448: 2nd Royal Tank Regiment War Diary.
21 TNA WO 167/411: 155th Brigade Headquarters.

By 1145 hours, contact with the enemy had been made by the French Army six miles to the east of Carentan, where trouble was to be expected from the advanced elements of the German divisions. The Beauman force was also in action and heavy fighting had broken out on the sector being held by the 157th Brigade. Its commander, Brigadier Sir John Laurie, sent a message to Lieutenant General Marshall-Cornwall informing him that the French troops on his flank were giving way and that the French artillery batteries that were supposed to be supporting him had ceased firing. Marshall-Cornwall gave the order to Laurie to extricate his Brigade and move it via Mortagne-au-Perche, Domfront, Mortain and Avranches, to reach Cherbourg. Similar instructions were also communicated to the remnants of the 3rd Armoured Brigade, which was to proceed to Domfront, Vire and to St-Lô.

When it was reported that the enemy had reached Évreux, a warning order was issued to the 4/5th Royal Scots Fusiliers at 1300 hours, that they must be prepared to withdraw to Cherbourg and then to embark for evacuation. This order came during the early evening and the battalion's troops either used motor transport or marched there by separate routes. They embarked two days later and returned to England having seen little enemy action during this brief period of service on the continent.[22]

D Company of the 6th Cameronians, commanded by Captain W. Taylor, was to take up the forward defensive positions at St Mere Eglise and the Company's main role there was to prevent the French Army from blowing up the bridges along this road until the 155th Brigade had passed through enroute to Cherbourg.[23] Having received orders to move during the previous morning, the 7th Cameronians had formed into a column and commenced the journey, arriving six miles to the south of Cherbourg at 0300 hours on 16 June. Later during that day, the battalion commander was told to move towards Cherbourg immediately and to immobilise the transport when they had reached their destination.[24] At 2130 hours, 156th Brigade was evacuated from the port of Cherbourg on the *SS Princesse Astrid* and the *Manxman*.[25]

At 2200 hours, the 3rd Armoured Brigade received confirmation that it was no longer to be placed under the orders of the French Army, but instead would now be under those issued by Lieutenant General Marshall-Cornwall, who had ordered it to move to Cherbourg forthwith. By this stage the Brigade was comprised of no more than 25 cruiser and light tanks and 50 other assorted motor vehicles and had been in the 10th Army reserve.[26] Thus, it had over 150 miles to travel before it reached Cherbourg but there was sufficient fuel to allow it to make the journey via Forêt d'Andaine, Domfront and Villedieu, so that it could take advantage of wooded concealment and it arrived at Cherbourg around midnight on the 17 to 18 June.

According to Brooke's account of these events, which was published after the war, the German forces had maintained their pressure on the French 10th Army throughout the day. During the evening a message from Marshall-Cornwall had set out his opinion, which was that the 10th Army would shortly disintegrate, were it to be seriously attacked by the enemy. This

22 TNA WO 167/817: 4/5th Royal Scots Fusiliers War Diary.
23 TNA WO 167/722: 6th Cameronians War Diary.
24 TNA WO 167/723: 7th Cameronians War Diary.
25 TNA WO 167/412: 156th Brigade Headquarters.
26 Bovington Tank Museum Archives: 2nd Royal Tank Regiment.

opinion was also to be corroborated by his GSOI, Lieutenant Colonel Raymond Briggs of the Royal Tank Regiment.[27]

17 June 1940

On 17 June, *The Times* published a article from its special correspondent that stated:

> The battle proper is entering into a state of extreme confusion. British armoured units and infantry are being rushed forward and fighting desperate rear-guard actions with their French allies, under a deluge of metal from German tank detachments which are filtering through gaps in the line.[28]

This was also the day on which the French Government's request for an armistice and to open peace negotiations reached Adolf Hitler's headquarters near to Sedan at 0300 hours. Later, at 1230 hours, *Maréchal de France* Pétain delivered his first message to the French people as their Prime Minister, when he spoke on the radio, telling them that 'It is with a heavy heart that I say to you that fighting must cease'.

As shown in Beauman Division War Diary, during the day news was heard from the radio that the French authorities had agreed to an armistice with the Germans.[29] This caused considerable alarm as it appeared entirely possible that the terms of any armistice might include the internment of British troops still in France. Lieutenant General Brooke was informed by Lieutenant General Marshall-Cornwall that the French 10th Army was now in full retreat in Laval and Rennes, and that he was withdrawing all his troops to Cherbourg for embarkation.[30]

At a meeting between the officer commanding the Cherbourg sub-area and Acting Major General Beauman, the former requested that the Beauman division hold the line between Lessay and Carentan to provide cover for the withdrawal of elements of the 1st Armoured Division and the 52nd Division. Beauman's response was to point out that his men had been fighting and marching continuously for nine days and that they were exhausted. He added that there were two brigades of the 52nd Division which were fresh and had never fired a shot in France, and that they should be used for this operation. It was thus arranged to withdraw both brigades to an area two to three miles from Cherbourg. The Beauman Division was ordered to retire at once to positions on the hills south of Cherbourg and the Royal Engineers were ordered to construct road blocks. Troops were then called in from the defensive line to the collecting centres and marched to the Quaie Normandie. By 1700 hours, the 3,500 men of the Beauman force had reached Cherbourg and began to embark on the *SS Belgravian*. All kit and arms were also embarked, including eight 18-pdr guns, 20 anti-tank guns and 4 Bofors guns, which had been constituted the Division's artillery.

Shortly thereafter, and despite the very long road journeys and a complete lack of spares and ordnance services, Brigadier Crocker's 3rd Armoured Brigade and its remaining 27 tanks, 11

27 *The London Gazette*, 22 May 1946, p.2436.
28 *The Times*, 17 June 1940.
29 TNA WO 167/1412: Beauman Division, Headquarters.
30 B. Karslake, *1940, The Last Act*, p.203.

Daimler Dingo scout cars and 49 lorries began to be embarked at Cherbourg.[31] Also to be boarded onto ships from this port, was the 157th Brigade, which had withdrawn via Auraches, and the Beauman Division.

At 0900 hours, Lieutenant Colonel G.G. Walker, the 5th KOSB's commanding officer, was summoned to the headquarters of the 52nd Division's at Tollevast Chateau. He was told to ascertain the position of the French forces around Caen and to contact the headquarters of 'Normanforce' (the 157th Brigade) to discover their disposition. A thorough reconnaissance was made of the defence's inner and outer perimeters. The outer perimeter meant holding the line of the river west of Carentan; the inner perimeter was the immediate defence of Cherbourg and was mainly concerned with setting up road blocks in and around the town. Proceeding to St Mere Eglise, he reconnoitred the defences at Les Veys and Carentan and instructed A Company of the 5th KOSB to take up position there. During this time there was considerable activity on the part of the *Luftwaffe*, including low level flying and strafing of positions. Lieutenant Ashton reported that French forces were holding a line on the River Orme as far south as Thury Harcourt. He reported that 'Normanforce' at Avranches was to withdraw and pass through the defences by midnight. The rest of the 5th KOSB was then ordered to St Mere Eglise. At 2230 hours, an attempt to demolish the bridge at Les Veys was made by Lieutenant Roughton of Royal Engineers. The first effort being unsatisfactory, this was re-attempted at 2359 hours and was successful.

After several days of successive withdrawals, the 2/4th KOYLI was ordered to withdraw via Caen to Vierville, to pick up the transport that had been provided by the Beauman Division. By 1400 hours, the Battalion was ordered to retreat immediately to Cherbourg and to be part of the defensive line there; however, later that day the Battalion was put aboard the *SS Duke of Atholl*, which then sailed for England.[32]

The 2/6th Duke of Wellington's Regiment proceeded to within three kilometres of Vitré and found the town to be empty of British troops, with the General Headquarters having moved out during the previous day. By managing to obtain trucks and sufficient petrol, the Battalion was to move to St Malo, some eighty miles away, and from there it embarked for Southampton at 2100 hours without incident.

On 17 June, Air Commodore Cole-Hamilton, the commander of the RAF's Air Component, was ordered to transfer two of the fighter squadrons and one flight of reconnaissance aircraft to the Channel Islands. The reasoning for this move was that from there they would be able to co-operate with the Army by carrying out a reconnaissance role and protect the troops who were embarking at Cherbourg. Once these tasks were completed, these RAF formations were to return to Britain. The remaining fighter squadron was detailed to cover the port of Brest whilst elements of the BEF were embarking from there. Thanks to the air cover provided, very little interference from the *Luftwaffe* was experienced, with only a few bombs being dropped close to troop ships but no damage was inflicted. The BAFF's headquarters at Nantes was closed at midday on 17 June and the staff and other personnel were ordered to La Rochelle for embarkation. Air Marshal Barratt returned to Britain leaving his senior air staff officer,

31 TNA WO 167/421: 3rd Armoured Brigade War Diary.
32 TNA WO 167/777: 2/4th KOYLI War Diary.

Air Vice Marshal Evill and his small staff to ensure that the necessary arrangements for the evacuation of 67 Wing were successfully carried out.

At 2130 hours, Lieutenant General Brooke left St Nazaire on the armed trawler HMT *Cambridgeshire*. This was because the vessel sent for his use by the Royal Navy's Commander-in-Chief, Western Approaches had become involved in the carrying off survivors of the HMT *Lancastria*, which had been sunk that afternoon following the critical damage caused by bombs dropped by a *Luftwaffe* Junkers Ju 88 bomber.

18 June 1940

Lieutenant General Marshall-Cornwall had hoped that the force covering the evacuation could be held on the line from St Sauveur to Carentan for three days, as this would have allowed all the vehicles remaining at Cherbourg to be embarked. However, the process had to be limited to 600 vehicles per day in the four transport ships available. Furthermore, the employees of the French power station had ceased work and no more electric power was available to work the port's loading cranes. At 0100 hours on 18 June, a War Office signal was sent to Lieutenant General Brooke and copied to Lieutenant General Marshall-Cornwall. It read as follows:

> French Army has been ordered to cease fighting. Normanforce should now withdraw for evacuation Cherbourg. You alone can decide degree of evacuation of material possible in accordance with information obtained by you.[33]

At 0230 hours, orders were issued for patrols of Dingo scout cars to be sent out to determine the position on the roads from La Haye du Puits to Lessay, from Carentan to Perriers and from Carentan to St Lo. Lieutenant Ashton of the 5th KOSB and three Dingo scout cars got through the French road blocks but their progress was impeded by demolition works. On the road from St Sauveur to Port he found there were lorries full of enemy infantry. Artillery and small arms fire were also reported in the area.

At 0900 hours on 18 June, having slipped past the French Marines who had been guarding the road at La Haye du Puits, some elements of the 7th Panzer Division had reached the covering position near St Sauveur. By now Rommel's troops had become known the 'Phantom Division' and had earned this title due to the remarkable advance they had made since the commencement of the Battle of France on 10 May, included 180 miles in a single day, and the capture of 97,648 prisoners of war, 277 artillery pieces, 438 AFVs and over 40,000 other vehicles.[34] Here, at a bridge to the north of the town of Carentan, the German 37th Reconnaissance Battalion's infantry were confronted by the 5th KOSB. This prompted the enemy troops to turn to the west, where they encountered French troops, but these offered little in the way of resistance and the Germans were able to outflank and infiltrate their position. At 1100 hours, the enemy units were reported as having penetrated the flank in the region of Denneville and being present in the area west of St Sauveur and proceeding north, with this being confirmed by the reports coming in from the British Dingo scout cars. The 5th KOSB was withdrawn without casualties

33 M. Glover, *The fight for the Channel ports: Calais to Brest 1940*, p.221.
34 A. Horne, *To Lose a Battle: France 1940* (London: Macmillan, 2012), p.643.

between 1200 and 1500 hours and was ordered to drive towards Cherbourg for immediate evacuation. By now the only passable road was the main Valognes Road, as the Briquebec road had been blown and the lanes were barricaded at every turn.[35]

The last company of the 5th KOSB rear-guard was withdrawn through the inner perimeter and the last barricade to the entrance to the town was then set on fire. By the time that the last troopship, the *SS Manxman*, left at 1600 hours during a *Luftwaffe* air raid, the German forces had penetrated to within three miles of the harbour. Aboard this vessel were Lieutenant General Marshall-Cornwall and his staff. When it was embarking, enemy aircraft that were flying overhead dropped their bombs from about 15,000 feet but these missed, landing in the water or hitting the buildings on the shore. It is reported that as well as from the French anti-aircraft batteries, every Bren and Lewis machine gun on the *Manxman* was fired at these aeroplanes. A naval demolition party successfully destroyed the dock and harbour installation as the final embarkation of troops took place form Cherbourg at 1615 hours on 18 June.

As German forces raced forwards, towards the area in which the AASF was located, it was planned for the RAF to move its squadrons to the Rennes and Nantes areas. This had been due to occur on 15 June, but instead they became part of the arrangements for the evacuation carried out under Operation Aerial. Once they had completed the tasks allocated for that day, all of the serviceable bomber squadrons flew directly to RAF bases in Britain. Whilst the fighter squadrons, did not return immediately, so that they were able to provide air cover for the evacuation, 17 and 242 Squadrons were despatched to Dinard and 1, 75 and 501 Squadrons remained at Nantes. These five RAF fighter squadrons had been an integral part of the AASF but were now to be placed under the command of the BAFF headquarters.[36]

During the day, there were four Blenheim reconnaissance flights over Caen, Argentan and Avranches, and seven patrols, which involved 37 aircraft, took place for local protection over Cherbourg but there was no combat with any *Luftwaffe* aircraft in this area.[37] Transport aircraft were sent to Nantes through an arrangement with the Air Ministry to allow various personnel to be returned to Britain by air. The Hawker Hurricanes from 1, 73 and 242 Squadrons (67 Wing) continued to carry out their operations until the embarkation at St Nazaire was completed. Following a last refuelling, the destruction of any unserviceable aircraft and the evacuation of the ground crews, the last British aeroplane left France at 1430 hours. In his dispatch report, Air Marshal Barratt referred to the last 24 hours of 67 Wing's operations and accorded them the highest praise. He noted that all personnel had been working under considerable strain, under intense conditions and were in danger of isolation due to poor communication and constant rumours of the approach of the enemy.[38] According to the *Manchester Guardian*, Air Vice Marshal Playfair, the AOC-in-C of the AASF had insisted that he would be the last member of the Force to leave France.[39]

On 19 June, the port of Cherbourg capitulated. *The Times* confirmed that nearly all of the BEF troops that were to be evacuated from north-western France had now arrived back in Britain. It added the account of a British Army officer commanding one of the very last units to

35 TNA WO 167/326 - 52nd Division War Diary.
36 TNA AIR 35/255: Report on the AASF in France, September 1939 - June 1940.
37 TNA AIR 35/192: Summaries of Operations 10 May – 16 June 1940.
38 TNA AIR 35/354: Barratt's Dispatch.
39 *Manchester Guardian*, 19 June 1940.

leave, who described how Fifth Columnists were posing as British officers and had attempted to detain him and his men by ordering them to wait for other troops. At the same time, the same time the sound of the German forces entering the town was audible, so these British troops made good their escape.[40]

40 *The Times*, 19 June 1940.

7

Final Evacuations

Planning and implementation

Operation Aerial (also known as Operation Ariel) was the codename allocated to the evacuation of all of the British military personnel and civilians still in France. This was carried out from several ports, including St Nazaire and Nantes, Cherbourg and St Malo, mainly between 15 and 18 June 1940, but was finally concluded on 24 June. This was in conformity with the armistice negotiated between France and Nazi Germany of 22 June. News of the French Government's request to open peace negotiations with Germany, and the implications this could have for the remaining British troops, also provided the impetus for an acceleration of the evacuations. Correspondingly, on the British mainland, several troop transit areas were prepared to receive those who had been evacuated and returned via Southampton, Portsmouth, Weymouth, Poole, Plymouth, Falmouth, Fowey, Avonmouth and Liverpool.[1]

The BEF withdrawal commenced during the early hours of 15 June. Even before he had communicated with Winston Churchill on 14 June, Lieutenant General Brooke had already instructed that the disembarkation of the remainder of the 52nd Division should be halted and for the men of the Canadian Division to be re-embarked. On that day, he received confirmation from the Secretary of State for War, Anthony Eden, that the British troops still in France would cease to be under French command. For all the British troops who had been under the control of the French 10th Army, Brooke determined that they should now be under the orders of Lieutenant General Marshall-Cornwall, and whilst they were to support their French allies in any actual fighting taking place, they were to proceed with all haste to Cherbourg and the other ports designated in Operation Aerial for embarkation and return to Britain. The CIGS, General Dill, telephoned Brooke on 16 June to confirm that all arrangements could now be made for the withdrawal of the 52nd Division, less any detachment that was still with the French 10th Army. Finally, on 17 June, and having been involved in the rear-guard actions at Conches-en-Ouche and Mortagne-au-Perche, the last unit to be in action, the 157th Brigade, received orders to disengage and evacuate.

1 TNA WO 197/88: Evacuation Progress Reports.

Orders having been received during the evening of 14 June for the AASF's Fairey Battle Squadrons to return to bases in Britain, and following their final sorties around Évreux, these aircraft then proceeded to Nantes, which was the first stage of the planned departure from France. Sixty Battles duly returned to Britain, whilst the Hurricanes of 1, 73 and 242 Squadrons continued to provide cover for the evacuations being undertaken from Brest, Nantes and St Nazaire. Fighters from 17 and 501 Squadrons performed a similar role during the evacuations taking place at Cherbourg and St Malo. Finally, on 18 June, 1 and 73 Squadrons, which had been the first RAF formations to go to France in 1939, were the last to depart, leaving behind those aircraft that were either unserviceable or without fuel. Following what had happened at Dunkirk, the *Luftwaffe* was determined that any further Allied evacuations should not be successful. Hence, *Generaloberst* Ulrich Grauert's *FliegerKorps I* was ordered to patrol both the areas of Normandy and Brittany, and by 15 June it had already dropped 15 tons of bombs on the port of Cherbourg alone. Despite this, when Operation Aerial was in progress, there was relatively little interference from enemy aircraft.[2]

Operation Aerial would be overseen by the Commander-in-Chief, Portsmouth, Admiral Sir William James, who had also supervised the conduct of Operation Cycle, whilst the evacuation from Brest, St Nazaire, La Pallice and the southern ports on the Bay of Biscay was led by the Commander-in-Chief, Plymouth Command and Western Approaches Command, Admiral Sir Martin Dunbar-Nasmith, VC.[3] As in the evacuations during Operation Cycle, the anticipated numbers to be extracted from each port fluctuated considerably and the rate of advance achieved by the German armoured and mechanised forces was still not fully appreciated.

However, lacking the quantity of vessels necessary for convoys to be maintained, James had to organise a continuous flotilla of troop ships, store ships and motor vehicles between Southampton and Cherbourg and Southampton and St Malo. Furthermore, it was arranged that coasters would operate between Poole and Cherbourg and Dutch schuyts would operate between Weymouth and St Malo. Preparations were also made for small boats and schuyts to ferry between the Channel Islands and St Malo in the event of a further deterioration of the situation, as larger vessels might not be able to enter these ports due to the state of the tides.

Given that speed was the principal consideration and because there were insufficient vessels available, sailing in convoy was deemed to be prejudicial to the success of the operation. Therefore, Admiral James made the decision that the Royal Navy's escort ships should patrol the various sea routes and provide a defensive screen for these other craft. The Royal Navy vessels to be made available included HMS *Vega*, HMS *Fernie*, HMS *Rosemary* and HMS *Foxglove*. HMS *Vega* was later to be relieved by HMS *Sabre*, and HMS *Laird's Isle* was also employed as transport. Offers of help from along the south-west coast were received by the Royal Navy, including from the fishermen of Brixham, Dartmouth, Exmouth, Falmouth,

2 H. Buckton, *Retreat: Dunkirk and the Evacuation of Western Europe* (Stroud: Amberley, 2017), p.218.

3 Admiral Sir Martin Eric Dunbar-Nasmith (1883-1965) received the Victoria Cross during the First World War when commanding Submarine E11 in the Sea of Marmara, Turkey. From 20 May to 8 June 1915, this craft destroyed one Turkish gunboat, two transports, one ammunition ship, three store ships and four other vessels. He was the Commander-in-Chief, Plymouth, from 1938 and Commander-in-Chief, Plymouth and Western Approaches Command, from September 1939.

Fowey, Teignmouth and Torquay, so that by 15 June this evacuation flotilla included some 50 merchant vessels, 20 armed trawlers and 23 Royal Navy destroyers.[4]

La Pallice and St Nazaire

La Pallice, the deep-water port of La Rochelle, is situated to the south of the port of St Nazaire. It was here on 16 June that Admiral Dunbar-Nasmith would discover that there was a considerable number of Allied troops, estimated to be approximately 10,000 men, but that there were no ships available for them to be evacuated because all of the suitable vessels were already bound for either Brest or St Nazaire. Fortunately, there were some cargo ships in the port at La Pallice and these were duly requisitioned by Dunbar-Nasmith, and so eventually 2,303 British personnel were taken off on 18 June and a further 4,000 Polish troops were evacuated the next day. Unfortunately, this meant that as in the other centres of evacuation, there was no choice but to leave behind valuable vehicles, equipment and stores.[5]

St Nazaire and Nantes were the locations of two of the BEF's main bases in the southern part of France. St Nazaire had been the Army's centre for the storage and distribution of ammunition and frozen meat, whilst Nantes was the base for motor transport and for the drivers of these vehicles. During the Battle of France, and so as not to be overrun by the swift advance of the enemy forces and sent into captivity, many of the British troops had already begun to retreat towards these locations. In doing so, it was their hope that once there, they might be able to re-group; or, if the situation continued to deteriorate further, be evacuated back to Britain. Contradictory information suggested that there could be as many as 40-60,000 men heading towards Nantes but there was no indication when they would arrive there.

With the evacuation initially estimated as a five-day process, there appeared to be no urgency on the part of the British garrisons.[6] However, the garrison stationed at St Nazaire was informed that if an evacuation was to take place, one of two signals would be sent out. It the signal PIP was received, this meant that arrangements were necessary to leave France in 24 hours; if the signal was PIP PIP, then garrison's departure should be within 48 hours. At 1000 hours on 15 June, the PIP signal came through. This prompted a degree of haste and, in panic that the enemy forces were closer than was actually the case in reality, resulted in large quantities of the BEF's valuable armaments and equipment being left behind, to fall into enemy hands.

In terms of the RAF presence, 67 Wing and its three squadrons had concentrated in Nantes, with the 12th Anti-Aircraft Brigade being deployed north and south of the estuary at Nantes to protect the port of St Nazaire. This small force continued to provide fighter cover for the evacuation from St Nazaire on the 16 and 17 June.

In his capacity as the Senior Naval Officer, Captain L.H.K. Hamilton provided a report on 26 June 1940 to the Admiral Dunbar-Nasmith on the evacuation of British personnel from St Nazaire.[7] In this document, it was pointed out that when the BEF was disembarked in France in 1939 there had not been an adequate movement control organisation at St Nazaire due to

4 J. Fenby, *The Sinking of the Lancastria: Britain's Greatest Maritime Disaster and Churchill's Cover-Up* (London, 2005), p.58.
5 H. Buckton, *Retreat: Dunkirk and the Evacuation of Western Europe*, p.232.
6 TNA WO 167/117: St Nazaire Garrison.
7 TNA WO 106/1739: Operation Cycle reports on evacuation.

the constant turnover in officer-level personnel. In June 1940, and despite this function now being carried out by four or five officers, it was evident that they lacked knowledge of the local situation, such as tidal complications, and what was actually required to embark a large number of troops. Prior to Hamilton's arrival at St Nazaire on 15 June, he had been told that the priority was to evacuate material, but when he arrived 48 hours later this had been reversed, as evidenced by the fact that the only ships in the port were large liners and thus insufficient and inappropriate for removing trucks, supplies and other material.

Admiral Dunbar-Nasmith assembled a force that consisted of the Royal Navy's destroyers HMS *Havelock*, HMS *Wolverine* and HMS *Beagle*, together with the liners *Georgic*, *Duchess of York*, *Franconia* and *Lancastria*, several cargo ships and the Polish ships MS *Batory* and MS *Sobieski*. These vessels were anchored in Quiberon Bay, which was approximately 20 miles to the north-west of the Loire estuary. Two more destroyers, HMS *Highlander* and HMS *Vanoc*, were subsequently involved in the evacuation operation. Due to their considerable size, the larger of these ships were particularly vulnerable to the air raids being carried out by the German aircraft. The RAF's fighter cover, with up to six sorties being flown each day, had been an effective deterrent in restricting the activities of the *Luftwaffe* to mine-laying, although this also meant that the Royal Navy's mine sweepers had to be used to clear the channels before any of the other ships could approach or depart from the port.

The evacuation from St Nazaire had commenced on 16 June, with 16,000 troops being placed aboard the *Georgic*, the *Duchess of York* and the two Polish vessels, in order that they could be taken back to Plymouth. An attack on these ships was subsequently made by a single *Luftwaffe* Junkers Ju 88 bomber and the bombs that it dropped had caused some damage to the former Cunard liner, the HMT *Franconia,* and this ship would have to be escorted back to Britain so that requisite repairs could be carried out.

The HMT *Cambridgeshire* had arrived off St Nazaire with a convoy of ships from the Bristol Channel on 16 June and on the morning of 17 June, there were estimated to be some 67,000 Allied troops still ashore, with many of them being situated in the port of St Nazaire. Anchored some miles away from the port at the wide estuary of the River Loire, were several merchant ships and railway ferries, but the largest of the vessels to be ordered to participate in the evacuation, was the HMT *Lancastria.*[8]

The *Lancastria* was constructed by William Beardmore and Company of Dalmuir, Scotland and launched on 31 May 1920 by the Cunard Line. By 1940, it was commanded by 55-year-old Captain Rudolph Sharp.[9] Originally it had been named the SS *Tyrrhenia,* which caused the ship to receive the nick-name of 'the soup tureen', and it was renamed in 1924, much to the consternation of a superstitious crew who believed this to be an ominous development that would inevitably lead to disaster. Originally it had been deployed in the Atlantic on the Hamburg – Southampton – New York service, and then became a cruise ship operating in the Mediterranean and the Norwegian Fjords. It was converted to a troop ship in 1940, becoming the HMT

8 During the Second World War, the designation HMT (His Majesty's Transport) replaced that of RMS (Royal Mail Ship), MV (Motor Vessel) or SS (Steamship) for those vessels which had been converted to troopship duty with the Royal Navy.

9 Rudolph Sharp had joined the Merchant Marine in Liverpool during 1908 and he had been the Captain the RMS *Lusitania* before it was sunk by the torpedoes from the German submarine U-20 on 7 May 1915.

Lancastria, and was provided with a 4-inch gun as its sole armament and then employed for conveying troops and supplies from Canada to Britain. Fitted with oil-burning Brown-Curtis turbine engines, the ship was 16,243 tons in weight, 582.5 feet in length and 70 feet wide, and required 1,380 tons of fuel oil.[10] Equipped with 580 cabins spread over five decks, normally it was permitted to carry only 1,700 passengers and 375 crew members but in the circumstances Captain Sharp was ordered to take on board as many Allied personnel as he could.

Rather than sailing into Brest, Captain Sharp had set a southerly course. Therefore, the *Lancastria* had travelled down the coast to the Bay of Quiberon, being accompanied by the *Franconia* and a Royal Navy destroyer, HMS *Wolverine*, which was acting as escort, and it was guided through the channels between the Quiberon peninsula and the island of Belle Île by a French trawler. During the early hours of 17 June, it entered the wide estuary of the River Loire and found there a number of other vessels, including the two destroyers, HMS *Havelock* and HMS *Highlander*, and the armed trawler, HMT *Cambridgeshire*, and it reached a point five miles south of the Pointe de Chémoulin and nine miles to the west of St Nazaire. It was there that the *Lancastria* dropped anchor and began to take on board those who were being ferried out to it in smaller vessels. This was due to the relative shallowness of the estuary near St Nazaire, with only the smaller vessels being able to gain access to the harbour. Also, there had been a delay to embarkations because the French authorities would not open the gates of the lock, thereby preventing troops being taken on board the smaller craft. Carrying at the most around 500 men, it took these vessels four hours to reach the *Lancastria's* position, during which they had to run the gauntlet of attacks from the bombs and machine guns of the *Luftwaffe's* aircraft. These were dropping mines into the water, but none of the ships were damaged by them.

At 1350 hours, a force of *Luftwaffe* bombers had attacked the liner SS *Oronsay*, which was a 20,000-ton liner from the Orient Steam Navigation Company, and although they had not sunk it, part of its bridge was destroyed by a bomb that killed several people, and caused damage to the ship's chart, steering and radio rooms.

At approximately 1500 hours, Captain Sharp had signalled that there were over 5,000 troops aboard and he could take no more but estimates of how many people were actually on board after this vary from 6,000 to 9,000. Incidentally, not all of these were military personnel, as some were civilians from the British Embassy and contractors from the Fairey Aviation Company who had also been put aboard. Concerned that it might be target for German U-Boats if sailed back to Britain alone, Sharp decided that it would be prudent to wait for the nearby *Oronsay* and the first available destroyer before doing setting off. By this time, HMS *Wolverine* had returned to its station, off Brest, and a squadron of Hurricanes from 73 Squadron was at the end of its patrol and low on fuel, necessitating a return to base in England. This was the moment when several of the twin-engine Junkers Ju 88 bombers from *II Gruppe, Kampfgeschwader 30*, a *Luftwaffe* squadron that specialised in attacking shipping and which was based at Louvain in Belgium, made their appearance.

The *Lancastria* was still at anchor, making it a far easier target for the bombers to hit than had it been moving, and at 1548 hours one of these aeroplanes dropped four bombs that achieved direct hits to the ship. Following the impact of the bombs, the *Lancastria* titled to its starboard and, as everyone aboard desperately tried to go to the port side, the ship then keeled over to

10 J.L. West, *The Loss of the Lancastria* (Lancashire: Rossendale, 1988), pp.2-3.

port. The bow of the ship sank and the stern came out of the water as it rolled over to port and by 1612 hours, it was submerged.

Lifeboats were launched, some sinking in the process after being swamped by the desperate, and then the order 'Every man for himself' was given. Others who had been on the deck and were wearing life jackets decided to take their chances and jump into the water. For many of them this resulted in instantaneous death, due to the height of the ship's deck in relation to the sea level, and when they hit the water the upward movement of their lifejackets violently jerked their heads back, breaking their necks. Whilst the *Lancastria* lay on its side, and for the next fifteen minutes until they either sank with the ship or through sheer exhaustion and despair allowed themselves to slip below the water, those who could not swim simply clung to the *Lancastria's* hull and sang songs, including 'Roll out the Barrel'. For those who were unable to escape from the ship's holds after the bombs exploded, their deaths were hellish, with one of the bombs rupturing the ship's boiler and causing many of them to be horribly scalded. In the shallow waters of the Loire estuary, the *Lancastria's* final resting place was at latitude 47.09 N, longitude 2.20 W.

Regarding those who had escaped the ship and were in the water, they were repeatedly strafed with machine gun fire by the squadron of *Luftwaffe* bombers which had come around again following the explosions. The *Lancastria* had also been carrying 1,400 tons of fuel oil that should have been taken off when the ship was undergoing repairs in the dry dock at Liverpool but, because of the urgency with which the evacuation was ordered, there had not been time to do so before sailing. As the enemy aircraft fired tracer bullets and dropped flares, they ignited the patches of leaking oil that were floating on the sea's surface, causing it to become a raging mass of fire that caused some of the 3,000 people in the water to be burned alive.

As soon as the *Lancastria* began to list, numerous boats attempted to rescue the ship's passengers and crew. The rest of those who were saved were rescued under continued air attacks. In the brief report submitted on 1 July by the commander of HMT *Cambridgeshire*, it was noted that it proceeded at full speed and was the first ship to arrive at the scene and able therefore to rescue between 800 and 900 survivors, most of whom were fished out of the water, at a time when enemy aircraft were continuing to bomb and machine gun those still in the water. When the *Cambridgeshire* reached and then exceeded its capacity, it had to withdraw and transfer some of the survivors to other vessels, such as the merchant ship *John Holt*, apart from the badly wounded who had been taken back into St Nazaire.[11]

Birmingham born and bred, from Bradford Street in the Digbeth area of the City, Thomas Patrick Smith was 18 year's old and had been serving with the Royal Army Medical Corps for six months. In early June, his unit had been making its way to Dunkirk for evacuation when it encountered an Army despatch rider who confirmed that the port was already in German hands. The men of the unit were then placed aboard a train that eventually arrived at St Nazaire when the evacuation from that port was underway. Private Smith was due to be part of a group to be ferried out and put on to the *Lancastria* but during the bombing of the quay he had suffered a wound to his hand. The delay, whilst his hand was bandaged, may well have saved his life. As part of the next group to be taken out on a fishing boat to where the *Lancastria* was anchored, when approaching the ship, he saw a German aeroplane fly overhead and drop its bombs. One

11 TNA ADM 1/12264: HMT *Cambridgeshire* in the rescue of survivors from the SS *Lancastria.*

of them appeared to Smith to have gone down the ship's funnel and almost immediately there was a huge explosion and within seconds there were people in the water.[12] As many of them were now completely covered in the fuel oil that was leaking from the ship, it was extremely difficult to lift them out of the sea. When trying to drag them into the fishing boat, for the first time during his wartime service, Private Smith would have to decide who could be saved and who could not. Subsequently, he was able to board a cargo ship, which arrived back in Britain two days later and he was disembarked in Plymouth.[13]

The evacuation from St Nazaire continued after the sinking of the *Lancastria*, with over 23,000 men being taken off by 18 June. With news that the arrival of the German forces at the port was imminent, this became increasingly frantic and a large amount of military equipment and supplies had to be left there to fall into enemy hands. In total, 57,235 men (54,411 of whom were British servicemen) were evacuated. As Operation Aerial approached its conclusion, HMT *Cambridgeshire* was boarded by officers of the BEF's General Staff, including Lieutenant General Brooke, and it then sailed for Plymouth whilst clearing the harbour during a continuous attack from the enemy's aircraft.

Only 2,518 were saved, and the exact number of armed forces personnel and the ship's crew to have lost their lives when the *Lancastria* sank is unknown, with estimates varying from between 4,000 to 9,000. This is because, contrary to the limits that were set by international law, Captain Sharp had been instructed by the Admiralty to load as many as possible. What is certain is that the number of Allied personnel perishing as a consequence was at least equal to the combined loss of life from the sinking of the RMS *Titanic* (1,522 lives) and RMS *Lusitania* (1,195 lives).

When presented with the reports of this disaster, and in view of the very probable negative consequences of this for the morale of the British people, the Prime Minister immediately prohibited the publication of this news by ordering that a 'D' Notice be issued. He observed, 'the newspapers have got quite enough disaster for today at least'. The news eventually reached the wider public some six weeks later after details were published in the press in the United States, initially appearing in the *New York Sun* on 25 July, before being briefly reported at home by the *Daily Mirror* on the following day. Winston Churchill was later to claim that he had fully intended to allow the information to be publicised within a few days, but then he further stated that the 'events crowded upon us so black and so quickly, that I forgot to lift the ban, and it was some time before the knowledge of this horror became public'.[14]

12 Several witnesses were to provide accounts in which they claimed to have witnessed one of the bombs dropped from a German Junkers Ju 88 aeroplane going down the funnel of the HMT *Lancastria*. However, if this had occurred, the resultant blast would have completely destroyed the ship's boiler room and the engine immediately below the funnel, which was not the case. Frank Bogden, who was the *Lancastria's* engineering officer considered that the bomb landed near to the funnel and entered the hold, which was immediately below the ship's bridge. The other bombs exploded in the other holds and in the water on the port side of the ship, resulting in the rupturing of the ship's fuel tanks, which were still full of fuel oil.

13 The author is indebted to Councillor Rose Martin of Walsall Metropolitan Borough Council, who told him about the wartime service of her late father, Thomas Patrick Smith. After his evacuation from France, he served with the British Army in the far east and, on 15 December 1943, was present when Lord Louis Mountbatten, the Supreme Allied Commander - South East Asia, told the British troops at Arakan, in northern Burma, 'You are not the forgotten army - nobody has ever heard of you'.

14 W.S. Churchill, *The Second World War* (London: Penguin 1959), p.172.

The families of those men believed to have died as a consequence of the sinking of the *Lancastria* received telegrams from the relevant military authorities which informed them that their loved ones were 'missing in action' but without providing any further details. Perhaps it was hoped that a few might somehow have made it back to land and were now being held captive in a German Prisoner of War camp. This was a forlorn hope and most of the families must have incorrectly concluded that the men had died on the French mainland during the final stages of the Battle of France.

Brest, Cherbourg and St Malo

The Royal Navy's liaison officer at Cherbourg was Captain Alan Twigg, who had sailed to Cherbourg on 12 June, and the following information has been taken from his report made to the Admiralty on 20 June 1940.[15] In his dealings with the senior French naval officer in Cherbourg, *Vice Amiral* Jean-Marie Charles Abrial and his chief of staff, *Rear Amiral* Leclerc, Captain Twigg was called upon to enquire whether the 52nd Division would be able to remain to assist in holding a line across the Cherbourg peninsula. Seeking an interview with the Division's GOC, Major General James Drew, Twigg was informed that the Division had been ordered to embark and even where that not the case, several divisions were required to hold the peninsula, the French forces being deemed to be quite inadequate. This, combined with the deteriorating political situation in France no doubt contributed to the decision to bring the date of the 52nd Division's return to Britain forward to 18 June.

There was a reluctance to accept that evacuation was necessary, and on 15 June Lieutenant General Brooke was told by General Dill that 'for political reasons', the two Brigades of Major General Drew's 52nd Division could not be embarked from Cherbourg. Discussions with General Dill and Anthony Eden were held, and permission to embark the Division's artillery (but not the infantry) was granted.

On the same day, Lieutenant General Marshall-Cornwall had requested that a fresh battalion of the 52nd Division with anti-aircraft guns be detailed to occupy a position 20 miles south of Cherbourg to provide protection from aerial attack for those units embarking and the ships taking them back to Britain. A demolition party comprised of personnel from the Royal Navy and the Army, and under the command of Commander Grindle, prepared in conjunction with the French authorities to assist them in blowing up the dockyard and other key points. The Maritime prefect for Cherbourg, *Vice Amiral* Jules Le Bigot, whilst making it quite clear that no destruction was to take place without his orders, offered every assistance in preparation. He also arranged for all the berths to be cleared to accommodate the berthing of transports. On 14 June, news had been received that there would be no further movements of troops and that the evacuation would commence on 15 June.

The 5th KOSB was also ordered to guard the approach roads and it carried out a reconnaissance and constructed road blocks for this purpose. On 17 June, a German motorised column including tanks was reported to be in the vicinity of Coutances. This was confirmed and orders issued for it to be attacked from the air but, before this could be carried out by the RAF, during the

15 TNA WO 106/1739 - Operation Cycle reports on evacuation.

following morning the German column had broken through the French line and was advancing towards Cherbourg.

Most of 52nd Division and what remained of the 1st Armoured Division were embarked between 15 and 17 June. Improvised formations, such as the Beauman Division and the 'Normanforce', left Cherbourg during the evening of 17 June and the rear-guard battalion was evacuated on the afternoon of 18 June. The demolitions were carried out by Commander Grindle and his party, who were the last personnel to leave on HMS *Fernie,* which departed at 1615 hours on 18 June, but returned to take off five stragglers from the quay at Cherbourg. In total, 30,630 men were evacuated from Cherbourg and taken by ship to Portsmouth.

The entrance to the harbour at Brest was closed due to magnetic mines having been dropped and orders were given for six mine sweepers to be deployed and ships were ordered to keep outside of the 50-fathom line until given permission to enter.[16] Here the French Army had tried to form two defensive lines, with the outer being 100 miles from the port and the inner line being 40 miles from it. Most of the British troops reaching there had been taken off by 17 June, but as was the case in the other ports from which the British troops were evacuated, there were enormous amounts of valuable materials which had to be left behind. This was so that sufficient space could be made on board the ships to rescue as many service personnel as was possible. A total of 32,584 men were evacuated from Brest, with a large number of these being from the RAF ground crews serving with the AASF squadrons.

Also anchored at Brest was the Atlantic Fleet of the *Marine Nationale* (the French Navy). Understandably Churchill was concerned at the possibility that it could easily fall into German hands and, by altering the balance of power at sea, it could pose an enormous threat to the Royal Navy in ensuring Britain's safety from invasion. Admiral Dunbar-Nasmith was therefore instructed to do all in his power to persuade the French naval commanders to sail their vessels to the safety of British harbours. Regrettably, only a small number did so on 17 June, with the remainder of the French fleet, including all its capital ships, transferring loyalty to the Vichy regime and sailing for the North African ports including Casablanca and Dakar, with most heading for the Algerian port of Mers El Kébir.[17] It is noteworthy that at the armistice, France still possessed over 6,000 aircraft of which at least 2,000 were still capable of being used on the front line, and which then fell into enemy hands.

The troops of 1st Canadian Division that had arrived in the concentration area were sent to Brest for embarkation, corps troops were to be embarked at St Malo and the various Line of Communications troops in the Le Mans area were moved to be nearer to the ports. 21,474 men, mostly from the 1st Canadian Division, were evacuated from St Malo between 16 and 17 June. To assist with this evacuation, the Royal Navy also called upon the authorities in nearby Jersey to render their assistance. As it was the potato season in the Channel Islands,

16 TNA ADM 199/2206: Operation Cycle, report.

17 On 3 July 1940, following the transfer of its allegiance to the Vichy regime and the rebuttal of Winston Churchill's demands that the French fleet should either join with the Royal Navy or be neutralised to prevent the possibility of any of its ships falling into enemy hands, as part of Operation Catapult, the Royal Navy attacked the French Navy's vessels at Mers El Kébir. In this action, the Royal Navy carried out a bombardment that sank one battleship and damaged two battleships and two destroyers, resulting in the deaths of 1,297 French sailors. Five aircraft from the Royal Navy's Fleet Air Arm were also shot down and two crew members were killed. This controversial incident soured Anglo-French naval relations for many years.

it was more than expedient that a number of large cargo vessels were harboured at the port of St Helier. Their organisation, together with that of a number of smaller vessels, was overseen by the Commodore of the St Helier Yacht Club and Solicitor of The Royal Court, William Le Masurier. The second piece of good fortune was that it had been arranged for those units of the *Heer* that were en route to St Malo to be diverted to take part in the assault being carried out on Rennes airport. The Canadian Division and other Allied troops there were consequently able to be evacuated without hindrance, and rather than being taken to Jersey, were conveyed to Plymouth, Dartmouth and other, smaller, ports on the south-west coast of England.

On 17 June, there were 9,014 (plus 357 casualties) evacuated from Cherbourg and St Malo. The total for the following day was 32,962 (plus 375 casualties). By 28 June, this increased to 135,663 (plus 2,626 casualties), of whom 16,558 were French, 20,477 were Polish, 483 were Czech and 66 Belgians. There were 21,474 (mainly the 1st Canadian Division) rescued from St Malo and 2,000 from La Pallice, and a further 19,000 were taken off from the smaller ports. The sum total of all of the evacuations was 191,870, of which 144,171 were British, 18,246 were French, 24,532 were Polish, 4,938 were Czechoslovakian, and 163 were Belgian.[18]

18 TNA WO 197/88: Evacuation progress reports.

Part IV

The Anglo-French Relationship

8

Haddock Force: Air Operations Against Mussolini's Italy

Planning

Italy declared war on Britain and France on 10 June 1940, during the final weeks of the Battle of France, and on the day in which the French Government fled from Paris. This action was strongly condemned by the US President, Franklin Roosevelt, who said that 'the hand that held the dagger has stuck it in the back of his neighbour'.

Although Italy's decision had little immediate military consequence, the British Government decided to implement an existing plan for RAF bombers to be sent to suitable airfields located in southern France in order to execute a mission to bomb key industrial targets situated in northern Italy. That it was Benito Mussolini's intention to declare war on the Allies and to enter the conflict on the side of the Axis powers had been known for some weeks. In a conversation with his Chief of Staff, Marshal Pietro Badoglio, Mussolini had, for fear that he would be left empty handed by the other Axis powers, claimed that 'I only need a few thousand dead to ensure that I have the right to sit at the peace table in the capacity of a belligerent'.[1] The British Government was well aware of such developments, due in the main to the radio transmissions that were being intercepted and decrypted by Station X at Bletchley Park. On 31 May, the Allied Supreme War Council had resolved that should Italy indeed declare war then the industrial targets and oil plants situated near to the northern Italian cities of Genoa and Turin should be attacked without delay. The official minutes recorded the determination of the British representatives:

> Mr Churchill said that the British view was that if Italy came in against the Allies, we should strike at her at once in the most effective manner, and all should be made to realise its severity. He proposed that we should strike at the North Western industrial triangle enclosed by the three cities of Milan, Turin and Genoa. Such an attack could be delivered without undue hardship to civilians. The British had four heavy Bomber squadrons available for the purpose and the French Government had already authorised the sending of an advance party, which had in fact left England for South-Eastern

1 A. Horne, *To Lose a Battle: France 1940*, p.648.

> France. The Royal Air Force believed strongly that great results would be gained by making this attack.[2]

At the meeting of the War Cabinet held on 1 June, it was reported that the intention of sending some of the RAF bomber squadrons to assist the French in attacking the Italian industries was already proceeding and had been communicated to the French Prime Minister, Paul Reynaud.[3] The same meeting received advice on whether the *Regia Aeronautica* (the Italian Air Force) would be capable of mounting a defence of their industries. It was concluded that this would not be the case, since the Italian aircraft were considered to be of inferior types, their reserves were inadequate, and there were no proper arrangements for anti-aircraft batteries and the defence of the industrial area. Advice had also been sought from the last British ambassador to Italy, Sir Percy Loraine, who was of the view that an assault by an RAF bomber force would make a very deep impression on the Italian Government.

The War Cabinet was informed that a plan had been devised for an air attack on the Italian industries. That it was vitally important to hit Italy a very hard blow right at the outset, with the intention of putting her out of the war as quickly as possible, was agreed by the Chief of the Air Staff, Air Chief Marshal Sir Cyril Newall.[4] Due to its reliance on the import of most of the basic raw materials, such coal and oil, Italy was deemed to be extremely vulnerable to the pressure of a sea blockade of the eastern and western Mediterranean. Moreover, half of the country's population and most of its industrial capacity, including the Fiat aero engine and motor works based at Turin and the Breda airframe and air component works at Milan, were concentrated in an area that could be reached by aircraft flying from the south of France. The typical weather conditions experienced also meant that these would tend to favour the attacker, with the nights being clear and cloud cover lying at around 4,000 feet making ideal conditions for evasive tactics by aircraft should this be required.

That same day, Air Marshal Barratt was tasked with organising a suitable base in the neighbourhood of Marseilles for the operation of 48 heavy bombers. As soon as the servicing units were established in southern France, the bombers could fly there directly and operations begin without delay; in the meantime, the bomber squadrons could remain in Britain to take part in the RAF's missions against Germany. It was recorded that 'The Prime Minister thought that a very much deeper impression would be made on Mussolini if the bomber squadrons were already there, the first blow could be struck within an hour or so of the opening of hostilities.[5]

It was known that if they were able to operate from an airfield in the Channel Islands, a force of the RAF's Armstrong Whitworth Whitley bombers would be able to reach the Italian targets. Were the force to be comprised of the Vickers Wellington bombers, however, the shorter range of these machines would necessitate that they be refuelled en-route. In view of

2 M. Gilbert, *Finest Hour: Winston Churchill, 1939-1941* (London: Heinemann, 1983), p.443.
3 TNA CAB 65/7/46: War Cabinet Minutes, 1 June 1940.
4 Sir Cyril Louis Norton Newall (1886-1963) was appointed as Chief of the Air Staff in 1937, the military head of the RAF. During the Battle of France, he resisted political demands to transfer more fighter squadrons to France, thereby preserving the RAF Fighter Command squadrons that would be vital during the Battle of Britain.
5 TNA CAB 65/7/46: War Cabinet Minutes, 1 June 1940.

this, the French Air Command had agreed to make the airfield at Salon-de-Provence, near Marseilles in southern France, available to the RAF for its use as a base for this mission.

On 3 June, a meeting was held at the French Admiralty in Paris, when the representatives of the British Admiralty and Air Ministry met with *Amiral de la flotte* François Darlan, *Capitaine de vaisseau* Gabriel Auphan and *Général d'Armée Aérienne* Joseph Vuillemin (the commander-in-chief of the French air force).[6] The minutes of this meeting record that its purpose was to discuss the fourth resolution reached by the aforementioned Allied Supreme War Council meeting on 31 May. *Amiral* Darlan began by noting that one-third of Italy's petroleum had been stored on the coast but that it had now been moved in land. The British opinion was in favour of an air attack against the aircraft and aero-engine manufacturing factories in the Milan and Turin areas, as this would also have an immediate effect on the morale of Italy's civilian population, and this was articulated by Air Vice Marshal William Sholto Douglas.[7] The French were still agreeable to the proposed mission and no great difficulty was expected, apart from allocating sufficient personnel, equipment and vehicles to establish the organisation required. Indeed, the decisions regarding the main defences of the area in which the advanced aerodromes were to be established rested with the French authorities and it was understood that three groups of French fighters would be available in the area, although *Amiral* Darlan was of the view that the duty of French fighters was to support the French line on the north-east front. It was also proposed that targets on Italy's coastline, between Genoa and Leghorn, should also be attacked by the French fleet and the French air force. Moreover, on the afternoon of 3 June, the executive order to create what was to be known as the 'Haddock Force' was issued verbally to Group Captain R.M. Field, who had been designated to be the commanding officer of the operation, by Air Vice Marshal Douglas Evill.[8] Hence, during the next day Group Captain Field, and the headquarters of the RAF's 71 Bomber Wing and the 16 and 17 Servicing Flights would fly to the Marseilles area. Upon their arrival they would establish the RAF's advanced organisation to prepare the reception and refuelling facilities that would be required by the British bombers, so that they were ready to launch their raids when Italy finally declared war, as it did at midnight on 10 June 1940.[9] Furthermore, and in accordance with correspondence dated 7 June from Air Vice Marshal Sholto Douglas to Bomber Command, which was on the subject of possible operations against Italy, it was emphasised that 'it should be understood that there is no intention of implementing the plan unless and until Italy enters the war against the Allies'.[10]

6 TNA AIR 35/157: Air action against Italy, Policy.

7 William Sholto Douglas (1893-1969) was appointed Air Vice-Marshal in 1938 and Deputy Chief of the Air Staff from 1940. In November 1940, he replaced Sir Hugh Dowding as the Air Officer Commanding-in-Chief of Fighter Command, with the temporary rank of Air Marshal, and with this rank being made substantive in 1942.

8 Douglas Claude Strathern Evill (1892-1971) was Australian-born and had served with the Royal Naval Air Service as a pilot and then a squadron commander during the First World War. Promoted to the rank of RAF Air Vice-Marshal during 1938, in February 1940 Evill was appointed as the Senior Air Staff Officer at the Headquarters of the RAF in France under the command of Air Marshal Sir Arthur Barratt, after which he returned to Fighter Command as the Senior Air Staff Officer.

9 TNA CAB 35/325: Haddock Force, Historical Diary.

10 TNA AIR 35/157: Air action against Italy, Policy.

Contact with the Enemy

In accordance with a secret cypher message dated 11 June 1940, during the night of 11 to 12 June, a force of 36 Armstrong Whitworth Whitley bombers selected from 10, 51, 58, 77 and 102 Squadrons, which were part of Bomber Command's 4 Group, proceeded to rendezvous in six groups before flying from Britain to airfields on the Channel Islands of Jersey and Guernsey, where they refuelled before flying directly to attack the targets in Italy. They were to return to Britain directly after the mission, landing at home bases or other bases as necessary. If the main target could not be reached then a substitute target was to be selected from a list of alternatives appended to the Operation instruction sheet at the direction of the AOC-in-C of 4 Group.[11]

The Armstrong Whitworth Whitley had entered service with the RAF in 1937 and was a medium bomber with a five-man crew (pilot, co-pilot/navigator, radio operator, bomb-aimer/forward gunner and rear gunner). It was 70 feet 6 inches in length with a wingspan of 84 feet and a maximum take-off weight of 33,500 lb. Powered by two Rolls-Royce Merlin X engines, it had a 230-mph maximum speed, a range of 1,650 miles and a maximum ceiling of 26,000 feet. A total payload of up to 7,000 lb of bombs could be carried in the fuselage and in its wing mountings. Its defensive armament was comprised of a 0.303-inch Vickers machine gun mounted in a nose turret and four 0.303-inch Browning machine guns housed in a tail turret. However, severe storms over the Alps made it impossible for these aircraft to reach their targets of the cities of Genoa and Turin. Hence, the majority of aeroplanes really had little choice but to return to their home bases with their mission incomplete. Only 13 of the Whitley bombers reached the objectives, and two of them failed to return home. In a remarkable display of navigational incompetence, several of these aircraft considerably overshot their targets and proceeded to drop their bombs on the Swiss cities of Geneva and Lausanne, where four civilians were killed and another 80 were wounded as a consequence. Nevertheless, in the edition of *The Times* dated 13 June, it was briefly reported that the RAF's heavy bombers operating from Great Britain had attacked targets in Turin and Genoa in northern Italy.[12]

Twelve Vickers Wellington bombers from 37, 75 and 99 Squadrons, which were part of Bomber Command's 3 Group, left their bases in Britain for France and arrived at Salon-de-Provence at 1530 hours on 11 June. The Wellington was famous for its geodetic airframe fuselage structure, which was principally designed by Sir Barnes Wallis. Introduced in 1938, this aircraft had a crew of five (pilot, co-pilot/navigator, radio operator and forward and rear gunners) and, as with the Whitley, the forward gunner was also the bomb-aimer. It was 64 feet 7 inches in length with a wingspan of 86 feet 2 inches and a maximum take-off weight of 28,500 lb. Powered by two Bristol Pegasus Mark XVIII engines, it had a maximum speed of 235 mph, a range of 2,550 miles and a maximum ceiling of 18,000 feet. A total of 4,500 lb of bombs could be carried in its fuselage and defence from hostile aircraft was to be achieved by between six and eight 0.303-inch Browning machine guns that were mounted in the turrets in the nose and the tail, and in waist positions on each side of the fuselage.

Later that day, as the time approached for the arrangements for the raid to be finalised, some of the French civilian authorities decided to take preventative action. Fearing that their own

11 Ibid.
12 *The Times*, 13 June 1940.

towns and cities, especially Marseilles and Lyon, were vulnerable to a retaliatory attack by the *Regia Aeronautica*, and with the petrol dumps on the Étang de Berre deemed particularly at risk, they obstructed the airfield's runway with lorries to prevent the RAF's bombers from taking off.[13] Indeed, the commander of the *Zone d'Opérations Aériennes des Alpes*, *Général de brigade* Jean-Baptiste-Benjamin Laurens, opposed the raid and refused to allow it to commence from any of the air bases under his command.[14] Therefore, whilst the Wellingtons were being refuelled, Group Captain Field was informed via a telephone call from the local French commander that the Italian targets were not to be attacked. Subsequently, Field received direct orders from the British Air Ministry countermanding this and demanding that his aircraft should take off, as per the agreed plan. Several heated telephone calls then took place, involving Air Marshal Arthur Barratt and the French Chief of the Air Staff, *Général d'Armée Aérienne* Vuillemin.[15]

Group Captain Field attempted to follow the orders from the British Air Ministry and from Air Marshal Barratt. At 1230 hours on 12 June, the RAF Wellingtons taxied into position ready to take off from Salon-de-Provence but found that French troops had again blocked the runway with lorries and carts. There was no choice but to abort the mission and most of the Wellingtons flew back to their bases in Britain the following day. During 12 June, personal visits to Group Captain Field were made by *Général de brigade* Paul-Jules-Joseph Gama and *Général d'armée* Jean-Paul-Marie Houdemon, both of the *Armée de l'Air*, and the representatives of the *Vice Amiral*, the Maritime prefect of Toulon and of the 3rd French Army.[16] He recorded that all of these officers expressed their profound regrets at having been compelled to intervene and to prevent the operation that was intended for 11 to 12 June.

On the evening of 11 June, the British diplomatic representatives in France had been informed that the RAF's bombers were being prevented from carrying out their planned mission and consequently strong protests were made to French Prime Minister Reynaud. Robust exchanges of views between the British and French Governments then took place and directives were sent from Paris to the French authorities on the ground ordering them to co-operate with the RAF. Consent was finally given following the bombing of the French city of Toulon and the naval base at Toulon by the *Regia Aeronautica* on 12 to 13 June. It was also learnt that the *Armée de l'Air* was to carry out their own operations on the following night.

On 13 June, and contrary to the earlier orders for the withdrawal of its aircraft, personnel and equipment, new orders were received by the Haddock Force for these to be countermanded. Therefore, on the night of 14 to 15 June, twelve further Wellingtons from 99 and 149 Squadrons flew from Britain to France.[17] This time their progress was not impeded by the French and, on 15 to 16 June, eight of these aircraft flew to Italy with the intention of bombing the Ansaldo engineering works at Genoa. Again, inclement weather prevented the aircraft from successfully executing their mission, as thunderstorms frustrated navigation, so that only one of the

13 P. Takle, *The British Army in France after Dunkirk*, p.84.
14 Jean-Baptiste-Benjamin Laurens (1884-1972) was a *Général de Brigade* in the *Armée de l'Air* and the Commanding Officer Air Forces, 3rd Army.
15 Joseph Vuillemin (1883-1963) was a *Général d'Armée Aérienne* and during the Battle of France held the position as the Chief of the Air Staff of the *Armée de l'Air*.
16 TNA AIR 35/354: Letter from Group Captain R.M. Field to the Secretary of the Air Ministry.
17 TNA CAB 35/325: Haddock Force, Historical Diary.

Wellingtons despatched on this sortie succeeding in reaching its target. This aircraft dropped two 500 lb and five 250 lb bombs, and forty 5 lb incendiary bombs.

Despite being hampered yet again by the poor weather, a further raid was carried out on the next night when the crews of six of the nine RAF aircraft despatched were despatched to carry out a final mission against the *Regia Aeronautica* aerodromes in Milan. It was subsequently reported that they had dropped a total of twelve 500 lb bombs, thirty-two 250 lb bombs and 416 of the 5 lb incendiary bombs on the city of Milan. During these operations, signals were received from the BAFF and the British Air Ministry that Haddock Force was to be kept in being until further orders were issued, and a detachment of the 708 Company of the Royal Engineers unexpectedly arrived by train in Avignon during the night.

Aftermath and Consequences

On 16 June, Group Captain Field travelled to the French port of Toulon, where he was to consult with Rear Admiral Geoffrey Watkins of the Royal Navy. The purpose of this meeting was to discuss the arrangements for the possible withdrawal from France of the Haddock Force. Field was informed by Watkins that currently there were thirteen British merchant vessels at anchor in Marseilles but he was of the opinion that embarkation at Toulon was to be preferred. This was because the port was more easily defended against the enemy and, therefore, it was considered that it should be possible to take off more stores and motor transport as well as the units of RAF personnel.

At 0430 hours on 17 June, a British Air Ministry signal was sent (subsequently confirmed by a cypher signal) which ordered the Haddock Force to be immediately evacuated. Accordingly, the Wellingtons were refuelled without interruption and at 0930 hours they were ready to return to Britain. At 0430 hours the following day, further orders were received for the evacuation of the ground crews and any additional stores. These orders were rescinded and then reinstated during the course of the day, and eventually convoys were ordered to proceed to Marseilles. Upon his return, Field received a further message to the effect that Rear Admiral Watkins wished the Haddock Force to remain in its present location so that it might supplement the efforts of the French air force and navy. Field attempted to contact the Rear Admiral, as he wished to inform him that he did not have the authority to disregard the direct order from the AOC-in-C, but he was unable to speak to him. In any case, it would not be possible to resume air operations immediately, as the men were exhausted and much of the confidential information had by now been destroyed. On 18 June, further orders were received at 0430 hours that following the embarkation of personnel and equipment (on board SS *Coultam*, which carried off 40 officers and 903 other ranks), the departure from Marseilles should be carried out as soon as possible and the sea convoy moved off at 0600 hours. On 20 June, the British War Cabinet was informed of developments and took note of the intelligence that the bomber force had returned to Britain some days before and that the RAF maintenance personnel were aboard vessels that were sailing from Marseilles to Gibraltar.[18]

Throughout its brief existence, the RAF's Haddock Force was prevented from achieving much of the potential material contribution it might have been able to make to the war effort at this

18 TNA CAB 65/7/68: War Cabinet Minutes, 20 June 1940.

stage. This was due to several factors, including the conditions it had to contend with, which were exceedingly difficult and, owing to the limitations of communication, the incomplete intelligence that had been supplied by the French in advance of the mission. There was also the impact made by the evacuation of the BAFF's headquarters. In his letter to Sir Arthur Street, the Permanent Under Secretary of State for Air, Group Captain Field reported that, having regard to the behaviour of the officers and men of this force, both from the RAF and the army units that were attached to Haddock Force, he could not write sufficiently highly. He emphasised that they were employed at very high pressure between 4 to 17 June in circumstances of considerable discomfort and continued improvisation, and during the last three days they had been subjected to rapid alterations in policy. This necessitated a speed of movement that was incompatible with the rapid embarkation of motor transport and the large quantities of stores that they then had at their disposal. Yet in spite of all of these considerations, Field reported that all ranks had worked with the greatest cheerfulness and willingness.[19]

19 TNA AIR 35/354: Letter from Group Captain R.M. Field to the Secretary of the Air Ministry.

9

Anglo-French Military Co-operation

Realities of the Situation

Pre-war liaison and the regular conversations that took place between their respective staffs should have ensured that the co-ordination of policy and strategy by the armed forces of Britain and France ought to have been achieved with at least some degree of harmony. Furthermore, following the outbreak of hostilities, a Supreme War Council had been established at Abbeville on 12 September 1939, to meet whenever it was necessary, either in Britain or France, although this body had no executive authority and left decision-making to the respective national governments. This development was followed by the creation of other committees and the conclusion of several agreements intended to cement co-operation between the two countries.[1]

Yet in reality, the relationship between the two nations was far from being so cordial, and it was influenced by the assumptions, myths and prejudices that both countries held about the other, and through which each viewed its ally. The French were resentful that they were dependent on the British but knew they could not do without them; whereas the British resented this situation, and that they could not let France down despite usually being at odds with much of French policy.[2] Therefore, the opinion of the French Government was that only the British could offer to France the type of military support it required, albeit a support constrained during the 1930s by a diminished popular support at home and British governmental cost-cutting. The French expectations were that a BEF, whilst it might be comparatively modest in size, should be mobile, well-equipped and able to play a significant role on the battlefield, so that it could fill in the gaps that existed in the French Army. The problem with this view was that the British Army had not fully embraced the doctrine and the new techniques necessary for modern warfare either. Indeed, those who were the foremost advocates of such thinking, particularly Basil Liddell-Hart and J.F.C. Fuller, were visionaries who had been marginalised and whilst their ideas may have been prophetic, they were not adopted. The inter-war British Army still

1 These were the Anglo-French Co-ordinating Committee; the Anglo-French Purchasing Committee; the Anglo-French financial agreement of December 1939; the Anglo-French trading agreement of February 1940; and the Anglo-French industrial agreement of March 1940.

2 J. Jackson, *The Fall of France: The Nazi Invasion of 1940* (Oxford: OUP, 2003), p.66.

clung to the virtues of the defensive strategy and had a distinct preference to have as its leaders those who were more gentleman-officer than professional soldier.

By 1940, the French Army's armoured units did not lack tanks, as more AFVs had started to become available to it during the autumn of 1939, but this late arrival did rather impede the operation of what were intended to be independent armoured formations. Many of the tanks that they possessed, such as the Renault R35 and Somua S35, had armour and a main firepower that were at least the equivalent to those of their German adversaries, and they were generally of a reasonable specification for the time. The key deficiencies of many of these French machines were evident in the housing of the tank's main armament in a turret within which all of the functions, including the loading, aiming and firing of the weapon, were performed by a single crewman, who was also the tank's commander. Moreover, many of the French vehicles lacked radio sets and so communication and co-ordination between tanks when under battle conditions became virtually impossible.

By May 1940, the French air force, the *Armée de l'Air*, was still in the process of reconstruction due to the delays in the production of more modern aeroplanes. Its most modern fighter aircraft was the Dewoitine D 520, which boasted a top speed of 350 mph and an armament of one 20 mm cannon and four 7.5 mm machine guns, making it a real threat to many of the *Luftwaffe's* machines, but it was not available in sufficient numbers for it to make the real impression of which it should have been capable.[3]

At the Supreme War Council, the French were of the opinion that the German *Luftwaffe* would quickly achieve complete air superiority, and that it would use its bombers in air raids that would break the morale of the French people. There can be no doubt that in arriving at this view, they had drawn heavily upon the recent events during the Spanish Civil War, such as the bombing of Guernica on 26 April 1937 by Nationalist forces, which had included participation by the German aircraft of the *Luftwaffe*'s Condor Legion. There was also considerable apprehension on the part of the French Government that any offensive actions that might be carried out by the RAF would result in retaliatory missions being mounted against French targets, especially the French aircraft factories that were clustered around Paris and deemed to be especially vulnerable. It was this fear that motivated the decision taken at the Supreme War Council on 17 November 1939 that, in the event of a German invasion of France, the RAF should only be able to attack military objectives in Germany.

French strategy and its Army's military doctrine continued to be based on an essentially defensive form of warfare with formations that, rather than being organised to instigate offensive operations, were configured in order to repel an invasion. Hence, it depended for its defence on the static fortifications of the Maginot Line and the apparently impassable terrain in areas such as the Ardennes forest. Even before its annulment in 1936 of the 1920 convention concerning joint military planning between Belgium and France, the Belgian Government was exhibiting

3 At this time during the Battle of France, the *Armée de l'Air* was in a considerable state of confusion and disorganisation, such that it was not possible to establish exactly how many aircraft it possessed, how many of them were operational and at which airfields and in which squadrons they were located. In all probability, there were at least as many modern French fighter aircraft as were being flown by the *Luftwaffe*, though none could compare with the Messerschmitt Bf 109. However, when added to the RAF's contribution of Hawker Hurricanes, it should have been possible for Allied air superiority to have been maintained in May-June 1940.

a preference for defence via neutrality rather than military strength and, consequently, France entered a very precarious position vis-à-vis its neighbour. Moreover, the French military was deeply affected by the devastation wrought on the men who served on the western front in the First World War and the conscripts to its Army during the inter-war years were often seriously lacking in any enthusiasm for military service. When faced with the prospect of invasion by the resurgent Nazi Germany, France was effectively paralysed by a sense of inferiority when comparing itself to its rival, and the objective of France's armed forces became principally one of survival rather than winning through outright aggressive or even counter-attacking action. As would be proved, it was incapable of waging the type of modern form of warfare required of it and of breaking the mobile German assault when it came.

In his Despatch, Air Marshal Barratt made reference to the wholly defensive attitude of mind on the part of both the land and air forces of France, with their high commands demonstrating on numerous occasions that they were disinclined to take any kind of action that might incur retaliation from the enemy:

> As regards the land, it is hardly my province to comment but I heard reports which led me to believe that this defensive attitude on the part of the High Command had percolated down throughout the French Army. As regards the air, the defensive attitude of mind was certainly most marked. I have already recorded how the French High Command refused to permit bombing of bottlenecks and German columns in Germany, even after the violation of the frontiers had occurred, until the Germans had seized the initiative and taken the first steps in this direction.[4]

Barratt's report also articulated his comments on the considerable reluctance often demonstrated by the French forces at the local level. He referred to the manner in which the French had prevented the departure from an airfield in the south of France of the RAF's bombers, which had been sent there as the Haddock Force to attack objectives in Italy once war had been declared on Britain and France by the Italian Government. Yet again, the French had, in wishing to wait until Italy had taken the first offensive step, been essentially reactive rather than proactive. This occurred despite the agreement that had been reached between the respective British and French Governments, the French Air Force's commander-in-chief and Air Marshal Barratt himself, and he confirmed that this was but one of the numerous examples of a failure to adhere to the arrangements which had been worked out beforehand between the Allies.

In Barratt's report to the Chief of the Imperial Staff, General Sir John Dill, which was submitted on 14 June, Lieutenant General Marshall-Cornwall also provided an assessment of the manner in which the techniques now being utilised during the *Heer's* onslaught in France had broken-down their opposition's defences with consummate ease and had upset all of the dominant pre-war military theories. On reflection, he considered that this was due to the moral rather than the technical factor. Furthermore:

> From what I have seen of the French troops, I have gained the opinion that, with certain brilliant exceptions, they have not really put up an obstinate resistance. The

4 TNA AIR 35/354: Barratt's Dispatch.

Frenchman's attitude seems to be that in the last war France was bled white on behalf of civilisation, and that this time it would be up to others – Poles, Norwegians, Dutch, Belgians or British – to do the fighting for him. Moreover, he has been infected for the last ten years with the Maginot psychosis, and has been trained to rely on the protection of steel and concrete. When he finds himself left out in the open to face tanks and dive-bombing, he develops a kind of agoraphobia and starts looking over his shoulder for a good "abri".[5]

Command and Control

Following his evacuation from Dunkirk on 30 May 1940, Lieutenant General Sir Alan Brooke had returned to Britain on 2 June. He had gone to the War Office, where he had been told by the CIGS, General Sir John Dill, that it was intended that he should be sent straight back to France in order to assemble a second British Expeditionary Force. In his War Diaries, Brooke expressed his feelings as follows:

> 'As I look back to the war, this was certainly one of the blackest moments. I knew only too well the state of affairs that would prevail in France from now onwards. I had seen my hope in the French Army gradually shattered throughout those long winter months. I had witnessed the realisation of my worst fears regarding its fighting value and morale, and now I had no false assumptions as to what its destiny must inevitably be. To be sent back into that cauldron with a new force to participate in the final stages of the French disintegration was indeed a dark prospect'.[6]

The plan was that the core of this formation would be the 51st Division and the two brigades of the incomplete 1st Armoured Division, both of which were still engaged in the fighting in France. Brooke had requested that the 3rd and 4th Divisions both be refitted and sent to France, so that at least some seasoned troops would be available, but he was told by Dill that there was not sufficient time for this. Therefore, the 52nd Division, augmented with the artillery and anti-tank guns of the 49th Division, and the 1st Canadian Division were then to be embarked for France. Dill made the concession that they would be followed by the 3rd Infantry Division, which had recently returned to Britain and was in the process of being re-equipped. Also intended for inclusion in the second BEF were the elements remaining in France of the 12th (Eastern) and 46th (North Midland and West Riding) Divisions, which were second line Territorial labour divisions and lines of communications formations. On 27 May, some of these had been improvised into the Beauman Division. Brooke was also informed that on his return to France, he would fall under the authority of *Général d'armée* Weygand and that his role was to support the French. As described earlier in this volume, the 51st Division's fate was determined at St Valery-en-Caux even before Brooke had been able to return to France and he only learnt of it upon his arrival at the British headquarters at Le Mans on 13 June.

5 TNA WO 32/9388, Overseas: Europe (Code O (V)), Despatches from BEF 12-19 June 1940. "Abri" – French for a shelter or dugout.
6 A. Danchev and D. Todman (eds), *War Diaries 1939-1945: Field Marshal Lord Alanbrooke* (London: Phoenix Press, 2003), p.74.

Given the serious implications for national defence, that the British Government should even contemplate sending these divisions out to France, constituting as they did arguably most if not all of the best equipped formations then based on the British mainland, was indicative of just how desperate were the choices being faced at that point, both in France and in Britain. As Winston Churchill later observed:

> That we should have sent out only two formed divisions, the 52nd Lowland Division and the 1st Canadian Division, over to our failing French ally in the mortal crisis, when the whole fury of Germany must soon fall upon us, must be set to our credit against the very limited forces we had been able to put into France in the first eight months of the war. Looking back on it, I wonder how, when we were resolved to continue the war to the death, and under the threat of invasion, and France was evidently failing, we had the nerve to strip ourselves of the remaining effective military formations we possessed. This was only possible because we understood the difficulties of the Channel crossing without the command of the sea or the air, or the necessary landing craft'.[7]

On 3 June, and further to the French Government's request to the British Government for the additional assistance which had been made at the Supreme War Council held on 31 May, the British War Cabinet approved the formation of the second BEF. It was envisaged that this new formation would operate to the south of the River Somme, and that it would have a 'good psychological effect on France' because it would be clear that Britain could not ignore 'the grave military consequences … which might arise should we give no further assistance to France'.[8]

Brooke advised both Dill and the Secretary of State for War, Anthony Eden, that in his view the enterprise was futile, apart from as a political gesture. He had seen the limitations of the French Army, its diminished fighting capability and lack of morale prior to Dunkirk, and he did not believe that the French stood a chance of holding back the German invasion. He was also concerned that the Territorials would not be able to stand up to the assault from the enemy's panzer divisions and dive bombers. In his meeting with Eden, he informed him that that from a military point of view, it had no value and there was no possibility of accomplishing anything. Given that a major disaster had only just been averted at Dunkirk, Brooke felt that a second disaster was now being risked and that any British troops remaining in France would be sacrificed for nothing. Brooke was also dismayed to learn that once the additional divisions had been sent to France, command of the second BEF was to be handed over to General Lord Gort.[9]

7 W.S. Churchill, *The Second World War*, p.284.

8 D. Newbold, 'British planning and preparations to resist invasion on land, September 1939 - September 1940', p.170.

9 In 1939-40, and especially during the BEF's retreat towards Dunkirk, before then being ordered to return to Britain by Lord Gort, Brooke had earned a deserved reputation for being a very effective commander of the II Corps. Lord Gort, who had previously been Commandant of the Staff College at Camberley, was effectively promoted by two ranks, rising from Major General to General, when promoted to be the CIGS in December 1937, and this created bad feeling amongst those Lieutenant Generals, such as Brooke and Dill, who had previously outranked him and who considered themselves to be superior to him in terms of both ability and experience. This was a grievance that would be compounded when Lord Gort was appointed to be the Commander-in-Chief of the BEF by Chamberlain in September 1939.

He did, however, obtain the promise that by the end of June an additional regular division, namely the 3rd Infantry Division commanded by Major General Bernard Montgomery, when re-organised and re-equipped, would be sent to join those already in France.

During 3 to 5 June respectively, the 52nd Division and the 1st Canadian Division were both ordered to make ready to proceed to the Continent. Departing on 7 June, the 52nd Division began to land in France from 9 June. The 1st Canadian Infantry Brigade of the 1st Canadian Infantry Division began its arrival at Brest on 11 June and was sent to Sablé-sur-Sarthe. This Division had initially been held back for political reasons but was finally despatched as it was deemed to be in the most advanced state of readiness, being fully trained and equipped, when compared to any of the other formations that were available at the time. This was despite the feeling on 2 June that 'it would be a grave military risk to let the Canadians go to France' since it was 'the most effective mobile reserve for the defence of this country and can consequently be less easily spared than for any other division'.[10] Despite the arrival of these additional Divisions, no sooner had they disembarked in France than it began an urgent matter to start sending the troops back to Britain before it became too late. The loss of the bulk of the 51st Division at St Valery was the starkest warning imaginable of the implications of losing more British troops in France.

For the British forces remaining in France after 4 June 1940, the command arrangements with their French allies were a matter of some confusion. The principal British infantry formation, the 51st Division was under the command of *Général de corps d'armée* Marcel Ihler of the French IX Corps, whereas the 1st Armoured Division, whilst being commanded by *Général d'armée* Robert Altmayer, was also receiving orders from *Général d'armée* Maxime Weygand. The improvised Beauman Division was under the orders of Lieutenant General Karslake (who had been given responsibility for the British L of C troops) but it also received orders from *Général d'armée* Joseph Georges, the commander of the French armies in the north-east. The French commanders 'traditionally regarded the British generals as amateurs who occasionally had more than their fair share of luck, and seldom bothered to explain their intentions or to give information about their dispositions'.[11]

The position held on the River Bresle by the British 51st Division and French IX Corps was particularly vulnerable due to the inherent danger of them being cut off in the Le Havre peninsula. The British liaison officer at the 10th Army HQ, Lieutenant General Marshall-Cornwall had already specified that there should be a policy to cover the routes of withdrawal for British troops in the event of an enemy breakthrough, especially given the risk to the 51st Division of being driven into the Le Havre – Fécamp headland and trapped there. On 6 June, Major General Fortune wrote to Lieutenant General Marshall-Cornwall to request reinforcements and permission for the 51st Division to retreat with the French 31st (Alpine) Division to the Bresle.[12] However, it was intended that one of the Brigades of the 52nd Division was to reach France by 7 June and the War Office urged the French Command to arrange a line of retreat to the south-east and away from Le Havre, towards the BEF's lines of communication, to the south of the River Seine. Such a retirement as that which had been requested by Fortune

10 TNA CAB 79/4/64: War Cabinet Chiefs of Staff, Despatch of additional forces to France.
11 M. Glover, *The fight for the Channel ports, Calais to Brest 1940*, p.19.
12 TNA WO 32/9388: Overseas: Europe (Code O (V)), Despatches from BEF 12-19 June 1940.

was expressly forbidden by *Général d'armée* Weygand, who had ordered that the current position should be held come what may.

At 0500 hours on 6 June, Lieutenant General Marshall-Cornwall had attended a meeting with *Général d'armée* Robert Altmayer's Chief of Staff. During this he received Altmayer's permission for the 51st Division to be withdrawn to the line of the River Bresle by the Forêt d'Eu. Major General Fortune therefore asked that the French 31st Division, which had been placed under his orders, now be removed from his command and that his own front line be shortened correspondingly.

In an immediate message to the CIGS, Marshall-Cornwall pointed out the gravity of the situation in relation to the 51st Division, advising him that this formation had been in action continuously and had as a consequence suffered heavy casualties. He urged that at least two more British divisions be sent to France as soon as possible. By midnight, Fortune had also reached the conclusion that the 51st Division was unable to hold the line of the River Bresle any longer and he therefore requested that it be relieved and placed into reserve. General Altmayer insisted that the line must be held and that the 51st Division could not be relieved as there was nothing in the reserve that could replace it. Marshall-Cornwall also pressed for permission to demolish some of the smaller road bridges over the River Béthune, which would have released a considerable number of the companies of the Royal Engineers for other duties. In response to this, Altmayer completely refused to agree to any demolitions being carried out at this stage. Marshall-Cornwall, who had no authority to give orders to the 51st Division directly, subsequently had to send a signal to the CIGS, who was the only officer of the British Army who could take this action:

> Situation of 51 Division is now serious. It has been fighting continuously for three days and has suffered heavy casualties. It has been forced to withdraw to the line of River Bresle from Gamaches to Eu. Enemy infantry have infiltrated across the Bresle into woods south of Eu. 51 Division is hardly fit for more fighting and may crack if seriously attacked even on Bresle position. If politically undesirable to withdraw all British troops from front line I would urge that two more British divisions with fighter support be urgently sent to France.[13]

Lieutenant General Karslake had already made representations to the CIGS concerning the lack of unity of command, but by this stage General Dill had written to Brigadier John George des Réaux Swayne, the Head of the British Military Mission to the French General Headquarters. This was to confirm that Lieutenant General Brooke was expected to reach France during the following week. In order that there could be a point of liaison for all the British commanders, and also to reassure the French of British determination to support them through the formation of the second BEF, Dill also sent to France Lieutenant General Sir Henry Pownall.[14]

With regard to the disembarkation in France of additional British and Empire forces, it was anticipated that 52nd Division would sail on 7 June, the 1st Canadian Division on 11 June

13 M. Glover, *The fight for the Channel ports: Calais to Brest 1940*, p.169.
14 Sir Henry Royds Pownall (1887-1961) was a Lieutenant General in the British Army and he had held the position of the chief of staff to the BEF until the fall of France, after which he became inspector general of the newly created Home Guard.

and the 3rd Division on 22 June. Upon his arrival, Pownall was advised by Karslake that the withdrawal of the 51st Division was wholly essential and he pressed him to seek to accelerate Brooke's arrival so that a Corps headquarters could be established to unify the command of all the British forces in France. At a meeting attended by Major Generals Beauman and Evans, and Lieutenant General Marshall-Cornwall, there was discussion of the isolated position now held by the 51st Division and doubts were also expressed about assurances that were being given about this by the French commanders.

On 7 June, Major General Evans of the 1st Armoured Division had been present at the 10th Army's headquarters when *Général d'armée* Weygand arrived and, following this, both he and Lieutenant General Marshall-Cornwall were afforded an interview with the French commander and *Général d'armée* Altmayer. During this meeting, Weygand remarked that the battle being waged by the 10th Army was to be considered the most decisive action of the war and given that the French Army was unable to make available any reserve forces, the outcome of the operations would depend upon the actions of the British 1st Armoured Division. To this end, Weygand ordered that the Armoured Division should hold the line of the River Andelle and the railway line from Holleval on the right of Serqueux. In turn, Major General Evans ventured to point out that in the absence of artillery, infantry, anti-tank weapons and mines, such a holding operation was impossible, especially given the lighter armour of the British tanks when compared with the heavier and better armed German tanks and vehicles. In what Evans subsequently described as an impassioned harangue, Weygand said to him 'that if he could not stop the enemy with his tanks then he must stop him with bare hands and bite him like a dog'.[15]

On 8 June, Lieutenant General Marshall-Cornwall informed the CIGS that he 'had lost all confidence in the ability of the French 10th Army to hold up the German drive to the Seine, and that there was every possibility of 51st Division being cut off by the panzer divisions'.[16] In addition to this, Marshall-Cornwall pointed out that the only real barrier was the 50 British tanks which were being used as blockhouses on the River Andelle, that the Germans had reached Forges-les-Eaux and that having requested that it be withdrawn to the River Béthune, the evacuation from Dieppe of the 51st Division should now be required. He also suggested that General Dill should travel out to France himself in order to discuss these crucial matters in person with *Général d'armée* Weygand.[17] In fact, within hours of this conversation, Marshall-Cornwall found that the French 10th Army headquarters had actually departed for an unknown destination (eventually it was found to be at Marines, a location that was 31 miles to the south-east of Paris) and that it had absented itself without either informing him of the intention to leave or providing any means of communication for him.

Eventually, Marshall-Cornwall re-established contact with the War Office when he reached the Howard-Vyse Mission, and he notified them that the 51st Division was now in imminent danger and consequently that it should be released from the French Army's command. Subsequent to this, and once he had found the re-located headquarters of the 10th Army, Marshall-Cornwall persuaded *Général d'armée* Robert Altmayer to allow the 51st Division to withdraw to the south of the River Seine (earlier to this, Altmayer had refused to even countenance such as withdrawal). At 2130 hours, Marshall-Cornwall relayed a message to the 51st Division

15 TNA WO 167/334: 1st Armoured Division War Diary.
16 J. Marshall-Cornwall, 'Normandy 1940', p.4.
17 M. Glover, *The fight for the Channel ports: Calais to Brest 1940*, p.158.

ordering its withdrawal south of the River Seine, via Rouen. Two liaison officers were sent to advise Major General Fortune of the 51st Division of this instruction, but unfortunately the message was never delivered as one of these officers was unable to make any progress beyond the French sentries who were guarding the River Seine Bridge in Rouen, and who refused to allow him to pass through, whilst the other officer was captured en-route by a German patrol. At 0200 hours on 9 June, Marshall-Cornwall sent a message to the CIGS to notify him that the French Army command was unable to communicate with either its own IX Corps, or with the British 51st Division. He suggested that in relation to continued communication with the 51st Division, this should therefore be via the Royal Navy or by aircraft.

At 1630 hours, Marshall-Cornwall endured a deeply unpleasant interview with *Général de corps d'armée* Benoît-Léon de la Laurencie, under whom the command of the 51st Division and the 1st Armoured Division had now been placed. In this meeting, de la Laurencie accused Acting Major General Beauman of treachery and cowardice and of dishonour to England by withdrawing his troops after promising to keep them on the Seine, and he described the British troops as 'a thoroughly undisciplined rabble'.[18] It was his intention to report to Weygand that he could no longer defend the Seine line as the British Army had failed him. Marshall-Cornwall responded that this was a grave accusation and there must have been some misunderstanding due to Beauman having been issued with the instructions for his exhausted and ill-equipped L of C troops to withdraw under orders from Lieutenant General Karslake, his superior officer, prior to Weygand's orders being received. In response, de la Laurencie stated that Weygand's orders as supreme commander took precedence over all others and were that there should be no retirement from the Seine. Marshall-Cornwall enquired whether Beauman had personally been given any orders that he had disregarded, and it was admitted that the communication with Beauman had been via his French liaison officer. Marshall-Cornwall informed the French general that his accusation was so grave that it would have to be reported to the CIGS. In his report, Marshall-Cornwall stated: 'My comment on the above is that the French having no Belgian scapegoat, will blame the British for failing to hold the Seine'.[19] On 9 June, Marshall-Cornwall sent a telegraph to the CIGS in which he emphasised how important it was for the 51st Division to be evacuated from Le Havre.

At 1830 hours on 11 June, during a meeting involving both Karslake and Marshall-Cornwall, it was decided that for political reasons both Brigades of the 1st Armoured Division should remain in the forward area in support of the French forces. However, in relation to the 3rd Armoured Brigade's vehicles, many of which now required heavy repairs, they should be transported by means of the railway line from Le Mans to Nantes where they could be re-fitted. On the following day, Major General Evans received a personal message from the CIGS, Sir John Dill. This informed him that he was to continue to receive and to follow the orders of the French 10th Army, and that this agreed with the views of *Général d'armée* Weygand.[20]

On 13 June, Lieutenant General Brooke reached France, disembarking in Cherbourg during a rainstorm, and proceeded to the headquarters of Major General de Fonblanque (commanding Line of Communication troops) which was situated at the important railway junction of Le

18 J. Fenby, *The Sinking of the Lancastria: Britain's Greatest Maritime Disaster and Churchill's Cover-Up*, p.32.
19 TNA WO 32/9388: Overseas: Europe (Code O (V)), Despatches from BEF 12-19 June 1940.
20 TNA WO 167/334: 1st Armoured Division War Diary.

Mans. Brooke met with him, Lieutenant General Karslake and Brigadier John Swayne (the Head of the British Military Mission to the French General Headquarters).[21] His arrival in France had been delayed by some days as he attempted to put together a team of staff officers to assist him but, nonetheless, Brooke had not rushed, presumably because of his own thoughts regarding the hopelessness of the British Army's position. His first action was to instruct Karslake to return to Britain, which he did by aeroplane that afternoon.[22] Brooke then took over command of all British troops still in France.[23]

On 14 June, Brooke met with *Général d'armée* Weygand who confirmed that the French Army was no longer capable of organised resistance and had, to all intents and purposes, broken up into four disconnected groups. Whilst these would continue to fight under the orders of their commanders, co-ordination was increasingly difficult due to the considerable distances separating the groups. One of these was the 10th Army commanded by *Général d'armée* Robert Altmayer, and within which the remaining elements of the BEF continued to operate. Weygand also advised Brooke that further to the decision of their respective Governments, the peninsula of Brittany was to be defended. Brooke estimated that the proposed holding line for this would be 150 kilometres in length and that at least fifteen divisions would be necessary to hold it. Therefore, this could do no more than lead to a further loss of British troops without any real hope of a positive outcome. In Brooke's discussions with *Général d'armée* Weygand and *Général d'armée* Georges, it had emerged that this project was not considered to be feasible by the military commanders. Following on from this, Brooke sent a telegraph to the CIGS, General Dill, and arranged for Major General Sir Richard Howard-Vyse of the British Military Mission to travel to Britain and to the War Office in order to advise Dill more fully on this matter.

At 2000 hours, Brooke was telephoned by the CIGS to discuss the position of the 52nd Division. Brooke assumed that General Dill was calling from the War Office but he was in fact at 10 Downing Street. When Brooke stated that he wanted this Division to be evacuated, Dill stated that 'the Prime Minister does not want you to do that' which elicited the response from Brooke of 'What the hell does he want?' Churchill then came on to the line and a difficult but rather forthright conversation took place between the two men, who had never met or even spoken before.[24] Churchill insisted that the Division should remain where it was, as it would be an asset to the French and could help to fill the gap between the French 10th Army and the Army of Paris. As this gap was 30 miles wide, Brooke was of the view that no useful purpose could be served by adding to these forces. Churchill indicated that Brooke had been sent to

21 Although only 54 years of age, Major General de Fonblanque was by this time a very sick man but as a consequence of this, together with his exertions during the BEF's withdrawal, following his evacuation from France he died on 2 July 1940.

22 Lieutenant General Sir Henry Karslake endured a rather unsatisfactory time in France in 1940. Firstly, he was given the impression by General Sir Edmund Ironside that he would be given command of all of the British troops currently there but, owing to Ironside's replacement as CIGS by General Sir John Dill, this action was never ratified and hence Karslake had to take charge of the L of C troops, which gave him the responsibility for the Beauman Division. However, this distraction caused him to neglect the remit should have carried out and the vast amount of equipment and stores accumulated since the BEF's arrival were not adequately prepared for return to Britain once evacuation of the remaining British troops became inevitable.

23 *The London Gazette*, 22 May 1946, p.2433.

24 A. Danchev and D. Todman (eds), *War Diaries 1939-1945: Field Marshal Lord Alanbrooke*, p.81.

France to give the French the feeling that the British were supporting them, which elicited Brooke's reply that 'it was impossible to make a corpse feel, and that the French Army was, to all intents and purposes, dead, and certainly incapable of registering what had been done for it'.[25] The conversation continued for over 30 minutes and Brooke, who certainly did not lack moral courage, had a difficult time in convincing Churchill of his case, with both men being on the verge of losing their tempers. Indeed, Brooke was even heard to say to the Prime Minister that 'You've lost one Scottish Division. Do you want to lose another?'[26]

Churchill subsequently acceded with Brooke's argument and it was decided that whilst continuing to fight for the present time, the rest of the 52nd Division would be ordered back to a defensive line near to Cherbourg in order to cover the BEF's planned withdrawal and evacuation.[27] Brooke was later informed that he was no longer under French command and that he should prepare to withdraw the rest of the British forces from France. As the French forces were retreating all along their line and their formations being forced apart by infiltrating German divisions, this development could not have been more welcome to the remainder of the BEF then in France. The British forces that had been under the command of the French 10th Army were now to be placed under the orders of Lieutenant General Marshall-Cornwall as 'Normanforce' and, whilst continuing to co-operate with the French Army, they were ordered to withdraw to Cherbourg. Marshall-Cornwall, who was based at Orbec, had been summoned to Brooke's headquarters at Le Mans, arriving there at 0230 hours and was received by Brigadier Neil Ritchie who conveyed Brooke's orders. At Marshall-Cornwall's insistence, Brooke was raised from his bed in order to receive a report on the position of the 10th Army. Marshall-Cornwall travelled to Mortagne-au-Perche to meet Brigadier Laurie of the 157th Brigade and to relate the orders that his Brigade was to act as the rear-guard for the evacuation.

That same evening, when he telephoned the CIGS to advise that the proposed plan to establish a redoubt in Brittany was quite impossible, Brooke learnt from Dill that the French Government and commanders were mistaken in their view that Churchill had taken a decision regarding the Breton redoubt at the Supreme War Council. Indeed, Dill maintained that no decision was made at the meeting and the Prime Minister had done nothing more than commit to an intention to study the redoubt proposal. Furthermore, given the French Army's state of disintegration, the movement of any more British troops and resources to France should be stopped and arrangements made for the evacuation of the BEF from the available ports as quickly as possible. In his diary and the account of events published shortly after the end of the war, Brooke recorded that the CIGS informed him that the orders had already been issued to stop the despatch of further troops and war materiel to France.[28]

At 2235 hours on 14 June, the CIGS further informed Brooke that the Brittany scheme was not to proceed and the Prime Minister had approved the evacuation, and that Brooke himself was no longer to come under the orders of *Général d'armée* Weygand. Furthermore, the remainder of the BEF was to act as an independent force, although Brooke and the BEF were

25 Ibid.
26 G. Stewart, *Dunkirk and the Fall of France*, p.127.
27 *The London Gazette*, 22 May 1946, p.2434.
28 A. Danchev and D. Todman (eds), *War Diaries 1939-1945: Field Marshal Lord Alanbrooke*, p.80.

still to continue to co-operate in every way possible with the French 10th Army.[29] In a telegram received from the Secretary of State for War, it was confirmed to Brooke that:

> You are no longer under French command but will co-operate with any French forces which may be fighting in your vicinity. In view of your report stating that organisational resistance has come to an end you must now prepare for the withdrawal of your force to the UK.[30]

On 15 June, considering his position at Le Mans to be too exposed given that there were no troops to cover this area, Brooke moved his headquarters back to Vitré, west of Laval. The following day, he moved again, this time from Vitré to Redon which was approximately 30 miles to the north of St Nazaire.

That same day, Brooke met with Lieutenant General Marshall-Cornwall and placed under his command the remaining British troops (codenamed 'Normanforce') that had been operating with the French 10th Army. As the French forces were in retreat everywhere, and had broken up into separate groups that could no longer communicate with each other, it was impossible to have a unified command. Brooke and Marshall-Cornwall were in agreement that the British forces should be detached and ordered to withdraw to Cherbourg from where they could be evacuated by the Royal Navy. Hence, Brooke ordered Marshall-Cornwall to co-operate as far as possible with the French until the opportunity arose to disengage from and to make a withdrawal to Cherbourg for evacuation.[31] Similarly, on 16 June, Lieutenant General Marshall-Cornwall wrote to Acting Major General Beauman, stating that:

> I thought that I had made it clear in my letter MC 43 that you were to continue your withdrawal slowly and steadily towards Cherbourg. You are not to take over a defensive sector on the Dives or any other line, except in so far as this may be necessary to cover your orderly withdrawal.
>
> I hope to visit General Fagalde to-day, to explain to him that you are under my orders not his, but you should co-operate with him as far as possible and fight a rear-guard action if attacked; I realise your troops are not suitable to be engaged in counter-attacks.[32]

On 16 June, *Général d'armée* Altmayer ordered French 10th Army, along with those British units still remaining in France, to withdraw to Brittany. In effect, this would create a gap of fifty miles between the 10th Army and the other French armies, and the ludicrousness of this persuaded Brooke that the only way in which these residual British troops could be saved from either death or captivity was for them to be ordered to Cherbourg and taken back to Britain at the earliest opportunity. Following the final evacuations of the BEF and upon his own return to England, surprisingly Brooke received an admonishment from the War Office because he

29 *The London Gazette*, 22 May 1946, p.2434.
30 L.F. Ellis, *The War in France and Flanders 1939-40*, p.300.
31 TNA WO 32/9388: Overseas: Europe (Code O (V)), Despatches from BEF 12-19 June 1940.
32 TNA WO 167/1412: Beauman Division, Headquarters.

had not saved more resources. This was in spite of his decisiveness, which contributed to saving almost 200,000 men who were able to carry on the fight against Germany.

10

The Anglo-French Political Relationship

Churchill and Reynaud

At the meeting of the British War Cabinet on 1 June, and whilst the evacuation of the BEF from Dunkirk was being carried out, consideration was given to the sending of further RAF fighter squadrons to France. The general feeling of the meeting was that should Paris fall into the enemy's hands, and because the French Government's resolve might collapse, a separate peace could be concluded between France and Germany. The possible implication of this was that a collaborationist French regime might be formed that was sympathetic to its former adversary and hostile to its former ally. In view of this, Britain should now concentrate on its own defence.

Clement Attlee, Leader of the Labour Party and now the Lord Privy Seal in the coalition Government, supported the idea that one or two British Army divisions should be sent 'as a token of sincerity' and to 'hearten the French'.[1] He also agreed with the Prime Minister that no further RAF fighter aircraft should be sent to France, so as 'not to impair the essential fighter defences of our country'.[2] Exercising caution, so that Britain's defence was not endangered, Churchill felt that France should be given the greatest possible support and he was, therefore, of the view that the RAF's bombers should be made available to carry out night-time missions to attack those targets which had been designated by the French Commander-in-Chief.

Two days later, the War Cabinet returned to the discussion of the French requests for further RAF fighter support and received a decisive presentation from the Air Officer Commanding Fighter Command, Air Chief Marshal Sir Hugh Dowding. This specified that of the 250 British aircraft that had already been sent to France, typically about 25 machines were being lost in combat each day, set against which four replacements were received direct from factory production. Dowding concluded that the evacuation from Dunkirk was placing a tremendous strain on Britain's home fighter resources. He was afraid that if the *Luftwaffe* instigated a heavy attack on Britain at this time, British air superiority could not be guaranteed for more than 48 hours.[3] The home defences had also suffered as a result of the operations conducted in France

1 TNA CAB 65/7: War Cabinet Minutes.
2 TNA CAB 65/13: War Cabinet Minutes.
3 M. Gilbert, *Finest Hour: Winston Churchill, 1939-1941*, pp.457.

and it was a formidable task to provide the depleted RAF squadrons with new aircraft and, just as importantly, trained and experienced pilots. Subsequently, Churchill telephoned General Edward Spears, who was the point of liaison with French Prime Minister, Paul Reynaud, and his commander-in-Chief, *Général d'armée* Weygand, informing him that 'You should prepare them for a favourable response regarding the Army but disappointment about the air'.[4] On 5 June, Reynaud was formally notified that the twenty RAF fighter squadrons he had previously requested were unable to be provided.

On the evening of 7 June, via his personal representative in London, Jean Monnet, and again on 8 June, Prime Minister Reynaud further implored Winston Churchill to send more of the RAF's fighter squadrons out to France. In response, Major General Hastings Ismay, Churchill's chief military adviser, expressed the opinion that, 'We should be insane to send them all our fighters because if they were lost the country would be beaten in two days, whereas even if France surrenders we should still win the war provided our air defences are intact'.[5]

When the War Cabinet met later that day, the losses that were being incurred by those RAF squadrons already in France were reported to it. The conclusion was reached that to commit any additional fighter resources in an attempt to shore up the deteriorating situation in France would, should it fail, lead inevitably to the surrender to the enemy of not just France but of Britain as well, and the war would be lost. However, even if France was forced into submission, and provided that its home fighter defences remained unbroken, Britain would be able to continue the struggle against Germany. On the same day, Churchill reiterated this message to the British Defence Committee, when he advised its membership that although the defence of France was important, it was not decisive; whereas maintaining an adequate force of fighter aircraft for the protection of the British mainland was decisive. The Committee concurred with his view and that by sending further fighter aircraft to France, it would jeopardise the defensive position of Great Britain at this time.

On 9 June, at Reynaud's request Churchill received in London the recently appointed French Under-Secretary for National Defence, *Général de brigade* Charles de Gaulle, who outlined the French plans for regroupment and urged that further British Army divisions be sent to France as soon as possible. This was their first meeting and Churchill was to later advise the War Cabinet of the favourable impression of determination given by this French General, who also agreed with the British policy in relation to the sending of more fighter squadrons to France.[6]

On 10 June, Churchill despatched a message to Prime Minister Reynaud in which he spoke of 'the maximum possible support being given by the British forces and of all available means being used "to give help on land, sea and in the air". He also referred to the RAF as having been continually engaged over the battlefields.[7]

Following an urgent invitation to him from Prime Minister Reynaud, Winston Churchill agreed to make the hazardous journey to Château du Muguet, which was situated near to Briare on the River Loire. This took place on 11 June, and Churchill was accompanied by the Secretary of State for War, Anthony Eden, the CIGS, General Sir John Dill, and Major General Hastings

4 TNA PREM 3/175: BEF: Evacuation.
5 TNA CAB 65/13: War Cabinet Minutes.
6 M. Gilbert, *Finest Hour: Winston Churchill, 1939-1941*, pp.486.
7 *The Times*, 11 June 1940.

Ismay and General Sir Edward Spears, the latter being the British Government's representative to the French Prime Minister.

Churchill's aircraft had been due to leave Hendon aerodrome when the news of the fall of the French capital and the departure of its Government to Tours had reached him in a telegram. Initially, Churchill had thought that this might be a positive sign of the French continuing to fight in the south rather than to sit and wait for the Germans to arrive in Paris so that they could surrender to them.[8] Thus, Churchill wanted to discover what the French Government was now intending to do and to discuss the measures necessary to meet the developing war situation. To this end, he consulted Prime Minister Reynaud, *Maréchal de France* Philippe Pétain (who had now been appointed as Reynaud's Vice Premier) and *Général d'armée* Weygand, the French Commander-in-Chief. At this meeting, Reynaud reiterated the opinion of the French High Command that a single large-scale attack upon the advancing German forces might completely reverse the situation and save the day.[9]

The British representatives were not in agreement with this opinion because they did not consider that the battle then being fought in France was really the decisive one, in spite of the scale of the French Army's losses since *Fall Rot*, the second phase of the German offensive, which had begun on 5 June. This view was motivated by a British distrust of the French politicians and understandable concerns about the capacity to continue to fight of the French armed forces, with contingencies already being put into place for the possibility that the French Government would collapse and seek to negotiate a separate peace with the Germans. In response to Weygand's assertions, made when demanding air support, that 'Here is the decisive point' and that 'this is the decisive moment' it was Churchill who immediately countered these by stating that 'This is not the decisive point; this is not the decisive moment'.[10]

For the British Government, the Battle of France was not the war and they were reluctant to commit such desperately needed resources as the RAF's fighter squadrons to what now clearly appeared to be a lost cause. Hence, Churchill spoke of the possibility 'that the Nazis may dominate Europe, but it will be a Europe in revolt, and in the end, it is certain that a regime whose victories are in the main due to its machines will one day collapse'. He also made reference to the prospect of a campaign of German air attacks on Great Britain and that it would be folly, therefore, to jeopardise the RAF's fighter strength. At the meeting of the War Cabinet held during the next day, and when referring to his discussions with Reynaud, Pétain and Weygand, Churchill noted how 'They had been studiously polite and dignified, but it was clear that France was near the end of organised resistance'.[11] Indeed, the official minutes of this meeting also record Churchill remarking:

> That the British commanders in the Havre peninsula must not accept any further orders from the French who had let us down badly. They had not allowed the 51st Division to retire on Rouen and had kept it waiting until it was no longer possible to

8 P. Warner, *Battle of France, 1940*, p.190.
9 *Manchester Guardian*, 13 June 1940.
10 J. Jackson, *The Fall of France: The Nazi Invasion of 1940*, p.98.
11 M. Gilbert, *Finest Hour: Winston Churchill, 1939-1941*, pp.48-49.

> reach Havre. Finally, they had compelled it to capitulate with their own troops. Any remaining troops must be evacuated that night without fail.[12]

On 13 June, Churchill attended the final gathering of the Anglo-French Supreme War Council, held at the Préfecture in Tours. At this meeting he was accompanied by Lord Halifax, the Foreign Secretary, Lord Beaverbrook, the Minister for Aircraft Production, Sir Alexander Cadogan, the Permanent Under Secretary of State for Foreign Affairs, and Generals Ismay and Spears. The atmosphere was quite different to that of the previous meetings because by then the British Chiefs of Staff were envisaging the very real possibility of France seeking a separate peace and that some of the French authorities might actively begin to collaborate with the enemy. Reynaud asserted that without help from the United States of America, the French would have little option but to surrender, and in this he was supported by *Général d'armée* Weygand, who felt that an armistice should be sought without delay.

In response to this, Churchill insisted that 'We must fight, we will fight, and that is why we must ask our friends to fight on'.[13] It was in this context, and in an attempt to prevent the French Government from seeking a separately negotiated peace with Germany, that Churchill suggested that a Franco-British Union could be established. This would have joint defence, foreign, financial and economic policies and a single war cabinet, as well as both of the national parliaments becoming formally associated. Fundamentally, this was little more than a desperate gesture to prevent the fall of Reynaud's Government and the proposal was rejected by the French.

On 14 June, the War Cabinet had further considered the immediate crisis in France and the proposal of the Prime Minister that once the British troops had been withdrawn to the port of Cherbourg then they should not be evacuated but they should remain there in case 'a fresh opportunity arose they could be ordered to proceed elsewhere in France'.[14] The War Cabinet also discussed the possible creation of a union between Britain and France. Although initially sceptical about this, Churchill did not dismiss the idea out of hand, but his main concern was to secure the French fleet in order to prevent it from falling into the enemy's hands, as the implications of this would be disastrous. On this day, *The Times* reproduced in full a message that had been sent to the French Government by the British Government:

> In this solemn hour for the British and French nations and for the cause of freedom and democracy, to which they have avowed themselves, his Majesty's Government desire to pay to the Government of the French Republic the tribute which is due to the heroic fortitude and constancy of the French Armies in the battle against enormous odds.
>
> Their effort is worthy of the most glorious traditions and has inflicted deep and long-lasting injury upon the enemy's strength. Great Britain will continue to give the utmost aid in her power. We take this opportunity of proclaiming the indissoluble union of our two peoples and our two empires. We cannot measure the various forms of tribulation which will fall on our peoples in the near future. We are sure that the ordeal by fire will only fuse them together into one unconquerable whole.

12 TNA CAB 65/7: War Cabinet, Minutes.
13 H. Buckton, *Retreat: Dunkirk and the Evacuation of Western Europe*, p.212.
14 TNA CAB 65/7: War Cabinet, Minutes.

> We renew to the French Republic our pledge and resolve to continue the struggle at all costs in France, in this island, upon the oceans, and in the air wherever it may lead us, using all our resources to the utmost limit, and sharing together the burden of repairing the ravages of war.
>
> We shall never turn from the conflict until France stands safe and erect in all her grandeur, until the wronged and enslaved States and peoples have been liberated, and until civilisation is free from the nightmare of Nazism. That this day will dawn we are more sure than ever. It may dawn sooner than we now have the right to expect.[15]

The French Government had, on 10 June, declared Paris to be an open city, meaning that it was undefended to prevent the destruction of its buildings and landmarks through artillery bombardment or aerial bombing and any violence being perpetrated against its residents. On 14 June, it fell into the hands of the German forces. The *Manchester Guardian* reported that on 16 June, the British Government, 'with the object of supporting France to the utmost and also in the hope of encouraging the French Government to continue in resistance,' had offered to enter into a solemn Act of Union arranged between the two countries. This provided for the joint organisation of defence, foreign, financial and economic policies, and there would be a single War Cabinet. The proposed declaration stated that 'France and Britain shall no longer be two nations, but one Franco-British union' thereby legalising a continuation of French military action, if necessary, from overseas.[16]

Moreover, on 16 June, the British Government had emphasised via a telegram that there was no possibility of it agreeing to the French authorities being released from the joint obligation not to make a separate peace with the enemy. In turn, the majority of the French Government rejected this and the aforementioned proposed Union in the belief that, if carried through, it would make France little more than a British dominion. Therefore, an armistice with Germany was sought by the new French Prime Minister, *Maréchal de France* Pétain, who had replaced Paul Reynaud following his resignation in protest at this decision.[17] In view of these developments, on 17 June the British War Cabinet had been in agreement that 'we would be sacrificing our men to no purpose if we told them to fight on'.[18] Lieutenant General Brooke learnt of the armistice from London rather than directly from any of the French sources, as *Général d'armée* Weygand, who had now been appointed as the Minister of National Defence, did not deem it necessary to inform him of it.

The French Government's request for an armistice was made to the German authorities at 0300 hours on 17 June. The meeting of the respective representatives was held at 1500 hours on 21 June at Le Francport, near Compiègne. This was in precisely the same location in the forest and in the same, historic *wagon-lit* railway carriage of the Allied Commander-in-Chief, *Maréchal de France* Ferdinand Foch that had been used for the signing of the armistice that had ended the First World War on 11 November 1918. The 1940 armistice was finally signed at 2050 hours on 22 June and came into effect at 0035 hours on 25 June, with the formal cessation

15 *The Times*, 14 June 1940.
16 *Manchester Guardian*, 16 June 1940
17 Ibid., 18 June 1940; E. Smalley, *The British Expeditionary Force, 1939-40* (New York: Palgrave Macmillan, 2015), p.35.
18 TNA CAB 65/7: War Cabinet Minutes.

of hostilities between France and Nazi Germany.[19] A similar armistice was then negotiated between France and Mussolini's Italy and signed by the representatives at the Villa Incisa in Rome on 24 June, and it also came into effect on 25 June.

At the meeting of the War Cabinet held on 17 June, general agreement was reached that 'now that the French Government under Marshal Pétain were suing for an armistice, we would be sacrificing our men to no purpose if we told them to fight on'.[20] It was agreed by the attendees that a telegram originally to have been sent to Reynaud, and insisting that the French fleet sail forthwith to British harbours, now be delivered to Pétain. Whilst this meeting was still in session, a message arrived confirming that the French troops had ceased fire at 1240 hours.

Thus, it was the conclusion of what had been a long and often considerably acrimonious period of disagreement between both the senior military ranks and the leading politicians in the governments of Britain and France, and the failure on both parties to create any real understanding and unity of purpose when they were faced with the German invasion during 1940. For the French it would be the, at the time was relatively unknown, *Général de brigade* Charles de Gaulle who would emerge from this chaos with any credibility, and it was announced on 28 June that the British Government had now decided to recognise de Gaulle as the leader of the French Government-in-exile and of Free France and the Free French armed forces.

Breton Redoubt

On 29 May, French Prime Minister Reynaud had rejected the recommendation of *Général d'armée* Weygand that an armistice should be considered. In turn, Reynaud had asked Weygand to prepare a study of the possibility of establishing a national redoubt. This was to be created at a port within the Brittany peninsula, in order to have access to the sea and to France's overseas possessions and its allies, and was in effect an updated version of the Lines of Torres Vedras. These were the forts and other defences constructed in Portugal during 1809/10 by the British commander during the Peninsula War, the then Viscount Wellington, to protect the Portuguese capital of Lisbon from the anticipated French offensive of 1810. On 31 May, the idea was initially discussed at a joint meeting of the British and French Governments.

On 5 June, an operational instruction was prepared by the British Government, which included the appointment of Lieutenant General Brooke as the commander of what would be known as the second BEF, which was to being prepared for despatched to France. This would employ the British Army's original 1939 Plan W for the landing of the BEF. To help stabilise the French Army's defensive efforts, upon its arrival the 52nd Division was to be directed to Cherbourg and assembled at Évreux to support the 51st Division, which was positioned to the north of the Seine. On 6 June, Weygand issued orders to commence work on the redoubt, with it being placed under the command of *Général de corps d'armée* René Altmayer, the younger brother of the commander of the 10th Army, *Général d'armée* Robert Altmayer.[21]

On 9 June, the Anglo-French Supreme War Council met at Briare and the new French Minister of War, *Général de brigade* Charles de Gaulle, was sent to Rennes in order to assess the progress that was being made with the redoubt's development. *Général de corps d'armée* René

19 A. Horne, *To Lose a Battle: France 1940*, pp.663-65.
20 TNA CAB 65/7: War Cabinet, Minutes.
21 B. Karslake, *1940, The Last Act*, p.264.

Altmayer had previously confirmed that the work had commenced on the construction of the redoubt's defences, as civilian labourers had been recruited and 3,000 Polish troops had also been allocated to the task. On 10 June, Reynaud suggested that there should be final stand in Brittany, and his view appeared to be supported by de Gaulle. Nevertheless, it transpired that the civil engineering machinery which was required for the construction of the defences was no longer unavailable. Returning to Paris on 12 June, de Gaulle reported that since the prospect of creating and maintaining a redoubt in Brittany was now not possible, Quimper, a city in Brittany, was an appropriate place for the French Government to retreat to because from there it could take a ship to either Africa or to Britain.

On 13 June, Winston Churchill had made at high personal risk what would be his last visit to France for four years. He met with Reynaud to attempt to dissuade the French Government from seeking an armistice with Germany. They also discussed the proposed redoubt. The following day, Lieutenant General Brooke met with *Général d'armée* Georges and *Général d'armée* Weygand at the former's headquarters in Briare to discuss this matter. Although Brooke and his team of staff officers had drawn up plans that anticipated having to defend a Brittany bridgehead, he observed that both of the French commanders considered the whole idea to be ridiculous. For example, if followed through, the *Luftwaffe* would have been able to position large numbers of its aircraft within easy striking distance of Brittany to attack not just the defending forces on the ground but also the Royal Navy's ships being sent to assist and supply them, and which, in their turn, would be vulnerable to attack from German U-boats. Furthermore, lacking radar coverage, any interventions by the RAF were likely to be costly in terms of pilots and machines.

Accordingly, Britain's home defences would have been fundamentally weakened and, by isolating a significant number of British Army divisions in this way, the remainder of the *Wehrmacht* would have stood a far better chance had Operation Sea Lion been launched in such circumstances. Regardless of these considerations, it was the will of the civilian leaders and that had to be respected by the military, and Brooke and the French commanders signed a memorandum confirming that British troops would be available for the defence of Brittany.[22] In doing so, it would appear apparent that Brooke not only fully appreciated the impossibility of the plan but that he clearly foresaw the imminent collapse of the French defences.[23]

Brooke had enquired how, given that the front to be defended would be 93 miles in length and this task would require at least 15 divisions, this was to be done as the British Army could only supply four divisions. When he asked where the additional divisions were to be obtained from, he was told that there were none.[24] Brooke stated that he would participate in the scheme, although he felt that it would needlessly risk the lives of more British troops, and he subsequently telephoned the CIGS, who was against the idea of the redoubt, claimed to know nothing about the plan and informed Brooke that no such agreement had been made between the British and French Governments. Instead, Churchill was now of the opinion that the new corps being assembled should remain in France, at least until the final collapse

22 This in itself was a most unusual action for these senior officers to take given the circumstances, and it perhaps indicates that the French commanders may have doubted Brooke's intentions and were trying to obtain a written commitment from him in order to justify their own positions.

23 P. Takle, *The British Army in France after Dunkirk*, p.116.

24 J. Thompson, *Dunkirk: Retreat to Victory*, p.292.

of the French armed forces, when it could be evacuated back to Britain via the nearest ports. However, according to Brooke's account published in *The London Gazette* in 1946, on 14 June he had contacted and had various telephone conversations with the CIGS, General Dill. In these discussions, he impressed upon Dill the view of the French commanders and himself that the Brittany plan was impossible given the troops available and the overall condition of the French Army. Initially, these conversations served to confirm that the Prime Minister knew nothing of this plan and that all of the arrangements were to start for the evacuation of those elements of the BEF still fighting on in France. Later, and in a further telephone call from the CIGS, Brooke was told that it was important for good relations with the French to be maintained to avoid the impression that the BEF was leaving them to their fate.[25]

25 *The London Gazette*, 22 May 1946, p.2434.

Conclusion

An Assessment of the Contribution of the British Armed Forces

The conventional explanations offered for the slow and ineffective rearmament of the British armed forces during the 1930s generally refer to a number of factors considered to be of relevance. There were the unhappy memories for many of the population that were associated with their experiences of the Great War; the Government-imposed financial constraints during a decade of economic depression; and other diplomatic and strategic priorities that weighed heavily on the governments of the day. In addition, and having regard to the armed forces of the other European countries, due to the poor intelligence assessments carried out before 1939, the British Government and the senior officers of its armed forces seriously under-estimated the military capability of Nazi Germany whilst over-estimating that of France.

Though the BEF should ideally have been larger in terms of the number of divisions sent to France, better prepared both operationally and tactically, and supplied with arms and equipment that could meet the requirements of fighting a modern war, it was nevertheless dependent upon the French High Command for direction. An alternative view, therefore, is that with strategy being dictated and imposed upon its commanders in this manner, the BEF could not avoid having to fight alongside allies whose expectations were of a campaign that would be defensive, reactive and slow. This was a contributing factor in the retreat that the BEF was forced to make, during both phases of the German offensive in France in 1940, and it was essentially a consequence of the BEF's allies on its flanks losing the battle.[1] The aim here is to examine the performance of the BEF, RAF and Royal Navy with the objective of reaching a set of balanced conclusions on this matter.

British Expeditionary Force

There have been many commentators who have expressed the view that in 1939 the British Army was not ready to confront a first-class adversary, particularly given that the BEF sent out to France 'was smaller than the British Expeditionary Force of 1914, less well-trained and badly deficient in vital equipment and stores'.[2]

1 J. Thompson, *Dunkirk: Retreat to Victory*, pp. iii-iv.
2 B. Bond, 'Introduction: Preparing the Field Force, February 1939 - May 1940' in Bond, B. & M. Taylor (eds), *Battle for France and Flanders Sixty Years On* (London: Cooper, 2001), p.1.

This has often been attributed to the British Army of the inter-war period having undergone a reversion to its previous role, by becoming again what was essentially an imperial police force. It was also due in part to insufficient funding but there was the fear of provoking either foreign governments or the pacifists at home should defence spending be increased. Indeed, prior to the outbreak of the Second World War, the Army's training had tended to be rather vague, inadequate and chronically under-resourced, with large-scale manoeuvres not being carried out for several years.[3] And, as with the regular army, the Territorial Army had been the victim of Government financial cutbacks and indifference. Although the number of territorials had been doubled in March 1939 (in an attempt to reach the target of 340,000 troops and the establishment of 12 new divisions), which was helpful in creating a logical framework for the overall expansion of the British Army as a whole, this initiative was rather too late in the day, and when deployed to France the TA divisions were certainly understrength.

Further constraints of receiving the minimum of training and having insufficient and obsolete arms and equipment for both men and officers also badly affected the effectiveness of those territorial units that were eventually to take part in combat in France. In contrast to this has been the view of some commentators that, whilst the inter-war British Army had long prepared for a future conflict against a first-class opponent, what it emphatically failed to do was to accurately anticipate what the principal characteristics of combat were likely to be by 1939-40.[4]

In 1940, the senior leaders of the British Army were generally the men who had been gallant and reliable junior or middle-ranking officers during the Great War. In view of the circumstances that they and their men had contended with in that conflict, and in the subsequent period, they attempted to acquit themselves as well as could reasonably have been expected. Moreover, because the regular British Army of the inter-war years had been considerably reduced in its numbers, many of these officers knew each other very well, both professionally and socially. By the standards against which they were judged prior to 1940, typically they were proficient full-time soldiers, who had received what was deemed to be the relevant training for a particular function or role. They trusted each other to carry out their duties and to obey the orders they received, but also to cope when they were faced with unfavourable situations and, most importantly, not to panic. As the official historian, Major Ellis, later observed, 'A cement of mutual confidence strengthened the whole Expeditionary Force and helped it to withstand the appalling shocks it had to suffer'.[5]

Regardless of the BEF's issues about how best to deploy what limited armoured and artillery support was available to it, and how to work in co-operation with the air power of the RAF, many valuable lessons had nonetheless been drawn from the earlier conflict. There were attempts to find out why, despite the detailed planning involved, offensives might actually achieve so little but be so costly in terms of the number of lives lost. Yet the British Army still appeared to be reliant upon its mass infantry divisions that were best suited to the types of conflicts that were essentially static and attritional in nature.

Following the Dunkirk evacuation, and until the arrival in France of Lieutenant General Sir Alan Brooke, the remaining BEF units had lacked a senior commander in the field who was capable of protecting the interests of his subordinates and their divisions and brigades. This was

3 E. Smalley, *The British Expeditionary Force, 1939-40*, p.15.
4 Ibid., p.1.
5 L.F. Ellis, *The War in France and Flanders 1939-40*, p.xv.

of importance, as they struggled to cope with the plethora of often contradictory orders received from the various French generals who had been placed in overall command of the British forces. A valiant attempt to do this was made by Lieutenant General Karslake but he was notably lacking in significant field experience and, due to this hindrance, was largely ineffective when trying to make the necessary interventions with the French High Command. The British Army's own command structure was publicly deemed to be fundamentally sound, although the operational framework was subsequently to be transformed and a number of the senior officers from the 1940 campaign would never see active field service again. However, others, such as Brigadier Richard McCreery and Brigadier John Crocker, the commanders of the 2nd and 3rd Armoured Brigades respectively, would make the progression to become successful Corps commanders before the end of the war.

In terms of the British Army's 'Other Ranks', when viewed in stark socio-economic terms, there was a noticeable tendency for many of these soldiers to have been recruited from British society's lower and often most-economically depressed social classes. Inevitably, they were the young men without an education or good prospects, for whom the unemployment and hunger of the depressed 1930s had often been the principal motivating factors for their enlistment in all branches of the British armed forces.

For this reason, it was believed that the quickest and most effective way to transform these recruits into a body of disciplined and efficient soldiers was to instil in them a blind obedience to the orders that were given to them by their superior officers. As recorded by the Official history, when in battle these British troops, 'though they fought with dogged tenacity were forced back, or overwhelmed as a result of mounting casualties, dwindling ammunition and the superior numbers of the enemy'.[6] Despite this, on 5 June, *The Times* commented on the fighting spirit of the BEF formations to the south of the River Somme in the following terms:

> Everywhere you go you see the same cheerful grins, the same expressions of philosophic doggedness on the faces of the men in battledress as you saw in the north right through the bad times.[7]

The downside of this approach was that when it became necessary for these troops to act decisively using their own initiative, the expectation of the rank-and-file and indeed many of their NCOs being ready and capable of doing so was debatable. Moreover, their junior and middle-ranking officers had not always been adequately prepared or given suitable training for the practical demands that were concomitant with the offensive operations dominated by the 1940-style deployment of armour and concentrated artillery firepower. This was due to the organisational cultures shaping strategies and the development of military doctrine during the inter-war years. Due to the political and social considerations that influenced its military leaders, both the British and the French armies failed to envisage just how the campaign of 1940 was likely to be fought and to make the requisite preparations for it.

On 14 June 1940, in a report that he prepared for the Chief of the Imperial General Staff, Lieutenant General Marshall-Cornwall highlighted how the British troops in France had

6 Ibid., p.271.
7 *The Times*, 5 June 1940.

developed the fatal habit of looking over their shoulder. He stated that since the last war, the British Army had never developed nor had it insisted upon an attack doctrine. Furthermore, he considered that British Army officers did not really believe that attacking infantry could successfully assault a well organised defensive position when it was protected by troops that were equipped with automatic weapons.

At the same time, insufficient attention was given to what the requirements of continental warfare might be, so that over six months after the outbreak of war not one British armoured division was ready for action. Tactical training during the inter-war years had concentrated on the implementation of a withdrawal in the face of the enemy, and this exercised a damaging influence on British military doctrine. In France, rather than the units allocated to the defence of a locality actually defending it, in practice, and owing to the thinness of troops on the ground, greater consideration was given to the achievement of a well-ordered withdrawal. Marshall-Cornwall pointedly contrasted this with Field Marshal Haig's order from 11 April 1918 that 'Every position must be held to the last man … with our backs to the wall and believing in the justice of our cause, each one of us must fight on to the end'.[8]

Even before the BEF had been embarked on to the ships destined for France in 1939, the then CIGS, General Sir Edmund Ironside, had warned his Vice-Chief, General Sir John Dill, and the BEF's Commander-in-Chief, General Lord Gort, of the importance of being prepared to defend the rear areas. This should have necessitated the non-combatant troops being suitably equipped and trained, and plans being formulated that could be implemented promptly for the communication centres to be garrisoned and any potential supply bottlenecks to be resolved. Yet, during what was termed the 'phoney war', very little would be done about this. However, on 19 June, the *Manchester Guardian* recorded the views of a young Yorkshire soldier, which demonstrated the views of the fighting men in the front line:

> We showed conclusively that tank for tank and man for man we were superior. But we did not have the support of a consecutive line behind us and we had to retreat.[9]

Eventually, Acting Brigadier (later promoted to Acting Major General) Beauman had been 'dug-out' of retirement and, insofar as anything could be accomplished in the circumstances, he was available to organise the Line of Communication troops that were south of the River Somme. Whilst discipline remained remarkably high when taking account of the circumstances they faced, it appeared to be the ancillary and service arms of the BEF (such as the Line of Communication troops) which tended to suffer most from deteriorating morale. Those located in the rear echelons, who were detached from the front-line fighting, became subject to a lack of communication and accurate information, leading inevitably to gossip and rumour. Those soldiers who were to subsequently find themselves placed in formations such as the Beauman Division had to manage whilst being insufficiently equipped when confronted by an adversary with superior weaponry and greater numbers of troops. Their light armaments were no match whatsoever for the German panzers, and then there was the constant hunger and exhaustion that would accompany their retreat.

8 TNA WO 32/9388: Overseas: Europe (Code O (V)), Despatches from BEF 12-19 June 1940.
9 *Manchester Guardian*, 19 June 1940.

In general, the units of the British Army surrendered only after they had been surrounded, outflanked and had run out of ammunition, and this was usually after putting up considerable resistance to the enemy. When this was combined with the sheer pragmatism of trying to limit unnecessary casualties and fatalities, and there was no alternative available, all these factors contributed to the eventual issuing of orders to lay down their arms and the resigned acceptance of being taken prisoners of war. Eventually, over 40,000 British servicemen would be compelled to surrender to the German armed forces during the campaign in France and Flanders and, for the men who had been hitherto disciplined and well-led troops, it was surely unavoidable that they would consider this to be anything other than an act of humiliation.

Once it became clear that the intended naval evacuation from St Valery-en-Caux was no longer possible, it was hardly surprising that the 51st Division had no other choice than to capitulate and thousands of British troops then passed into enemy captivity.[10] The circumstances of how this was carried out still remains the subject of continued debate. At the time, it was certainly implied that the men of the 51st Division had held on to their positions for far longer than was prudent, but this was done to assist the French 31st Division which was on its flank, and by doing so they had allowed themselves to be cut off and encircled by the 7th Panzer Division.

Furthermore, there remain unanswered the questions of whether Churchill deliberately sacrificed the 51st Division to keep the French Army fighting on? Or if the capitulation was actually instigated by the French commander, *Général de corps d'armée* Ihler? Churchill certainly attributed the loss of the 51st Division to the French Army's refusal to allow it to retire towards Rouen when this was possible. In reality, the Allied troops at St Valery had very little option other than to lay down their arms. As it was to have provided the core around which the second BEF would be assembled, the surrender of the 51st Division was both a profound blow to British esteem and the ambition to retain a fighting force on the Continent and a warning that a similar fate could befall the other British divisions still arriving in France.

When Lieutenant General Brooke returned to the Continent with orders to take command of the remaining British formations in France, he made it clear that he had little faith in either the arrangements then in hand for the creation of a second BEF or the prospects for its military operations in France. Hence, his determination to end the British presence in France as quickly as possible.[11] His diary refers to the difficulties being contended with of trying to balance the political considerations, of which he was not fully informed, and the military necessities staring him in the face, and that these were frequently diametrically opposed.

Whilst politically it was desirable to support the French Army, militarily this would have led to sheer annihilation and catastrophe when it was evident that a force as small as the remnants of the BEF were being expected to undertake tasks well beyond their capacity. The difficulty was to extricate the British troops without giving the impression of just abandoning the French and it was their request for an armistice with Germany which provided the essential outcome to the situation. Brooke stated that 'The last week has been very trying for me, and I hope never to be entrusted with a similar task again'.[12] It was his acute and accurate assessment of the fate that would befall France and its armed forces, together with his steadfastness when standing

10 M. Connelly and W. Miller, 'The BEF and the Issue of Surrender on the Western Front in 1940', *War in History*, October 2004, Vol. 11, p.434.

11 B. Karslake, *1940, The Last Act*, pp.240-41.

12 A. Danchev. and D. Todman (eds), *War Diaries 1939-1945: Field Marshal Lord Alanbrooke*, p.87.

up to the politicians, which meant that in 1940 no other British Divisions would suffer the humiliation that was to be the lot of the 51st Division.

Similarly, in a report on the 1st Armoured Division's operations, Major General Evans stated that the Allied inability to hold the German advance at the River Seine, in conjunction with the German drive on Paris, had the most serious consequences. Evans was critical that 'The French troops – even after the tardy and piecemeal arrival of "fresh" divisions – were thin on the ground and in little heart for the fight'.[13] He added that it was not uncommon to find the French units that were due to be in position either had not materialised at all, or were taking cover in woods without making much pretence of tactically disposing themselves. As this had occurred south of the Somme, no defences were prepared, no wire or anti-tank mines were sited and no trenches were dug. Nor was there any offensive spirit among the French troops or their commanders, as reconnaissance to confirm or refute the generally inaccurate and exaggerated reports by local civilians was neglected. The French units continued to move southwards, in many instances being inclined to move off at the first rumour of the enemy's approach, and an atmosphere of inevitable defeat was growing. Evans noted that in Normandy, British reinforcements were arriving and a British GHQ under Lieutenant General Brooke had been created but it was obvious that the situation required further reaching measures than these if the situation was to be stabilised. In default of the arrival of more British divisions, all troops in the area of operations, whether French or British, would have no choice but to continue to fall back or be destroyed.[14]

Acting Major General Beauman, in his report of 21 June 1940, set out a number of points about the operations both north and south of the River Seine between May and June 1940. He asserted that to combat the type of warfare which had been evolved by the *Wehrmacht*, a considerable force of all arms, fully equipped, was required for the protection of the Line of Communication. He speculated that had such a force been stationed in the Amiens area from the outset, then the Battle of France's outcome could have been very different.

Beauman also believed that a definite effect on operations was made by the defensive line held on the rivers Andelle and Béthune and to the north of Rouen. During the period when the German forces were first on the Somme, with a detachment on the Bresle, and there was nothing between them and the important base installations surrounding Rouen and Le Havre, this line, thinly held though it had been, but combined with a vigorous policy of patrolling, probably bluffed the enemy into believing that there was a much larger British contingent present than was the case. Consequently, although the enemy could have employed quite a small force to seize and destroy these installations, they had not attempted to do so. A captured German operation order clearly indicated that the objectives of the panzer divisions on 7 June, which was the rear of the British line. Therefore, when the German units approached on the afternoon of 7 June and met with opposition, they broke off the engagement and did not resume their attack until 1000 hours on 8 June. This then provided a breathing space to evacuate the most valuable of the stores.

Beauman recounted how the successful defence of the divisional reserve position at Isneauville, between 1800 and 1900 hours on 8 June by the Beauman Division's 4th Reinforcement (Syme's)

13 TNA WO 167/334: 1st Armoured Division War Diary.
14 Ibid.

Battalion, considerably delayed the entry of the enemy's forces into Rouen. Indeed, the German troops were so roughly handled during this action that they waited until the early hours of the following day before resuming battle. However, had the Syme's Battalion failed to hold the enemy at bay, they would have assaulted that part of Rouen earlier and captured a large number of Allied troops and prevented them and much valuable equipment from being transferred to the south of the river, as occurred during the night of 8 to 9 June. The original defensive line was not very strong and was thinly held, but time and work were devoted to strengthening it so that the weaker parts were heavily mined. Beauman emphasised that this action supported his view that when a position was selected with care and appropriately reinforced with machine guns and anti-tank guns, the British infantry had little to fear from the German *Wehrmacht* and its panzers. Unfortunately, this did not take full account of the *Luftwaffe's* ground support role, and especially the Stuka dive bombers when they made attacks on such positions.

Beauman also noted that although a prolonged resistance against the panzer units could not realistically be expected when they attacked on a narrow front, a delay might have been caused in several locations had the German forces not used trickery to infiltrate and pierce the British line. For example, the overwhelming evidence of the use by the *Heer* of captured French AFVs that were flying French flags and which had their turret hatches open. In some of these cases the British troops actually guided these tanks through their own minefields only to find that they were being followed by German tanks. Understandably, Beauman considered it problematic to find an answer to a deception of this type, which it was difficult to anticipate.

The practice of placing small 'packets' of British troops and tanks under French command was mostly disastrous. Beauman pointed out that he was ordered to send one of the battalions to be placed under the orders of the French Army. This unit was situated astride a French inter-Corps boundary, resulting in it receiving conflicting orders from both of the French commanders in the field. Eventually this battalion was moved so far from the rest of the Beauman Division that providing supplies became impossible and it ran out of ammunition and food.

Conversely, it was noted that throughout these operations, constant contact with the enemy was being maintained by means of officer patrols mounted on motor cycles, as they could cover more ground than any of the dismounted patrols. These proved to be of the utmost value and enabled commanders to have an appreciation of the situation in good time. Little or no information about the enemy's movements was provided by other sources as, so far as could be ascertained, the French sent out no patrols and were always hours if not days behind in their knowledge of the situation. It was acknowledged by Beauman that some gallant British officers undertaking this role were lost when performing what was a most important duty.

In a report to Lieutenant General Marshall Cornwall made on 29 June 1940, the commander of 5th KOSB raised a number of points following his Battalion's experience in the operations carried out during the period 16 to 18 June 1940.[15]

First, regarding enemy tactics, he noted the initial response of German troops on gaining contact with the British positions was to bring up mortars to fire against them, this taking precedence over the use of rifles or light automatic weapons. To counter this, Marshall-Cornwall suggested that every defensive position should include a counter-attack detachment,

15 TNA WO 167/775: 5th King's Own Scottish Borderers War Diary.

which could be brought into action as soon as contact with the enemy was made and that this would prevent the German troops from using their mortars.

Second, regarding the use of road blocks, demolitions and anti-tank mines, the closure of roads also denied British troops the use of the roads to send out patrols or to mount counter-attacks. Furthermore, the premature closure of roads was a major source of inconvenience and it impeded any chance to reconnoitre and gather information about enemy intentions. These difficulties were aggravated because the French forces were in charge of the demolitions and the roadblocks generally.

Third, the Allied rear-guard force was never fully in control of Cherbourg and there was no military unit that had such control. Hence, the military police and staff officers in Cherbourg gave orders directly to the sub-unit commanders without informing unit commanders but, to prevent commanders losing control of their units, the correct channels for orders should have been used even during an emergency.

Fourth, there had been the regrettable loss of two of the 5th KOSB platoons and other casualties, which was attributable to lorry drivers and navigators losing their way. The method of company tactical groups was otherwise used successfully but the incidents emphasised the necessity for the close control of all vehicles in the group.

Fifth, the difficulties of controlling a military force over such a wide area were successfully overcome through the employment of motor cycle despatch riders and the military police, and this had contributed to the success of the withdrawal.

In November 1940, a report from the Committee on the evacuation of the BEF from the French ports, chaired by Lieutenant General Sir Geoffrey Howard, was presented to the War Office.[16] This Committee was established with the remit of enquiring into the lessons to be learnt from the evacuation, with special reference to the possibility of whether the extraction of arms, equipment, vehicles and stores (both for the fighting formations and the Line of Communication troops) could reasonably have been increased under the existing circumstances.

In terms of the Line of Communication, the Committee acknowledged that the headquarters of the L of C had of necessity become the nerve centre of the British forces in France. However, given the tasks being imposed upon them, the staff of the L of C was not adequate for it was not prepared for operational as well as administrative duties, nor for the crisis of an emergency evacuation. From the headquarters to the various bases, all of the L of C officers had large numbers of personnel under their command and they should have been better prepared for dealing with those emergency situations that were to be expected in a modern war.

In relation to the 1st Armoured Division, this arrived in France under-equipped and insufficiently trained, with many AFVs either not fit for purpose or which were rushed into service and lacked reliability under battlefield conditions. It required a reserve to replace casualties, and there was a severe shortage of spare parts for the maintenance and repair of battle-damaged vehicles. Furthermore, it was required to act without the co-operation of a support group, had no assistance from ground-support aircraft and was deployed on an improvised and piecemeal basis. Hence, it was unable to achieve success against superior opposition.

Evacuation back to Britain on such a large scale did not commence until 10 June, and the whole series of operations was mainly completed by 18 June when the last parties left Cherbourg

16 TNA WO 33/2384: Report of Committee on Evacuation of BEF from French ports.

and St Nazaire. The Committee's assessment was that the organisation of the evacuations tended to be over-centralised, with those on the ground being unable to exercise their own initiative, and too much attention was given to the unauthorised and unsubstantiated reports of the German advance that led to a fear of being caught in France that was exaggerated. The Committee considered that such fears had an impact on civilians in particular, and that if allowed more time the evacuation could perhaps have been more orderly and successful.

It was noted that a whilst a reason for the delay in embarking supplies was to avoid the appearance of deserting their French allies, the steps taken had been inadequate and that the leadership of the L of C had not done all that was to be expected of it. The Committee concluded that it was necessary for the Line of Communication to be competent and efficient, that there was a need to cultivate the offensive spirit, and for there to be better communication during evacuations between the senior naval officers at the ports and the naval authorities at home.

There can be little doubt that had the British troops been under the command of a single British commander with sufficient authority and a fully manned operational headquarters, the divisions and other units could have been deployed more effectively and been able to use their strengths to their advantage. This would have minimised them being frittered away to little effect, or being misused or squandered, as had occurred with the 51st Division. Given the quality of this Division's constituent elements, it should have been a formidable adversary to the German panzer divisions had it been furnished with the air and artillery support that it needed.

British Air Forces in France

For the RAF, just as for the French *Armée de l'Air*, the air campaign during the Battle of France was disastrous, and the contribution of the British Air Forces in France highlighted many of the inadequacies and shortcomings in pre-war planning, coupled with the inappropriateness of doctrine and organisation. During the battle, the commanding officer of the AASF was completely independent of the BEF's ground forces, and received his orders from Bomber Command. On this point, it prompted recognition of the need for a single authority to command and co-ordinate the operation of all RAF functions carried out in a theatre of war.

This would have been beneficial to matters of higher policy, including the disposition, employment and strength of the RAF squadrons in the field, and in liaison with their allies, regardless of whether more fighter squadrons ought to have been made available. Air Marshal Barratt was of the opinion that the BAFF's performance in France was impaired due to the absence of a commander-in-chief who could demand and appropriate the necessary facilities from the allies.[17] He maintained that the French authorities were always too slow in allocating new aerodromes or airfields to the RAF squadrons, and that they appeared to know remarkably little of the characteristics of their own grounds, making a reconnaissance necessary before it was certain that these were even serviceable.

From the inter-war years, the RAF's commitment was to a policy of independent strategic bombing. Given that the AASF's intended objective was to carry out bombing missions in Germany, especially against industrial targets in the Ruhr, the BEF's ground forces received little close support from the air. This was in marked contrast to the final battles of the First

17 TNA AIR 35/354: Barratt's Despatch, BAFF.

World War, such as during the Hundred Days campaign, and it gave credence to the view that 'the RAF had forgotten how to support the army'.[18] The prevailing opinion in the RAF was that air strikes should be carried out before the need for ground support became evident and, moreover, aircraft capable of co-operating effectively with the ground forces were not available.

In June 1939, the War Office had called for 1,440 aircraft to be allocated to the roles of close support and to short-range, tactical bombing, but the Air Ministry had strenuously objected to this request. The rationale for the Ministry's opposition was that this initiative was considered unrealistic, that close support was more effective when carried out against a retreating enemy rather than an advancing one, and that the proposal was for the close support aircraft to be placed under Army rather than RAF control. The Chief of the Air Staff, Air Chief Marshal Sir Cyril Newall had warned that 'the dissipation of bomber squadrons into small packets over a wide front would prevent the concentration of maximum effort at the decisive point'.[19]

Formation flying had received a higher priority for RAF pilots than the skills of dog-fighting, air gunnery and observation, including during the so-called 'Phoney War' prior to the commencement of *Fall Gelb* on 10 May 1940. When compared with the *Luftwaffe*'s pilots, many of whom had experienced real combat during the Spanish Civil War and in Poland, this was far from satisfactory. In consequence, few of the RAF's pilots fighting in France actually saw the German fighter that shot them down due to the *Luftwaffe's* avoidance of conventional aerial combat tactics and the practice of attacking their opponents from 'out of the sun'.

In the RAF, the selection of tactics was, as far as possible, left to the discretion of the squadron commanders and formation leaders. On balance, there were no radically new lessons to be learnt from the AASF's bombing operations; the principal one being that attacks against targets that were well protected by anti-aircraft guns and which had defensive fighter cover tended to result in substantial aircraft loss and high casualty rates. Indeed, the AASF was sent to France so that its short-range bombers could reach Germany and, in due course, other aircraft with a longer-range capability and flying from bases in Britain were to have replaced this effort. When the AASF's squadrons were tasked with the types of missions that should otherwise have been carried out by the artillery or the infantry, heavy losses tended to ensue. In the AASF's report on operations, the methods used to attempt to reduce casualties were outlined.[20] These included the provision of fighter cover for bombing operations (although this could be limited for the lesser endurance of the RAF's fighter aircraft, such as the Hawker Hurricane, when compared with the bombers), the use of concealment using cloud cover, when this was possible (however, in June 1940 there were cloudless skies for several days), and night operations, notwithstanding that this meant often resulted in greater difficulty in locating targets.

Yet the primary function of the RAF's fighter aircraft remaining fairly constant throughout the campaign, namely, to seek out and destroy the enemy's aircraft and, by competing with the *Luftwaffe* for air superiority, this could have offered support to the Allied cause. There were concerns from the outset that should an increased number of RAF aircraft be drawn into and lost during a prolonged air battle on the Continent then it would be detrimental to the defence of the British mainland. The demand for more fighter aircraft to be made available

18 J. Terraine, *The Right of the Line: The Royal Air Force in the European War, 1939-1945*, p.383.

19 B. Bond, 'Introduction: Preparing the Field Force, February 1939 - May 1940' in Bond, B. & M. Taylor (eds), *Battle for France and Flanders Sixty Years On*, p.4.

20 TNA AIR 35/255: Report on the AASF in France, September 1939 - June 1940.

was a persistent feature of the Battle of France that continued after the Dunkirk evacuation. Although extra resources were committed, after 12 June the bases used by the AASF were increasingly threatened by the pace of the German advance and it became evident that the attempts to support the French armed forces were increasingly futile.

Air Marshal Barratt's dispatch reached a number of firm conclusions from the AASF's experiences.[21] Firstly, that the use of dive-bombing techniques increased the necessity for fighter support; secondly, that the French were considerably below British standards with respect to the organisation and training of both their fighter and bomber forces, although this could be attributed to the limited pre-war organisation and training of France's air force; thirdly, that whilst the overly academic approach of the French yielded some excellent projects, they were often out of touch with the day-to-day requirements; and fourthly, that there were differing British and French approaches to operational orders/instructions, with the latter being less able to cope with fast moving mechanised warfare. Barratt emphasised the need to concentrate the available fighter strength wherever the enemy's air attacks were temporarily most intense, and that to achieve this there had to be greater flexibility in organisation, especially when the range of the fighter aircraft was so restricted.

The primary fighter aircraft used by the RAF during the Battle of France was the Hawker Hurricane Mk 1. According to the AASF, its operation in the field exceeded expectations, particularly once a modification to the rotor airscrew had been made. This ensured that it performed very well when it had to engage with the *Luftwaffe*'s main bomber and reconnaissance aircraft, and also against the Messerschmitt Bf 110 twin-engine heavy fighter (unless it was overwhelmed by large numbers of them). The faster and well-armed Messerschmitt Bf 109 E single seat fighter was a different proposition, however, and the Hurricane Squadrons sustained some heavy losses as a consequence of this adversary. In the fighter-escort role, it was also hindered because its endurance was mostly lower than the bombers it was seeking to protect.

The Fairey Battle light bomber was used for tactical missions against centres of communication, concentrations of enemy troops and AFVs, and fuel and ammunition dumps. Effectiveness in this role was at best mixed due to its comparatively low speed (attributable to the combined weight of its three-man crew and payload) and its fuel capacity that made it unsuitable for short-range, low altitude missions. Furthermore, its chief drawback was its inability to effectively defend itself and whilst extra armour and self-sealing fuel tanks were sent to France they were not fitted. Hence, when flying at high level it became easy prey for the *Luftwaffe's* fighters; when flying at low level, it was frequently brought down by anti-aircraft fire from the ground, and when flying at night the limited visibility of the pilot and observer led to navigational problems when locating and attacking objectives. The Battle's crews did not lack courage but their inexperience was a factor, as they often took far too long to approach and bomb a target until they learnt how to utilise the terrain and make short approach runs to better effect.

There was some improvement from 5 to 15 June, when compared with May, as 264 sorties were flown with only 23 Battles being lost in air combat.[22] With regard to the losses incurred during low-flying attacks, in his Dispatch Air Marshal Barratt concluded that the improvements were attributable to both the experience gained by the bomber crews and also the weakening

21 TNA AIR 35/354: Barratt's Despatch, BAFF.
22 This is likely to be an under-estimate owing to the loss of the RAF's records.

of the German anti-aircraft defences as these became over-extended during the later stages of the Battle of France.[23] The necessity of carrying out missions by night, with the number of day operations being reduced to those that were absolutely essential, was also discussed by Barratt and he noted that there had been a very material decrease in the numbers of casualties.

Throughout the campaign, the AASF gravitated towards the coast, as the RAF depots and stores were moved by long convoys of lorries and the squadrons then flew to the new aerodromes or airfields. Nevertheless, the units continued to operate as previously until they were required to move back to Britain by circumstances over which their control had been limited. On 19 June, the *Manchester Guardian* highlighted:

> The feats of salvage carried out by the RAF under constant danger of being bombed and machine gunned by German aircraft and of being cut off by a lightning German tank thrust were considerable. One stores park got away with 100 per cent of its effectives in men and material. It is the ninth such achievement since 10 May.[24]

In terms of the discipline and morale of the BAFF in France, Air Marshal Barratt was of the opinion that this was most satisfactory and he felt proud to be associated with the officers and airmen who had shown such loyalty to their commanders and conducted themselves in such a way as to be a credit to their service.[25] He praised the gallantry of both the air crews and the ground support personnel, and the standard of morale was reflected in the tasks which were undertaken by the them with a cheerfulness and devotion to duty that was commendable. He noted the frequency with which the various formations had to move from location to location, including the final evacuations from the French ports, and that often unavoidably this was performed without an officer being in charge. Barratt expressed the view that such discipline could have been severely tested were it not for the good conduct of all ranks, and through independent thinking, which was of great credit to them.

In terms of the RAF's presence in France, there was a commitment to ensuring this was maintained with aircraft and pilots being allocated from the British-based squadrons, despite this weakening the home defence due to the casualties that were sustained and the aircraft which were lost. The demands of the battle in France were such that there was nearly always an insufficient quantity of aircraft available to be sent on sorties, as compared with the numbers sent into action by the *Luftwaffe*. From 10 May to 24 June the AASF lost 229 aircraft and a further 279 were lost by the Air Component. Because the squadrons had to move from one airfield to another to avoid being overrun by the German advance, this meant that much equipment was destroyed or had to be left behind, limiting the effectiveness of squadrons to continue to operate from bases behind the front line.[26] They were also inhibited by operating from improvised airfields of variable quality, which could lead to aircraft being damaged when taking off or landing. Moreover, these airstrips were often quite unprotected from roaming enemy fighter aircraft. Yet, regardless of the *Luftwaffe's* air superiority, the Battle of France was

23 TNA AIR 35/354: Barratt's Despatch, BAFF.
24 *Manchester Guardian*, 19 June 1940.
25 TNA AIR 35/354: Barratt's Despatch, BAFF.
26 TNA CAB 120/246: BEF, Evacuation from France.

not lost in the air. As stated by Air Marshal Barratt, 'The RAF could not win the war if the French infantry had lost it'.[27]

Royal Navy

In the official history, Major Ellis stated that by the end of the evacuations that were carried out in 1940 by the Royal Navy during Operation Cycle and Operation Aerial, a further 191,870 personnel could be added to those that had already been evacuated from France during Operation Dynamo. This figure was comprised of 144,171 British, 18,246 French, 24,352 Polish, 4,938 Czech and 163 Belgian troops and others. When taken with the 366,162 that were extracted from Dunkirk during Operation Dynamo, it amounted to 558,032 of whom 368,491 were British service personnel.[28]

Operation Cycle was conducted at a considerable distance from the British mainland. In order for it to succeed, it was imperative that all of the vessels involved should rendezvous at the evacuation areas in sufficient time. Unfortunately, many of these vessels did not possess radio sets, making even the most basic communication between them very difficult, if not impossible. Furthermore, there was a constant stream of conflicting information and orders regarding which places, times and the numbers of people expected to be rescued from France.

The evacuation from Le Havre was largely successful in taking off all of the British troops possible, but there were a number of factors that nevertheless served to hinder the operation. These included doubts as to when and where the evacuation was to take place, with delays in decision-making also contributing to the situation at St Valery-en-Caux; the insecure defence of the port, due to inadequate command of the forces at Le Havre, with the Garrison commander having no instructions regarding the evacuation; a failure of communications due to an over-reliance on despatch riders; and a loss of substantial quantities of military equipment, stores and other war material, including vehicles and guns that could have been saved and taken back to Britain, but which were abandoned and allowed to fall into enemy hands.[29]

Having examined the situation at Le Havre, Admiral James decided to move the smaller vessels to St Valery once it became obvious to him that the 51st Division was being forced towards the coast in that vicinity. Unfortunately, the harbour and beach of that port became overwhelmed with intense enemy artillery fire. In his report on the completion of Operation Cycle, Admiral James stated that he had not anticipated that the enemy would be able to reach the coast so quickly, with his ships being bombarded by the German shore batteries between St Valery-en-Caux and Fécamp.[30] Whilst it was investigating beaches to the west of St Valery, HMS *Ambuscade* was hit and HMS *Boadicea* was engaged when taking 60 soldiers from Veulettes-sur-Mer. This provided him with confirmation that the German Army had already cut through to the coast and had isolated the 51st Division by cutting it off from Le Havre.

Admiral James also noted that the artillery fire of the German shore batteries was extremely accurate throughout, with HMS *Codrington* being straddled by shells at 18,000 yards and the

27 J. Jackson, *The Fall of France: The Nazi Invasion of 1940*, p.214.
28 L.F. Ellis, *The War in France and Flanders 1939-40*, p.305.
29 TNA ADM 179/158: Operation Cycle, Information on British and French troops in Havre district.
30 TNA ADM 267/126: Operation Cycle, Report.

motor boat MTB 69 being hit while it was steaming at 35 knots on 11 June.[31] In addition to the damage that was caused to the Royal Navy's ships, a number of other vessels were lost during Operation Cycle. These included the passenger vessel *Bruges* and the No. 2 train ferry (both as a consequence of aerial attacks rather than artillery fire from land), two Dutch schuyts (one due to contact with a mine and the other sunk by German shore batteries), and six small motor craft.

What was attempted at St Valery fell greatly short of the Royal Navy's early positive expectations, but the enemy had established artillery positions on the high cliffs that commanded the small narrow beaches, the harbour and the town. As the merchant ships, lifeboats and various other craft proved to be unsuitable due to the considerable distance they had travelled, other transports and smaller craft were available in sufficient numbers and had assembled off the coast in time. However, fog prevented them from reaching the harbour at St Valery and even when the weather improved, these ships then had to be withdrawn due to bombing by enemy aircraft, and artillery and machine gun fire. Admiral James was of the view that even if more craft had reached St Valery, no more troops could have been evacuated.[32]

Notwithstanding, Admiral James praised their bravery, as their crews had endured three days of hardship and in some cases were subject to attack from both the air and from the shore-based artillery, stating that he could not 'speak too highly of those fishermen and yachtsmen who came forward so eagerly'. Furthermore, he added that the behaviour of the officers and men of the Royal Navy was in accordance with the highest traditions of the service, and that 'the embarkation from the beaches under fire was conducted with coolness and fine courage'. In recognition of their services at Le Havre and at Veules-les-Roses, Commander C.A.N. Chatwin was awarded the Distinguished Service Order, whilst Sub-Lieutenants D.A. Killan and L. McLernon of the beach party were both awarded the Distinguished Service Cross. There were also 16 recipients of the Distinguished Conduct Medal.[33]

In terms of accountability, and the responsibility for the disastrous attempt to evacuate the 51st Division, Winston Churchill was profoundly affected by its loss, and believed that it could have been rescued had the French High Command allowed it to be sent to Le Havre earlier, before it was cut off and trapped at St Valery. A share of the blame must also be placed on Churchill himself, though, as well as on the British Government, which was aware of the position, as was the French Army's High Command. This was because the 51st Division was allowed to remain under the dogmatic orders and inflexible arrangements of the French commanders who would not countenance strategic withdrawal, and which both prolonged delay and indecision when decisive advances were being made by the *Wehrmacht's* Panzer and infantry divisions.

The British politicians feared that following the Dunkirk evacuation, the French Army and Government would use another withdrawal of British troops as the excuse they were looking for to justify their breaking the joint agreement that neither Britain nor France would seek the negotiation of an armistice without the other's permission. This was despite all of the counsels from the various British commanders then in France, including Fortune, Karslake and Marshall-Cornwall, who had all warned them that the 51st Division was in explicit danger of being cut off and, with its back to the sea, would be sacrificed for political not military ends. Surrounded, vastly outnumbered and starved of essential resources, with fighting often of the

31 Ibid.
32 TNA ADM 1/10481: Operations Cycle and Ariel.
33 Ibid.

most brutal kind resulting in its soldiers being killed or captured and then forced into years of enemy captivity, the fate of the 51st Division at St Valery-en-Caux is perhaps even analogous to that of the Texans during the epic 13-day siege of the Alamo in 1836.

Operation Aerial was almost entirely completed by the late afternoon of 18 June, and the RAF's fighter patrols that were maintained over the areas concerned undoubtedly contributed to its relatively successful conclusion. In doing so, they prevented many of the *Luftwaffe's* aircraft, and especially its dive bombers, from mounting sustained attacks on the ports and vessels. Had this happened, there would have been even more serious loss of lives and shipping than occurred towards the end of the Operation, with the damage caused to *HMS Fernie* and *HMS Sabre*, and the tragedy of the sinking of *HMT Lancastria* at St Nazaire. Admiral James, in his report to the Secretary to the Admiralty paid a full tribute to the large numbers of the Royal Navy's officers and men who worked unremittingly and carried out their tasks with professionalism and efficiency, both afloat and on shore when under enemy fire.

Aftermath and Implications: Consequences for Future Operations

For the British Army, the 1940 campaign in France and Flanders was to carry an enduring legacy because, at this point in the Second World War, it did not have the requisite doctrine, equipment, tactics and training to oppose, halt and defeat the rapid advance of the German *Wehrmacht.* Even if it had been possible for a larger BEF with greater mechanisation to have been sent to France, it might have won a few more successes on the battlefield but it is highly unlikely that it would have been able to anticipate and prevent the humiliating capitulation and defeat of the French armed forces during 1940.

There were far too many deficiencies in the capacity to fight and win of France's army and air force. These included the Allied advance into Belgium and southern Holland in May 1940 that assisted the *Heer's* offensive successes in *Fall Gelb* so effectively, an over-reliance, even on a psychological level, on the static fortifications of the Maginot Line and the largely undefended Ardennes forest, and an inflexible chain of command and military doctrine that dispersed two-thirds of armoured resources to an infantry support role.

The French air force, the *Armée de l'Air*, was certainly no match for the *Luftwaffe*, either in terms of the performance of its aircraft or the tactics being employed by its pilots and squadrons. On the other hand, whilst it was often outnumbered during combat conditions, and had to frequently and urgently withdraw its squadrons to new airfields to avoid being overrun by the German ground forces, the BAFF had at least attempted to provide the enemy with a worthy adversary during the air battle over France.

Even though only sixteen of the *Wehrmacht's* infantry divisions were motorised, with the majority still reliant on horse-drawn transport, *Blitzkrieg* evolved during the Battle of France, especially at the operational and tactical levels. This was through the development of close support from the *Luftwaffe*, the use of infiltration tactics and bypassing of the French 'hedgehogs' and other strongpoints. With the infantry mopping-up, the panzer divisions were able to penetrate deeply to seek out and destroy communications, control and command structures, causing paralysis and disorder in the armed forces of their opponents.

However, and in spite of its ostensible standing in 1940, the battlefield performance of the *Wehrmacht* was not quite as superlative as has subsequently been presented. Importantly, it lacked the manpower and resources that the Kaiser's Army had possessed in 1914. It was heavily reliant upon the *Luftwaffe* to tackle the French Army and frustrate the Allied attempts to concentrate their ground forces for fear of attacks from the air. Had the battle become protracted and the *Blitzkrieg* tactics diminished in their efficacy, then a major re-organisation would have been required of both the *Heer* and the *Luftwaffe*. Indeed, there has been much speculation about the effectiveness of *Blitzkrieg* as a strategy manifestly designed to allow a series of successive blows to be executed in order to knock out its adversaries, and whether it was in fact a solution to the inferiority of Germany's industrial complex when assessed against that of the Allies. There was also the added benefit that it would not necessitate the German economy becoming a war economy which, for both political and social reasons, was something Adolf Hitler was extremely reluctant to do.

Equally, many of the problems experienced by the British and French armies were essentially self-inflicted. This was due to the 'inappropriate strategic planning, poorly conceived doctrine and inadequate adequate equipment, but also to blame was a general malaise in Allied leadership and an inability to use the available resources effectively'.[34] Yet, on the occasions when they were not considerably outnumbered, facing the armour of the Panzer divisions and subject to attack from a *Luftwaffe* enjoying air superiority and then air supremacy, and when they were opposed by the ordinary German Army divisions, even the most unprepossessing units and troops of the BEF were able to prove that they were more than capable of holding their own.

As it became increasingly obvious that the French Army was utterly demoralised and that it had insufficient reserves to make the counter-attacks needed to challenge and halt the German breakthroughs, the decision was taken to attempt to hold a line on the River Somme. Since the key British Divisions had been committed to the main battle in Belgium and northern France during May 1940, and were subsequently evacuated during Operation Dynamo, there were few fighting formations available at this point. Thus, the 51st Division and the remaining elements of the 1st Armoured Division had to be called upon and transferred to the area to attempt to relieve the heavy burden placed on the hastily formed units of Line of Communication troops.

Therefore, in order to stand any chance of holding this position of the Somme, it was essential that the French forces were rapidly put into the line. This was not carried through and, as a direct consequence, the German armoured and mechanised divisions were able to capture key bridgeheads and to decisively cut through the makeshift Allied defences. Although the 51st Division and the 1st Armoured Division were under French command, they received no orders to move and remained at the River Bresle long after the French 10th Army's front was broken by the enemy. The lack of orders compounded their difficulties and hindered what could have been a co-ordinated withdrawal towards Rouen, and this effectively sealed their fate.

During the Battle of France, 68,111 men of the BEF were killed (including those who died from their wounds), were wounded, or reported missing or captured. A further 599 men were reported to have died from illness or other non-combat related injuries. The French losses were approximately 90,000 dead, 20,000 wounded and 1,900,000 taken prisoner. The German Army's losses were 27,074 killed, 111,034 wounded and 18,384 missing. During the first phase of the battle, *Fall Gelb*, the *Heer* suffered an average of 2,500 casualties per day; but during the

34 J. Buckley, 'The Air War in France' in Bond, B. &M. Taylor (eds), *Battle for France and Flanders Sixty Years On*, p.117.

second phase, *Fall Rot*, this increased to an average of 5,000 per day.[35] In spite of the collapse of the French forces and the various evacuations of the British troops during Operation Cycle and Operation Aerial, the *Wehrmacht* paid for its victory in 1940 with the blood of its troops, especially when the fighting became increasingly desperate and intense.

The BEF had from its arrival in France anticipated that it would be required to engage in a drawn-out and defensive war. Owing to this perception, when the urgent need to withdraw from the Continent came, it had little option but to leave behind vast quantities of arms, equipment and ordnance. This was estimated to include over 2,300 guns, 90,000 rifles, 8,200 Bren light machine guns and 7,000 tons of ammunition of all calibres. In terms of vehicles, approximately 400 tanks and 63,900 vehicles of all types were left behind. Of the 4,739 vehicles that were returned back to Britain, most had belonged to either the 52nd Division or the 1st Canadian Division. The remainder had been embarked before the orders had been issued to the ports. The 1st Armoured Division had lost practically everything it had possessed except the personal equipment, light machine guns and anti-tank rifles carried by its men. All anti-aircraft guns were lost, and only four anti-tank guns, fourteen cruiser tanks (out of 154) and eleven light tanks (out of 138) were returned from France.[36]

By 13 June, a serious attempt to begin to disperse these supplies with a view to taking them back to Britain, and so that they did not fall into German hands, was to have been organised. Crucially, there was a failure to stop any further shipments of equipment and stores from being sent to France, even at this stage. Between May and the end of June 1940, the RAF lost 959 aircraft (477 of which were fighters). Detailed by formation, there were 229 from the AASF, 279 from the Air Component, 219 from Fighter Command, 166 from Bomber Command and 66 from Coastal Command. During the same period, the *Luftwaffe* lost 1,284 aeroplanes.

Despite the BEF having failed to meet the objectives that were initially set for it, many thousands of its soldiers and other servicemen were rescued from France and the likelihood of years of enemy imprisonment. This was due to the skillfuil implementation of the evacuations of Operations Dynamo, Cycle and Aerial. During Operation Cycle, the number of military personnel evacuated from Le Havre was 11,059 British troops, with 9,000 men from the Beauman Division's A Brigade and the 154th Infantry Brigade, who were then taken to Cherbourg before eventually being returned to Britain. A total of 2,137 British and 1,184 French soldiers were evacuated from Veules-les-Roses.

It is impossible to estimate with accuracy how many men of the 51st Division might have been evacuated had the weather and the communication difficulties not prevented the Royal Navy's ships from attempting to rescue them at St Valery-en-Caux. Due to the German artillery and machine guns being positioned on the steep cliffs overlooking the harbour of the small port, it is highly probable that even more death and destruction would have been inflicted on British soldiers and sailors than was the case. Even in ideal weather conditions, such an enterprise would have been difficult; the fog made it impossible. The remainder, including over 6,000 men of the 51st Division were taken prisoner on 12 June. The conduct of Operation Aerial ran more smoothly but the loss of the *HMT Lancastria* on 17 June was more than just a maritime disaster;

35 P. Caddick-Adams, 'Anglo-French Co-operation during the Battle of France' in Bond, B. & M. Taylor (eds), *Battle for France and Flanders Sixty Years On*, p.49.

36 M. Gilbert, *Finest Hour: Winston Churchill, 1939-1941*, p.127; D. Newbold, 'British planning and preparations to resist invasion on land, September 1939 - September 1940', p.169.

however, in the circumstances of war, and given the limited coverage in the press, this tragedy soon passed into obscurity with an indecent haste.

Addressing the House of Commons on 18 June, the Winston Churchill provided an appraisal in which he surveyed the events of the preceding fortnight. He pointed out that what had happened in France had not surprised him. Indeed, he reiterated his declaration that whatever happened Great Britain and the British Empire would fight on, 'if necessary for years, if necessary alone'. The evacuations from France would mean that should a German invasion occur, there would be some 1,250,000 British troops and 500,000 volunteers of the Local Defence Force, together with those troops from other units of the British Empire that had also been evacuated to defend the British mainland.[37]

Following the BEF's 1940 campaign, there was a major investigation to consider and evaluate the lessons 'which could be applied usefully to our present organisation and training'. This resulted in the publication in July 1940 of the report of a committee chaired by General Sir William Bartholomew, a former commander of the Imperial Defence College and the recently retired GOC-in-C of Northern Command. In this document, the Bartholomew Committee identified four major lessons.[38] Firstly, the Army's offensive spirit had been blunted by the BEF allotting too much time to defensive positions, especially given that the Germans appeared to dislike being attacked. Secondly, discipline and physical fitness were lacking. Thirdly, urgent action was required to achieve co-operation between the Army and the RAF. Fourthly, anti-tank defence was key and an increased issuing of tanks and anti-tank weapons was necessary. The steps required to address these lessons were to contribute considerably to the transformation of the British armed forces by the time of Operation Overlord four years later.[39]

Reviews such as this would ultimately lead to root-and-branch changes, such as the transformation of operational command, in the British armed forces. There was a recognition that the British tanks sent to France were mechanically unreliable, needed thicker armour to provide better protection, and a larger calibre weapon that could fire high explosive as well as armour-piercing shells. However, due to the small number of tanks that had returned from France, modification to the production process was deemed to be inadvisable at this time, as to institute such major changes would slow down the production of tanks at a moment when they might be needed to repel a German invasion.[40] Regarding the war in the air over France, this was affected by numerous factors relating to doctrine, equipment and organisation, together with the rapidly changing circumstances of the campaign. Even though the *Luftwaffe's* capabilities appeared limited when compared to those of the BAFF and the *Armée de l'Air* when they were considered jointly, for the Germans 'the Allies arrayed against them were weaker still in doctrine, resources and ambition'.[41]

37 *The Times*, 19 July 1940.
38 J. Drewienkiewicz, 'The influence of the Battle of France on British Military Doctrine' in Bond, B. & M. Taylor (eds), *Battle for France and Flanders Sixty Years On*, p.163.
39 TNA CAB 106/1775: Final report of the Bartholomew Committee on lessons to be learnt from the operations in Flanders.
40 J. Drewienkiewicz, 'The influence of the Battle of France on British Military Doctrine' in Bond, B. & M. Taylor (eds), *Battle for France and Flanders Sixty Years On*, p.167.
41 J. Buckley, 'The Air War in France' in Bond, B. &M. Taylor (eds), *Battle for France and Flanders Sixty Years On*, p.126.

On 20 June, Major General Hastings Ismay (the Prime Minister's chief staff officer and his military adviser) produced a report for the British War Cabinet's Joint Intelligence Committee. This paper provided a summary of all of the main developments in the naval, military and air situation up to 18 June and it included data on the numbers of personnel evacuated from the French Ports. It stated that 111,505 British personnel (including wounded) had been extracted and that there were approximately 16,000 who could not be accounted for or had been left behind (included the men of the 51st Division captured at St Valery-en-Caux). In addition to these British servicemen, it was reported that also evacuated from France were some 17,062 French, 24,353 Polish, 4,938 Czech and 163 Belgian nationals.[42]

Throughout the campaign there was a constant reproach from the French authorities that the British Government and its armed forces were not fully committed to the battle being waged in France and that they wished to evacuate their troops as soon as possible. The evidence presented gives the clearest indication that this criticism was both unfounded and unjustified. It can perhaps be attributed to an obliviousness on the part of the French politicians and Government regarding the limited resources available to the British armed forces at this point, when there was a very real threat to the British mainland from Nazi Germany, perhaps combined with a desire to find a convenient scapegoat for France's hardships and misfortunes.

Indeed, Viscount Hood, the British Government's Minister of Information, had received a telegram dated 27 July 1940 that was forwarded to him by the Ambassador to the United States, Philip Kerr the 11th Marques of Lothian:

> One story sedulously being spread here is that after evacuation of Dunkirk Britain refused to send fighter squadrons vitally needed to the Somme front and that the first breach in that front was due to precipitate flight to the Channel coast leaving Chasseurs Maritimes exposed and with their retreat cut off. These failures to support France are being quoted as justification for French acceptance of armistice terms about the fleet. Can you send me authoritative answer before that legend gets established in the American mind?[43]

A response to Viscount Hood was prepared on behalf of Major General Ismay by Colonel E.I.C. Jacob of the Office of the War Cabinet. This succinctly pointed out that following the BEF's withdrawal from Dunkirk, it had become clear that a German attack might take place against the French line established on the Aisne and Somme Rivers. The French Government had pressed for all forces to be made available, particularly in the air, but the British Government had been unable to make any specific promises in view of the events which had taken place, and their effect upon the British land and air forces. Telegrams had been sent to the French Prime Minister, Paul Reynaud, to offer him the assurance that Britain was giving all the support that it could short of ruining the capacity of this country to continue the war.

Following the armistice, France's capitulation and the surrender to Nazi Germany of the French Government and armed forces, for many British people the feeling of defiance was most eloquently illustrated in David Low's cartoon entitled 'Very Well, Alone' which was published

42 TNA PREMIER 3/75: BEF, Evacuation.
43 TNA CAB 120/246: BEF, Evacuation from France.

in the *Evening Standard* on 18 June 1940. By coincidence this was also the day during which most of those British servicemen remaining in France had been evacuated through Operation Aerial. A similar judgement to that propounded by Low's cartoon was articulated on 27 June, when in his correspondence with his mother, Queen Mary, King George VI wrote 'Personally, I feel happier now we have no allies to be polite to and to pamper'.[44]

44 P. Caddick-Adams, 'Anglo-French Co-operation during the Battle of France' in Bond, B. & M. Taylor (eds), *Battle for France and Flanders Sixty Years On*, p.49.

Epilogue

A Forgotten Campaign and its Rightful Place in History

The idea for this book emerged from the realisation that for many people their appreciation and understanding of the Battle of France was based on the belief that the involvement of the British armed forces ceased with the evacuation from Dunkirk carried out by the Royal Navy and the civilian small ships during Operation Dynamo. Clearly, this was not the case and the research underpinning this work has endeavoured to demonstrate the extent to which the British forces continued to fight on until the fall of France. Indeed, in one of the most important speeches in British history, on 4 June 1940, the day on which Operation Dynamo was concluded, Winston Churchill referred to the continuing battle in France.

> I have, myself, full confidence that if all do their duty, if nothing is neglected, and if the best arrangements are made, as they are being made, we shall prove ourselves once more able to defend our island home, to ride out the storm of war, and to outlive the menace of tyranny, if necessary for years, if necessary alone. At any rate, that is what we are going to try to do. That is the resolve of His Majesty's Government – every man of them. That is the will of Parliament and the nation. The British Empire and the French Republic, linked together in their cause and in their need, will defend to the death their native soil, aiding each other like good comrades to the utmost of their strength. Even though large tracts of Europe and many old and famous States have fallen or may fall into the grip of the Gestapo and all the odious apparatus of Nazi rule, we shall not flag or fail. We shall go on to the end. We shall fight in France, we shall fight on the seas and oceans, we shall fight with growing confidence and growing strength in the air, we shall defend our island, whatever the cost may be. We shall fight on the beaches, we shall fight on the landing grounds, we shall fight in the fields and in the streets, we shall fight in the hills; we shall never surrender, and if, which I do not for a moment believe, this island or a large part of it were subjugated and starving, then our Empire beyond the seas, armed and guarded by the British Fleet, would carry on the struggle, until, in God's good time, the New World, with all its power and might, steps forth to the rescue and the liberation of the old.[1]

1 *Hansard*, Vol. 361, Columns 787-98, 4 June 1940.

Churchill's speech galvanised the fighting spirit of the British people because, in the words of the American broadcaster and journalist, Ed Murrow, 'he mobilized the English language and sent it into battle to steady his fellow countrymen and hearten those Europeans upon whom the long dark night of tyranny had descended'.[2]

In 1940, the initial belief of the British armed forces and their Allies was that the war would probably be waged in a similar manner to the First World War with trench warfare, protracted offensives and with superior resources ultimately proving decisive. Such notions were quickly dispelled, however. During the Battle of France, the sheer speed of the campaign waged by the *Wehrmacht*, combined with a more effective doctrine and the flexibility to capitalise on the errors of its adversaries, gave its Allied opponents the impression that the German Army was invincible. The loss of men was considerable and the collapse of the French armed forces made it inevitable that this would be a major disaster for the Allied cause. If there had been greater co-ordination then perhaps the loss of materials and men would not have been as high as it was. Furthermore, the command structure, doctrine, equipment and tactics of the Allied armies generally left much to be desired so that, rather than being out-fought, they were comprehensively out-thought and out-manoeuvred by a more flexible enemy.

Although it had taken a mere six weeks for France to fall in the most humiliating military defeat in French history, Germany's victory was far from being a bloodless one. Although it was not afflicted by the widespread deterioration of discipline and morale that infected the French Army, the BEF of 1940 was never to have the opportunity to demonstrate what its true capabilities and qualities really were.

As has been demonstrated, a significant number of military personnel from the British Army and the RAF remained in France after Dunkirk to face the German onslaught. Whilst all of them had received the basics of military training, many of these men were not from what would be considered as first-rate fighting regiments or units but were the reservists or rear echelon troops from the Line of Communication detachments. And they had to face a highly motivated enemy whose professional army possessed greater numbers of men, armour and better equipment. Despite this, and to their considerable and lasting credit, they continued to fight on with both defiance and determination in what were often the most challenging and personally dangerous circumstances. Regardless of the conditions in which it was obliged to engage in combat with the *Wehrmacht*'s panzer and mechanised divisions, in his subsequent report on the 1st Armoured Division's operations during the Battle of France, Major General Evans reported that all ranks of the Division had kept fighting to the end:

> There is one feature, characteristic of the operations which I cannot sufficiently emphasise – the spirit and endurance of the troops. After the advance to the Somme and the understandable failure to force a crossing there, the Division was continuously engaged in operations which obviously afforded no prospect of a major tactical success. Day after day, our troops saw a stream of not only destitute refugees but also fit French soldiery steadily pouring to the rear, and they looked in vain for any sign which

2 In the 2017 film, '*Darkest Hour*', this statement has been portrayed as being delivered by Churchill's rival, the arch-appeaser, Viscount Halifax, immediately following the Prime Minister's speech in the House of Commons on 4 June 1940. There appears to be no evidence of Halifax actually saying these words, which are in fact to be found in Edward R. Murrow's 1954 biography, *Winston Churchill*.

> betokened a real spirit of resistance on the part of our Allies. No attempts to prepare defensive positions were made; the formidable obstacle of the River Seine was so feebly defended as to afford scarcely more than a few hours respite from the advance of an enemy whom they know to be vastly superior to them in numbers both on the ground and in the air.[3]

One of the primary objectives of the British formations that fought on in June 1940 was to support the French Army and to try to prevent its commanders and Government from capitulating and surrendering to the Germans. This proved impossible but, whilst holding off the enemy for as long as they could, and until withdrawal became unavoidable, the BAFF and BEF units bought for the rest of the British armed forces that most valuable of commodities, namely the time to prepare the home divisions and those already evacuated to resist a possible invasion. Given, their sheer effort and courage when facing overwhelming odds, this might bear some comparison with an earlier historical event, for there are some similarities. This was in 480 BC when, for at least three days before being overrun, the warrior-king Leonidas I and his 300 Spartan Hoplites and 900 Helots blocked the pass of Thermopylae preventing the advance into Greece of the army of Xerxes I. This act enabled the Persian invasion to eventually be repulsed by the other Greek City States.

The evacuation of the BEF via the successive Operations Dynamo, Cycle and Aerial was of the greatest significance to the defence of the nation. It was not merely an indicator of Great Britain's morale but, once the bulk of the Army had returned from France, of its determination to hold out against Nazi Germany at a time of the utmost peril, when the prospect of an invasion was very real. The success of all of the evacuations must be attributed to the professionalism of the respective armed services and to the bravery of the crews of the vessels, whether Royal Navy or civilian, who put themselves and their ships in the way of danger in order to bring the troops home to safety. Speaking in the House of Commons on 4 June, Winston Churchill would remind the British people that the BEF was the 'whole root and core and brain of the British Army' and with its return to Britain there was a great increase in confidence that a German attack could be resisted and with the sheer determination to fight on until the end to secure the nation's independence and its integrity.[4]

However, unlike the earlier evacuation from Dunkirk, when the troops returning to Britain were often received with public adulation, those who came home as a result of Operations Cycle and Aerial were largely ignored and their contributions remained unacknowledged or were even treated with some distain. This was despite their having continued to fight courageously and now being available in their thousands should a German invasion of Britain be attempted.

Regrettably, not all of the BEF made it back to Britain. Comprised of over 6,000 men, the core of the 51st Division was cut off and surrounded by the enemy in the small port of St Valery-en-Caux. The gallant Highlanders fought on but were unable to contend with the sheer scale of the assault on their positions by the German panzer divisions. Eventually, on 12 June 1940, the Division faced the reality of its situation, which was that the Royal Navy was unable to rescue it and there was no choice but to surrender to the German forces. One of the main streets in

3 TNA WO 167/334: 1st Armoured Division War Diary and Bovington Tank Museum Archives: Report on the operations of the 1st Armoured Division in France.
4 *Hansard*, Vol. 361, Columns 788-91, 4 June 1940.

St Valery is named *L'Avenue de la 51eme* in honour of the 51st Division's troops and a granite monument has been erected near to the beach from which they were unable to be evacuated and where so many lives were lost. Its inscription states 'In proud and grateful memory of the 51st (Highland) Division who gave their lives during the war, 1939-45'.

There can be little doubt that to have complied with the French Government's entreaties to despatch more fighter aircraft to France, and to have kept the divisions of the BEF that were still resisting the German advance any longer in a France that was on the verge of defeat would have been catastrophic for Britain. That this did not occur was due to clear-sighted military leaders, such as Air Chief Marshal Sir Hugh Dowding and Lieutenant General Sir Alan Brooke, and to those who organised the evacuations, including Admiral Sir William James and Admiral Sir Martin Dunbar-Nasmith. The nation rightly owed a huge debt to these men for the thousands of troops who were returned to Britain to continue the struggle against Nazi Germany.

Throughout May and June 1940, at the outset of the campaign, the similarities of the British, French and German armies arguably outnumbered their differences. Where the latter were most evident was in communication, leadership and training, combined with the German force's capacity to take advantage of the continuing mistakes made by the Allies. Military success, and the growing belief that no other army could defeat it, would lead to the *Wehrmacht's* eventual downfall, when some of its Generals began to believe that Adolf Hitler had been right all along and that he could make Germany invincible. Whilst most of the Continent had been rapidly subjugated to its rule, or became Nazi satellite states, Britain did not capitulate. Instead, the nation rallied and was united in its defiance. This was because it could still rely on the Royal Navy, an RAF Fighter Command equipped with excellent aircraft and a defensive radar network that enabled them to be used efficiently, and the high-quality troops in the British Army and in the armies of the Commonwealth and Empire countries.

As Lieutenant General Marshall-Cornwall stated when he subsequently referred to his departure from France on 18 June, 'It was the 125th anniversary of Waterloo but it was more like Corunna'.[5] Yet, in spite of all that had happened in France, the evacuations during Operations Dynamo, Cycle and Aerial had shown the spirit of the British armed forces and the people at their very best. Describing the mood of the country on 14 June, the Prime Minister's Personal Private Secretary, John Colville, confided to his diary that 'If we can hold on until November, we shall have won the war'. At the secret session of Parliament that took place on 20 June, Winston Churchill similarly stated, 'If we get through the next three months, then we can get through the next three years'.[6] On 18 June, as Operation Aerial was being concluded, Winston Churchill addressed the Home of Commons and the nation:

> What General Weygand has called the Battle of France is over … the Battle of Britain is about to begin. Upon this battle depends the survival of Christian civilisation. Upon it depends our own British life, and the long continuity of our institutions and our Empire. The whole fury and might of the enemy must very soon be turned on us. Hitler knows that he will have to break us in this island or lose the war. If we can stand

5 J. Marshall-Cornwall, 'Normandy 1940', p.9.
6 M. Gilbert, *Finest Hour: Winston Churchill, 1939-1941*, pp.578-79.

> up to him, all Europe may be freed and the life of the world may move forward into broad, sunlit uplands.
>
> But if we fail, then the whole world, including the United States, including all that we have known and cared for, will sink into the abyss of a new dark age made more sinister, and perhaps more protracted, by the lights of perverted science. Let us therefore brace ourselves to our duties, and so bear ourselves, that if the British Empire and its Commonwealth last for a thousand years, men will still say, "This was their finest hour".[7]

Although it was overshadowed at the time by the rescuing of the largest element of the BEF from Dunkirk, which was completed during Operation Dynamo, and undoubtedly eclipsed by it in terms of the accounts that have subsequently been published since, the evacuations carried out during Operation Cycle and Operation Aerial were largely successful in achieving what was their primary objective. This was the return to the British mainland, before the fall of France and its surrender to and occupation by Nazi Germany, of as many members of the British armed forces as it was possible to arrange.

These servicemen would contribute to the safeguarding of the nation, ensuring that it was not defenceless and with little choice but to plead for what would surely have been the most humiliating peace imaginable. Instead, and although it achieved an operational victory during the campaign in France and Flanders in 1940, in the longer term this would be a strategic defeat for a Nazi Germany that had to enter into a prolonged and attritional war that Britain, its Empire and its Allies were in a far better position to wage. Nevertheless, the armed forces of Britain had a great deal to learn from the very many harsh lessons that would lie ahead on the long road that eventually led to victory in 1945.

7 *Hansard*, Vol. 362, Columns 51-64, 18 June 1940; *The Times*, 22 June 1940.

Appendix I

BEF Order of Battle, 5 to 18 June 1940

12th (Eastern) Division, Major General R.L. Petre

35th Brigade, Brigadier V.L. de Cordova

- 2/5th Queen's Royal Regiment
- 2/6th Queen's Royal Regiment
- 2/7th Queen's Royal Regiment

36th Brigade, Brigadier G.R.P. Roupell

- 5th Royal East Kent Regiment
- 6th Queen's Own Royal West Kent Regiment
- 7th Queen's Own Royal West Kent Regiment

37th Brigade, Brigadier R.J.P. Wyatt

- 2/6th East Surrey Regiment
- 6th Royal Sussex Regiment
- 7th Royal Sussex Regiment

Divisional Troops

- 262nd, 263rd, 264th Field Companies, Royal Engineers
- 265th Field Company, Royal Engineers

23rd (Northumbrian) Division, Major General A.E. Herbert

69th Brigade Brigadier, The Viscount Downe

- 5th East Yorkshire Regiment
- 6th Green Howards
- 7th Green Howards

70th Brigade, Brigadier P. Kirkup
- 10th Durham Light Infantry
- 11th Durham Light Infantry
- 1st Tyneside Scottish

Divisional Troops
- 233rd, 507th Field Companies, Royal Engineers
- 508th Field Park Company, Royal Engineers
- 8th Royal Northumberland Fusiliers (Motorcycle)
- 9th Royal Northumberland Fusiliers (Machine Gun)

46th (North Midland and West Riding) Division, Major General H.O. Curtis

137th Brigade, Brigadier J.B. Gawthorpe
- 2/5th West Yorkshire Regiment
- 2/6th Duke of Wellington's Regiment
- 2/7th Duke of Wellington's Regiment

138th Brigade, Brigadier E.J. Grinling
- 6th Lincolnshire Regiment
- 2/4th King's Own Yorkshire Light Infantry
- 6th York and Lancaster Regiment

139th Brigade, Brigadier R.C. Chichester-Constable
- 2/5th Leicestershire Regiment
- 2/5th Sherwood Foresters
- 9th Sherwood Foresters

Divisional Troops
- 270th, 271st, 272nd Field Companies, Royal Engineers
- 273rd Field Park Company, Royal Engineers

51st (Highland) Division, Major General V.M. Fortune

152nd Brigade, Brigadier H.W.V. Stewart
- 2nd Seaforth Highlanders
- 4th Seaforth Highlanders
- 4th Queen's Own Cameron Highlanders

153rd Brigade, Brigadier G.T. Burney
- 4th Black Watch
- 1st Gordon Highlanders

5th Gordon Highlanders

154th Brigade, Brigadier A.C.L. Stanley-Clarke

1st Black Watch

7th Argyll and Sutherland Highlanders

8th Argyll and Sutherland Highlanders

Divisional Troops

17th, 23rd, 75th Field Regiments, Royal Artillery

51st Anti-Tank Regiment, Royal Artillery

26th, 236th, 237th Field Companies, Royal Engineers

239th Field Park Company, Royal Engineers

1st Lothians and Border Yeomanry

1st Royal Horse Artillery

97th Field Regiment, Royal Artillery

51st Medium Regiment, Royal Artillery

213th Army Field Company, Royal Engineers

7th Royal Northumberland Fusiliers

1st Princess Louise's Kensington Regiment

7th Royal Norfolk Regiment

6th Royal Scots

52nd (Lowland) Division, Major General J.S. Drew

155th Brigade, Brigadier T. Grainger-Stewart

7/9th Royal Scots

4th King's Own Scottish Borderers

5th King's Own Scottish Borderers

156th Brigade, Brigadier J.S.N. Fitzgerald

4/5th The Royal Scots Fusiliers

6th The Cameronians

7th The Cameronians

157th Brigade, Brigadier Sir J.E. Laurie

1st Glasgow Highlanders

5th Highland Light Infantry

6th Highland Light Infantry

Divisional Troops

70th, 71st, 78th Field Regiments, Royal Artillery

54th Anti-Tank Regiment, Royal Artillery
202nd, 241st, 554th Field Companies, Royal Engineers
243rd Field Park Company, Royal Engineers

1st Armoured Division, Major General R. Evans
2nd Armoured Brigade, Brigadier R.L. McCreery
The Queen's Bays
9th Queen's Royal Lancers
10th Royal Hussars
3rd Armoured Brigade, Brigadier J.G. Crocker
2nd Royal Tank Regiment (2 RTR)
3rd Royal Tank Regiment (3 RTR)
5th Royal Tank Regiment (5 RTR)
1st Support Group, Brigadier F.E. Morgan
101st Light Anti-Aircraft and Anti-Tank Regiment
Divisional Troops
1st Field Squadron, Royal Engineers
1st Field Park Squadron, Royal Engineers

Line of Communication Troops, Major General P. De Fonblanque
3rd Anti-Aircraft Brigade, Brigadier W.R. Shilstone
2nd, 8th, 79th Anti-Aircraft Regiments, Royal Artillery
4th Light Anti-Aircraft Battery, Royal Artillery
104th, 106th, 110th, 212th, 218th Army Troops Companies, Royal Engineers
4th Royal East Kent Regiment
14th Royal Fusiliers
12th Royal Warwickshire Regiment
4th Border Regiment
1/5th Sherwood Foresters
12th Anti-Aircraft Brigade, Brigadier W.T.O Crewdson [With the AASF]
53rd, 73rd Anti-Aircraft Regiments, Royal Artillery

Beauman Division, Acting Major General A. Beauman
A Brigade (Until 7 June 1940 known as 'Beauforce'), Brigadier M.A. Green
4th Royal East Kent Regiment

1/5th Sherwood Foresters

2/6th East Surrey Regiment

4th Border Regiment

B Brigade (Known as 'Vicforce'), Brigadier A.L. Kent-Lemon

1st Provisional Battalion ('Merry's Rifles')

2nd Provisional Battalion ('Davies's Rifles')

3rd Provisional Battalion ('Newcombe's Rifles')

4th Provisional Battalion

C Brigade (Known as 'Digforce'), Lieutenant Colonel J.B.H. Diggle

P Battalion Auxiliary Military Pioneer Corps

Q Battalion Auxiliary Military Pioneer Corps

R Battalion Auxiliary Military Pioneer Corps

2/4th King's Own Yorkshire Light Infantry

2/6th Duke of Wellington's Regiment

23rd Anti-Aircraft Battery, Royal Artillery

Divisional Troops

Divisional Tank Company

E Anti-Tank Regiment, Royal Artillery

X Field Battery, Royal Artillery

Appendix II

BAFF Order of Battle, 5 to 18 June 1940

Air Officer Commanding in Chief, Air Marshal A.S. Barratt
Senior Air Staff Officer, Air Vice Marshal D.C.S. Evill

Air Component, Air Vice Marshal C.H.B Blount
No 14 Group, Group Captain P.F. Fullard
No 60 (Fighter) Wing, Wing Commander J.A. Boret
 85 and 87 Squadrons
No 61 (Fighter) Wing, Wing Commander R.Y Eccles
 607 and 615 Squadrons
No 70 (Bomber Reconnaissance) Wing, Wing Commander W.A. Opie
 18 and 57 Squadrons
No 52 (Bomber) Wing, Wing Commander A.F. Hutton
 53 and 59 Squadrons
No 50 (Army Co-operation) Wing, Wing Commander A.R. Churchman
 4, 13 and 16 Squadrons
No 51 (Army Co-operation) Wing, Wing Commander A.H. Flower
 2 and 26 Squadrons
 81 (Communication) Squadron

Advanced Air Striking Force, Air Vice Marshal P.H.L. Playfair
No 71 (Bomber) Wing, Air Commodore R.M. Field
 105, 114, 139 and 150 Squadrons

No 75 (Bomber) Wing, Group Captain A.H. Wann
    88, 103 and 218 Squadrons
No 76 (Bomber) Wing, Group Captain H.S. Kerby
    12, 142 and 226 Squadrons
No 67 (Fighter) Wing, Wing Commander C. Walter
    1 and 73 Squadrons
    212 (Photographic Reconnaissance) Squadron

Appendix III

Heer Order of Battle, June 1940

Army Group A, *Generaloberst* Gerd von Rundstedt

4th Army, *Generaloberst* Günther von Kluge

II Corps, *General der Infanterie* Adolf Strauss
12th and 32nd Infantry Divisions

V Corps, *General der Infanterie* Richard Ruoff
211th, 251st and 263rd Infantry Divisions

VIII Corps, *General der Artillerie* Walter Heitz
8th, 28th, 87th and 267th Infantry Divisions

12th Army, *Generaloberst* Wilhelm List

III Corps, *General der Artillerie* Curt Haase
3rd, 23rd and 52nd Infantry Divisions

VI Corps, *General der Pioniere* Otto-Wilhelm Förster
16th and 24th Infantry Divisions

XVIII Corps, *General der Infanterie* Eugen Beyer
5th, 21st and 25th Infantry Divisions; 1st Mountain Division

16th Army, *General der Infanterie* Ernst Busch

VII Corps, *General der Infanterie* Eugen Ritter von Schobert
36th and 68th Infantry Divisions

XIII Corps, *Generalmajor* Heinrich von Vietinghoff
10th, 15th and 17th Infantry Divisions

XXIII Corps, *Generalmajor* Albrecht Schubert
26th, 34th, 58th and 76th Infantry Divisions

Panzergruppe Guderian, *General der Panzertruppen* Heinz Guderian

XXXIX Corps, *Generaloberst* Rudolf Schmidt
the 1st and 2nd Panzer Divisions and the 29th Infantry Division

XLI Corps, *Generalmajor* Georg-Hans Reinhardt
6th and 8th Panzer Divisions and 20th Infantry Division

Reserves

XXXX Corps, *Generalmajor* Georg Stumme
6th, 4th, 9th, 27th, 71st and 73rd Infantry Divisions

Army Group B, *Generaloberst* Fedor von Bock

6th Army, *Generaloberst* Walther von Reichenau

IV Corps, *General der Infanterie* Viktor von Schwedler
205th Infantry Division

XI Corps, *Generalmajor* Joachim von Kortzfleisch
7th, 11th, 31st and 253rd Infantry Divisions

18th Army, *General der Artillerie.* Georg von Küchler

X Corps, *General der Artillerie* Christian Hansen
227th Infantry Division, 1st Cavalry Division and 1st SS Panzer Division *Leibstandarte Adolf Hitler*

XXVI Corps, *General der Artillerie Albert Wodrig*
254th and 256th Infantry Divisions and SS *Verfügungstruppe* Division, *Der Führer* Regiment

Panzergruppe Kleist, *General der Kavallerie* Ewald von Kleist

XIV Corps, *General der Infanterie* Gustav von Wietersheim
9th and 10th Panzer Divisions and 9th and 13th Infantry Divisions

XVI Corps, *General der Kavallerie* Erich Hoepner
3rd and 4th Panzer Divisions, 33rd Infantry Division and units of the SS-*Verfügungstruppe* and the *Leibstandarte Adolf Hitler* Regiment

Panzergruppe Hoth, *Generalleutnant* Hermann Hoth

XV Corps, *Generalleutnant* Hermann Hoth
5th and 7th Panzer Divisions and 62nd Infantry Division

Reserves

207th, 208th, 225th and 526th Infantry Divisions
SS *Verfügungstruppe* Division
7th Airborne Division
22nd Air Landing Infantry Division
9th Panzer Division

Army Group C, *Generaloberst* Wilhelm Ritter von Leeb

1st Army, *Generaloberst* Erwin von Witzleben

XII Corps, *General der Infanterie* Gotthard Heinrici
75th, 198th and 268th Infantry Divisions

XXIV Corps, *General der Kavallerie* Leo Geyr von Schweppenburg
60th, 168th and 252nd Infantry Divisions

XXX Corps, *General der Artillerie* Otto Hartmann
79th, 93rd and 258th Infantry Divisions

XXXVII Corps, *General der Kavallerie* Hans Feige
257th Infantry Division

XLV Corps, *General der Infanterie* Kurt von Greiff
95th and 167th Infantry Divisions

7th Army, *General der Artillerie* Friedrich Dollman

XXV Corps, *General der Infanterie* Karl Ritter von Prager
557th Infantry Division and 6th Mountain Division

XXVII Corps, *General der Infanterie* Alfred Wäger
218th and 221st Infantry Divisions

XXXIII Corps, *General der Kavallerie* Georg Brandt
239th and 556th Infantry Divisions

Reserves

197th, 213th, 215th, 246th, 262nd, 554th and 555th Infantry Divisions

Bibliography

I. Archive Sources

1.1 Admiralty Papers, The National Archives, Kew

ADM 1/10481	Honours and Awards (85), Operations Cycle and Ariel
ADM 1/10481	Strategies and Tactics (82), Operations Cycle and Ariel
ADM 1/12264	HMT *Cambridgeshire* in rescue of survivors from SS *Lancastria*
ADM 179/158	Operation Cycle, British and French troops in Havre district
ADM 199/2206	Operation Cycle, Report
ADM 267/126	Operation Cycle, Report

1.2 Air Ministry Papers, The National Archives, Kew

AIR 35/157	Air action against Italy, Policy
AIR 35/192	Summaries of Operations, 10 May – 16 June 1940
AIR 35/253	67th Wing, AASF Combat reports
AIR 35/255	Report on the AASF in France, September 1939 – June 1940
AIR 35/325	Haddock Force Historical Diary
AIR 35/354	Barratt's Despatch, BAFF
AIR 50/31	73 Squadron (67 Fighter Wing, AASF) Combat reports
AIR 50/175	615 Squadron (61 Fighter Wing, 14 Group) Combat reports

1.3 Cabinet Papers, The National Archives, Kew

CAB 65/7	War Cabinet Minutes
CAB 65/13	War Cabinet Minutes
CAB 66/7	War Cabinet Memoranda
CAB 69/1/1	War Cabinet Defence Committee
CAB 79/4/64	Chiefs of Staff Committee, Despatch of forces to France
CAB 79/4/65	Chiefs of Staff Committee, Evacuation of Allied troops
CAB 106/1775	Final report of the Bartholomew Committee
CAB 106/244	BEF Operations, Despatch by Sir Alan Brooke
CAB 106/1739	Operation Cycle, evacuation of troops in Havre area
CAB 120/246	BEF, Evacuation from France

1.4 Premier's Papers, The National Archives, Kew

PREM 3/175	BEF, Evacuation
PREM 3/188/5	Despatches on operations of British Expeditionary Force

1.5 Treasury Solicitor's Papers, The National Archives, Kew

TS 26/207	Brutality to prisoners on the march from St Valery-en-Caux

1.6 War Office Papers, The National Archives, Kew

WO 32/9388	Overseas: Europe (Code O (V)), Despatches from BEF
WO 33/2384	Report of Committee on Evacuation of BEF from French ports
WO 106/1608	Evacuation from St. Valery and area
WO 106/1739	Operation Cycle, Reports on evacuation
WO 167/117	St Nazaire Garrison
WO 167/244	48th (South Midland) Division War Diary
WO 167/314	51st Division, General Staff War Diary
WO 167/326	52nd Division, General Staff War Diary
WO 167/334	1st Armoured Division, General Staff War Diary
WO 167/383	37th Brigade, Headquarters War Diary
WO 167/411	155th Brigade Headquarters War Diary
WO 167/412	156th Brigade Headquarters War Diary
WO 167/419	2nd Armoured Brigade War Diary
WO 167/421	3rd Armoured Brigade War Diary
WO 167/448	2nd Royal Tank Regiment War Diary
WO 167/704	7th Argyll & Sutherland Highlanders War Diary
WO 167/705	8th Argyll & Sutherland Highlanders War Diary
WO 167/711	4th Black Watch War Diary
WO 167/714	4th Borders War Diary
WO 167/722	6th Cameronians War Diary
WO 167/723	7th Cameronians War Diary
WO 167/736	2/6th Duke of Wellington's Regiment War Diary
WO 167/737	2/7th Duke of Wellington's Regiment War Diary
WO 167/775	5th King's Own Scottish Borderers War diary
WO 167/777	2/4th KOYLI War Diary
WO 167/810	2/6th Queen's Royal Regiment War Diary
WO 167/817	4/5th Royal Scots Fusiliers War Diary
WO 167/1412	Beauman Division, Headquarters War Diary
WO 167/1417	Beauman Division, Tank Company War Diary
WO 197/88	Evacuation Progress Reports
WO 197/124	Movements of 51st Highland Division, April to June 1940
WO 311/923	Deliberate exposure to fire from own lines of British prisoners of war after capture St Valery-en-Caux, France, 12 June 1940

1.7 Archives of the Tank Museum, Bovington, Dorset

War Diaries of the 2nd and 3rd Royal Tank Regiment (2 RTR and 3 RTR)

II. Printed Sources

2.1 Books

Bond, B. & M. Taylor (eds), *Battle for France and Flanders Sixty Years On* (London: Cooper, 2001).

Buckton, H., *Retreat: Dunkirk and the Evacuation of Western Europe* (Stroud: Amberley, 2017).

Churchill, W.S., *The Second World War* (London: Penguin 1959).

Danchev, A. and D. Todman (eds), *War Diaries 1939-1945: Field Marshal Lord Alanbrooke* (London: Phoenix Press, 2003).

David, S., *Churchill's Sacrifice of the Highland Division, France 1940* (London: Brassey, 1994).

Ellis, L.F., *The War in France and Flanders 1939-40* (London: HMSO, 1953).

Fenby, J., *The Sinking of the Lancastria: Britain's Greatest Maritime Disaster and Churchill's Cover-Up* (London, 2005).

Gilbert, M., *Finest Hour: Winston Churchill, 1939-1941* (London: Heinemann, 1983).

Glover, M., *The Fight for the Channel Ports: Calais to Brest 1940* (London: Leo Cooper, 1985).

Horne, A., *To Lose a Battle: France 1940* (London: Macmillan, 2012).

Jackson, J., *The Fall of France: The Nazi Invasion of 1940* (Oxford: OUP, 2003).

Karslake, B., *1940, The Last Act* (London: Cooper, 1979).

Longden, S., *Dunkirk: The Men They Left Behind* (London: Constable & Robinson, 2008).

Sebag-Montefiore, H., *Dunkirk: Fight to the Last Man* (London: Penguin, 2006).

Smalley, E., *The British Expeditionary Force, 1939-40* (New York: Palgrave Macmillan, 2015).

Stewart, G., *Dunkirk and the Fall of France* (Barnsley: Pen & Sword, 2008).

Takle, P., *The British Army in France after Dunkirk* (Barnsley: Pen & Sword, 2009).

Terraine, J., *The Right of the Line: The Royal Air Force in the European War, 1939-1945* (Ware: Wordsworth Editions, 1997).

Thompson, J., *Dunkirk: Retreat to Victory* (London: Sidgwick & Jackson, 2008).

Warner, P., *Battle of France, 1940* (Simon & Schuster, 1990).

West, J.L. (ed), *The Loss of the Lancastria* (Lancashire: Rossendale, 1988).

2.2 Book Chapters

Bond, B., 'Introduction: Preparing the Field Force, February 1939 – May 1940' in Bond, B. & M. Taylor (eds), *Battle for France and Flanders Sixty Years On* (London: Cooper, 2001).

Broadhurst, R., 'The Royal Navy's Role in the Campaign' in Bond, B. & M. Taylor (eds), *Battle for France and Flanders Sixty Years On* (London: Cooper, 2001).

Buckley, J., 'The Air War in France' in Bond, B. &M. Taylor (eds), *Battle for France and Flanders Sixty Years On* (London: Cooper, 2001).

Caddick-Adams, P., 'Anglo-French Co-operation during the Battle of France' in Bond, B. & M. Taylor (eds), *Battle for France and Flanders Sixty Years On* (London: Cooper, 2001).

Drewienkiewicz, J., 'The influence of the Battle of France on British Military Doctrine' in Bond, B. & M. Taylor (eds), *Battle for France and Flanders Sixty Years On* (London: Cooper, 2001).

2.3 Journals

Caddick-Adams, P., 'Phoney War and Blitzkrieg: The Territorial Army in 1939-40', *RUSI Journal*, 1998, Vol. 143 (2).

Connelly, M. & W. Miller, 'The BEF and the Issue of Surrender on the Western Front in 1940', *War in History*, October 2004, Vol. 11.

Johnson, D.W.J., 'Britain and France in 1940', *Transactions of the Royal Historical Society*, 5th Series, Vol. 22, December 1972.

Marshall-Cornwall, J., 'Normandy 1940', *War Monthly*, Vol. 45, 1977.

Philpott, W. & M.S. Alexander, 'The French and British Field Force: Moral Support or Material Contribution', *Journal of Military History*, Vol. 71, No. 3, July 2007.

Porch, D., 'Military Culture and the Fall of France in 1940: A Review Essay', *International Security*, April 2000, Vol. 24 (4).

Sixsmith, E.K.G., 'The British Army in May 1940: A comparison with the BEF in 1914', *The RUSI Journal*, 09/1982, Vol. 125, Issue 3.

2.4 Theses

Esnouf, G., 'British government war aims and attitudes towards a negotiated peace, September 1939 to July 1940' (PhD Thesis, University of London, 1988).

Newbold, D., 'British planning and preparations to resist invasion on land, September 1939 -September 1940' (PhD Thesis, University of London, 1988).

2.5 Newspapers and Periodicals

London Gazette Operations of the BEF, from 12 June to 19 June 1940. (Supplement) no. 37573, 2433–2439. 21 May 1946

Manchester Guardian

The Times

2.6 Parliamentary Papers

Hansard War Situation: 4 June 1940; 18 June 1940; 25 June 1940

Index

General Index

A13 Cruiser Tank 32-33, 70-71, 83, 117, 124
AASF combat reports 58, 61, 72, 87, 211
Abbeville 23, 47-48, 50-51, 62, 66, 68, 72-74, 78, 99, 120, 154
Abbeville bridgehead 40, 52, 66, 78
Abrial, *Vice-Amiral* Jean-Marie 142
Acquigny 82
Admiralty 22, 94-97, 101, 104, 109, 141-42, 149, 189
Admiralty reports 95, 97, 101, 104
Aigneville 57
Ailly 68, 82, 99
Air Component 27, 186, 191, 206
Air Ministry 27, 30, 61, 108, 133, 149, 151, 153, 184
Airaines 68, 99
Alençon 84, 127-28
Allied Supreme War Council 147, 149, 154-55, 158, 164
Alost 110
Altmayer, *Général d'armée* Robert 26, 32, 48, 50, 127, 159, 161, 163, 172
Altmayer, *Général de corps d'armée* René 172
Amiens 48-49, 56-59, 62-63, 67-68, 78, 81, 99, 180
Angers 28, 125, 127
Anglo-French co-operation 143, 145, 154-55, 157, 159, 161, 163, 165, 167, 169-73
Ardennes 35, 48, 58, 155, 189
Argentan 124, 133
Argueil 59, 78
Armistice 17, 37, 130, 135, 143, 170–73, 179, 188, 193
Armstrong Whitworth Whitley 148, 150
Arques 68-69, 77, 99
Arques-la-Bataille 93-94
Arrest 53-54
Attlee, Clement (Leader of the Labour Party and Lord Privy Seal) 167
Auberville 59
Aumale 59, 62-63, 66, 68, 72, 99
Avranches 129, 131, 133

Badoglio, Marshal Pietro 147
BAFF (British Air Forces in France) 21, 27, 32, 84, 152, 183, 185–86, 189, 192, 197, 211
BAFF headquarters 61, 133
BAFF Order of Battle 206-207
Barratt, Air Marshal Sir Arthur 27-28, 30-31, 58, 116, 125, 131, 133, 148, 151, 156, 183, 185-87, 206
Bartholomew Committee 192
Bartholomew, General Sir William 192
Bataille 68, 77, 93-94, 99
Battle of Britain 34, 44-45, 87
Battle of France 23-24, 26-27, 30-31, 34, 36, 38-39, 43-46, 51, 147-48, 169, 180, 185-86 189-90, 192, 195-96
BEF (British Expeditionary Forces) 21-34, 78, 157, 171, 175-76
BEF Order of Battle 201-205
Beauman, Brigadier (later Acting Major General) Archibald 25-26, 87, 125, 130, 162, 165, 168, 180
Beaumont 86, 88, 126
Belgian Government 155
Belgium 35, 139, 155, 189-89
Belloy 56
Bernay 73, 82, 88
Bernières-sur-Seine 75
Blades, Troop Sergeant 65-66
Blangy-sur-Bresle 59
Bletchley Park 147
Blitzkrieg 21, 31, 39-40, 44, 189-89
Blois 84
Blount, Air Vice-Marshal Charles 27, 206
Bock, *Generaloberst* Fedor von 38, 74, 209
Bolbec 73, 92
Boos 58, 62, 68-70, 99
Bordeaux 37, 90

Boulogne 35, 104
Bouvray 56
Brauchitsch, *Generaloberst* Walther von 36
Brest 37-38, 71, 86, 124, 128, 136-37, 139, 142-43, 159
Breton/Brittany Redoubt 164, 172
Briare 168, 172-73
Bristol Blenheim 27, 62, 88, 109, 188
British defence spending 40, 176
British prisoners of war 109-110
British War Cabinet 22, 148, 167–70, 172, 193
British War Cabinet Joint Intelligence Committee 193
Brittany 24, 125, 127–28, 136, 163–65, 172-74
Brooke, Lieutenant General Sir Alan xvi, 32, 72, 113, 124, 128, 130, 135, 141, 157-58, 160, 163-65, 171-76, 179-82, 198
Buchanan, Lieutenant Colonel E 53-54
Buchy 68, 70, 99

Cadogan, Sir Alexander 170
Caen 84, 125, 131, 133
Calais 26, 35, 38, 59, 71, 104, 132, 159–61
Camm, Sidney 34
Cany-Barville 73, 100
Carentan 126, 128–32
Case Red 35–37
Case Yellow 21, 35
Catenay 65
Catigny 53-55
Caubert 50
Chamberlain, Neville (Lord President of the Council) 21, 41, 158
Channel Islands 17, 28, 131, 136, 143, 148, 150
Channel Ports 38, 59, 71, 132, 159–61, 213
Chartres 37, 125, 127
Cherbourg 24, 28, 31, 37, 41, 95–97, 123–33, 135–36, 142–44, 162, 164–65, 172, 182
Chief of the Imperial General Staff (CIGS) 25, 32, 41, 57, 96, 135, 157–58, 160–64, 168, 173–74, 177–78
Christie, Walter 33
Churchill - sacrifice of 51st Division 51–52, 55, 64, 72, 93
Churchill, Winston (British Prime Minister) 22, 41, 135, 137, 141, 147-48, 158, 162-64, 167–70, 173, 179, 188, 191–92, 195–98
Colville, John (Prime Minister's Personal Private Secretary) 198
Composite Armoured Regiment 56, 59, 64–65
Conches 86-87, 89-90, 124, 126, 135
Conches-en-Ouche 124, 126, 135
Corunna 198
Crocker, Brigadier John 26, 66, 130, 177, 204
Cruiser tank 26, 29–30, 32–33, 61, 65, 71, 83, 191
Cruiser tank concept 30
Cunard Steam Company 138

Daily Mirror 141
Daimler Dingo scout car 61, 71, 83, 131-32
Dargnies 60
Darkest Hour 196
Denneville 132
Dewoitine 155
Dieppe 63–64, 67, 74, 77, 82, 85, 87, 92, 94–95, 99–100, 107
Diggle, Colonel J 25, 205
Dijon 37, 74
Dill, General Sir John 25, 41, 96, 135, 142, 156–58, 160-64, 168, 174, 178
Dinant 35
Domfront 127, 129
Dornier Do 17 45, 58, 61
Doudeville 94
Doullens 110
Dowding, Air Chief Marshal Sir Hugh 149, 167, 198
Drew, Major General James 24, 142
Dunbar-Nasmith, Admiral Sir Martin 115, 136-38, 143, 198
Dunkirk 18, 21–33, 35–36, 91-92, 94, 96, 100, 102–103, 107–109, 125, 136–37, 157–58, 167, 173, 175-76, 185, 188, 193, 195–97, 213
Dunkirk evacuation 18, 22, 27, 91, 96, 125, 176, 185, 188

Échemines 58, 62, 86
Eden, Anthony (Secretary of State for War) 135, 142, 158, 168
Elbeuf 73, 76, 88
Elkins, Commander RN 104
Eu 56, 59, 64, 66-68, 99, 160
Evans, Major General Roger 51, 59, 65–66, 69, 76–77, 83, 161–62, 180, 196
Evill, Air Vice Marshall Douglas 149, 206
Évreux 76, 86, 88, 91, 124–26, 129, 136, 172

Fairey Battle 27-28, 31, 33–34, 57–58, 62, 66, 72, 78, 84, 86, 88, 90–91, 125-26, 136
Fall Gelb 21, 36, 57, 184, 189–90
Fall Rot 28, 40–42, 48–49, 52, 78, 126, 169, 191
Farnes, Paul 28
Fécamp 23, 49, 69, 73, 92–97, 101, 105, 187
Feuquières 55
Field, Group Captain R 149-53
Fields, Colour Sergeant Edwin 111
Flixecourt 49
Fonblanque, Major General Philip de 24-25, 162-

63, 204
Fortune, Major General Victor 23, 48, 50, 77–78, 81, 92–94, 96, 98, 100-101, 104–107, 114, 144, 159–60, 162, 188
Franco-British Union 170-71
Franleu 53-54
French Army 35, 47–48, 73, 75, 89–91, 100, 102, 124–25, 128–29, 154–58, 161–64, 169–70, 179, 190, 196–97
French AFVs employed by German Army 71, 181
French Air Force (*Armée de l'Air*) 27–28, 42, 52, 67, 149, 152, 155–56, 189
French Government 17, 130, 135, 147, 151, 154–56, 158, 167, 169–73, 193, 198
French High Command 32, 52, 72, 96, 106, 156, 169, 175, 177, 188
French Navy 17, 143

Gaillon 71, 76–77, 88
Gamaches 57, 63, 67–68, 99, 160
Gamelin, *Général d'armée* Maurice 47
Gaulle, *Général de brigade* Charles de 168, 172–73
Geneva Convention 110-12
Genoa 147, 149–51
Georges, *Général d'armée* Alphonse-Joseph 26, 159, 163, 173
Gort, General Lord 158, 178
Gournay-en-Bray 65
Gravigny 91
Guderian, *General* Heinz 36-37, 39, 48,74, 308
Guernsey 150

Halder, *General* Franz 36
Hangest-sur-Somme 49, 56
Hansard 195, 197, 199
Hawker Hurricane 22, 27, 34, 42, 44, 52, 58, 62, 66, 72, 78, 84, 87, 89, 118, 126, 133, 136, 139, 185
Haye 128, 132
Hazebrouek 110
Hedebrauville 71
Hedgehog defences 47, 49, 189
Heer (German Army) 35–36, 40–42, 47–48, 65, 72–73, 78, 85, 123, 125, 127, 190
Heer Order of Battle 208-209
Heinkel He 111 45-46, 58, 89
Heinkel He 113 89
Heudebouville 82
Heve 95
Hitler, Adolf 36, 38, 42, 48-49, 190, 198
HMCS *Restigouche* 95, 104
HMCS *St Laurent* 95
HMS *Ambuscade* 95-97, 108, 187
HMS *Beagle* 138
HMS *Boadicea* 95-97, 108, 187
HMS *Broke* 95, 101
HMS *Bulldog* 95–97, 108
HMS *Codrington* 95, 105, 109, 187
HMS *Fernie* 95, 136, 143, 189
HMS *Foxglove* 136
HMS *Gardenia* 95
HMS *Hampton* 95, 104
HMS *Harvester* 95
HMS *Havelock* 138-39
HMS *Highlander* 138-39
HMS *Laird's Isle* 95, 136
HMS *Rosemary* 136
HMS *Sabre* 136, 189
HMS *Saladin* 95, 108-109
HMS *Vanoc* 138
HMS *Vega* 92, 136
HMS *Wolverine* 128-139
HMT *Cambridgeshire* 132, 138-41
HMT *Franconia* 138
HMT *Georgic* 138
HMT *Lancastria* 17, 46, 119, 132, 138, 141, 189, 191
Hoth, *Generalleutnant* Hermann 48, 67, 74, 209
Howard-Vyse, Major General Sir Richard 96, 163

Ihler, *Général de corps d'armée* Marcel 50, 101, 106-107
Imperial Defence College 192
Incheville 56, 60–61, 63–64
Ironside, General Sir Edmund 25, 163, 178
Ismay, Major General Hastings 163, 168-70, 193
Isneauville 70, 180
Italian Government 148, 156
Italy 37, 147–51, 156, 211

James, Admiral Sir William 94–96, 98, 104–109, 115, 136, 187–89, 198
Jersey 143-44, 150
Junkers Ju 87 Stuka 44, 57, 62, 72
Junkers Ju 88 xvii, 45-46, 58, 72, 132, 138, 141

Kampfgeschwader 30 138
Karslake, Lieutenant General Sir Henry 25–26, 29, 32, 51, 57, 77, 86, 96, 130, 159–63, 172, 177, 179, 188, 213
King George VI 194
Kleist, *General* Ewald von 37, 49, 74, 209
Kluge, *General* Günther von 38, 48, 125, 208
Kriegsmarine 22

Laon 38, 49, 62, 66, 72, 78
Laurencie, *Général de corps d'armée* Benoît-Léon de la 76, 127, 162

Laurie, Brigadier Sir John 24, 129, 203
Laval, Pierre 127, 130, 165
Le Bigot, *Vice Amiral* Jules 142
Le Havre 67, 73, 77–78, 84, 87, 89, 91–98, 100–101, 109, 159, 162, 187–88, 191
Le Mans 24, 27–28, 77, 88, 124, 126, 143, 157, 162–65
Le Masurier, William 144
Le Tôt 100, 102, 111
Leeb, *Generaloberst* Wilhelm von 38, 210
Lemelsen, *Generalmajor* Joachim 48
Les Andelys 48, 67, 70–71, 73, 75–76, 82, 86, 88–90
Liddell-Hart, Basil 154
Lillebonne 92, 95–96
Lockie, Regimental Sergeant Major W.S.I. 53
Loire 27, 31, 37, 74, 78, 84-85, 96, 127, 138, 140
Longpré 48, 72
Louviers 70, 76, 81–84, 87-88, 91
Luftwaffe 30–31, 34–36, 39, 41–42, 44–47, 59, 89, 91, 93, 97, 123, 131, 136, 184–86, 189–91
Luftwaffe air raids 67, 92, 133
Luftwaffe air superiority 94, 186
Luftwaffe Condor Legion 45–46, 155
Luftwaffe doctrine 42
Luftwaffe ground support role 181

Maginot Line 21, 23, 27, 38–39, 47, 90, 155, 189
Maillard, *Général de brigade* Marie-Michel-Gustave-Louis 75, 81
Manchester Guardian 48–49, 57, 61, 73, 77, 81, 109–10, 133, 169, 171, 178, 186
Marchainville 127
Marne 37, 74, 91
Marseilles 148, 151–52
Marshall-Cornwall, Lieutenant General James 41, 54, 57, 71–72, 77, 113, 125, 127, 129–30, 132–33, 135, 142, 156, 159–62, 164–65, 178, 181, 188, 198
Martigny 77, 94
Mathonville 68, 99
McCreery, Brigadier Richard 26, 82-83, 124, 177, 204
Mers El Kébir 143
Messerschmitt Bf 109 34, 45, 62, 66-67, 72, 87, 89
Messerschmitt Bf 110 45, 58, 67, 87, 185
Milan 147–49, 152
Mistreatment of British Prisoners of War 110-111
Monnet, Jean 168
Mons 53
Montgomery, Major General Bernard 159
Mortagne-au-Perche 124, 127–29, 135, 164
MS *Batory* 138
MS *Sobieski* 138
Murray-Grant, Major James 102, 111
Murrow, Edward 196,
Mussolini, Benito 147-148

Nantes 28, 37, 90, 125–26, 131, 133, 135–37, 162
Neufchâtel 67, 70–71, 95
Neuville 82
Newall, Air Chief Marshal Sir Cyril 148, 184

Oberkommando des Heeres (OKH) 36, 38, 57
Oise 74, 81, 85
Oisemont 57, 59, 62, 68, 99
Operation Aerial 17–18, 24, 120–21, 133, 135–36, 141, 187, 189, 191, 194, 198–99
Operation Catapult 143
Operation Cycle 93, 95, 97–98, 101, 104–105, 108, 136-37, 142–43, 187–88, 191, 211–12
Operation Dynamo 17–19, 22, 187, 190–91, 195, 197–99
Operation Overlord 17, 192
Orbec 164

Pallice 136–37, 144
Panzer 37, 39–40, 42–44, 48–49, 65, 67, 70, 73, 77, 82, 91, 95, 102
Panzer 35(t) 44
Panzer 38(t) 44, 65
Panzer I 40, 42-43
Panzer II 40, 42-43
Panzer III 33, 43–44
Panzer IV 33, 40, 42–43
Panzerwaffe 40, 48
Péronne 62
Pervitin 39
Pétain, *Maréchal de France* Philippe 169, 172
Petiet, *Général de division* Robert 83, 88
Picquigny 48
Planches 124
Playfair, Air Vice-Marshal Sir Patrick 27-28, 116, 133, 206
Plymouth 135–36, 138, 141, 144
Poix 59, 63, 66, 68, 72, 99, 110
Poland 31, 35, 39–40, 42–43, 184
Polish Campaign -- *Wehrmacht* tactics 42–43
Pont de l'Arche 73, 75–77, 83, 86
Pont Remy 68, 99
Pont-l'Évêque 125
Ponts-et-Marais 59
Poole 135-36
Portsmouth 94, 104–5, 135–36, 143
Pownall, Lieutenant General Sir Henry 160-61
Prady, Lance Corporal Edward 110
Praga 44

Quai Nord 97
Quaie Normanie 130
Quesne 126, 128
Quesnoy-le-Montant 30
Quiberon 138-39
Quimper 173

RAF (Royal Air Force) 28, 148, 184
RAF Air Raids 31, 62, 88, 91, 149–52
RAF Bases 127, 133
RAF Bomber Command 27, 34, 57, 91, 149–50, 183, 191
RAF Coastal Command 28, 191
RAF Depots 186
RAF Fighter Command 17, 28, 97, 198
RAF Ground Crews 143
RAF Tangmere 28
Redon 128, 165
Redoubt 164, 172–73
Regia Aeronautica 148, 151-52
Reims 31, 38, 74, 85
Rennes 24, 28, 37, 126–27, 130, 133, 172
Rethel 67, 74
Reynaud, Paul (French Prime Minister) 47, 148, 151, 167–70, 172–73, 193
Rheims37-38
River Aisne 38, 48, 66, 72, 78, 91
River Andelle 64–67, 69, 161, 180
River Béthune 48, 67, 94, 160–61
River Bresle 56–57, 59–64, 66–67, 77, 159–60, 190
River Durdent 73, 94, 100–101
River Loire 17, 127, 138–39, 168
River Marne 85, 90–91
River Meuse 35, 38, 84
River Oise 38, 81, 85
River Rhine 124
River Risle 87
River Somme 23, 26, 35, 38, 47–50, 56–58, 62, 64, 69, 78, 85, 177–78
River Yères 60
Rochelle 131, 137
Rocque 126
Romilly 83
Rommel, *Generalmajor* Erwin 23, 49, 103, 107, 114, 125
Rouen 23–27, 48–49, 52, 58–59, 62–63, 65, 67–74, 76–77, 85–87, 93–96, 99, 162, 179–81
Rouvray 56
Royal Navy (RN) 17–18, 22, 95–98, 100–105, 109, 136–39, 142–43, 162, 165, 173, 175, 187–89, 191, 195, 197–98
Royal Navy Fleet Air Arm 143
Roye 58, 62
Royroi 62

Ruhr 30, 34, 78, 183
Rundstedt, *Generaloberst* Gerd von 38, 74, 208

Saar 22, 50
Saigneville 53,
Sallenelle 53, 55
Salom-de-Provence 149-51
Sarreguemines 38
Saumur 28, 37
Schlieffen Plan 49
Secretary of State for Air 153
Secretary of State for Foreign Affairs 170
Secretary of State for War 135, 158, 165, 168
Sedan 35–36, 47, 57, 130
Seeckt, *Generaloberst* Hans von 39
Senarpont 59–60, 63–64, 68, 99
Serqueux 64, 66, 69–71, 161
Sharp, Captain Rudolph 138
Sholto Douglas, Air Vice Marshal William 149
Sigy-en-Bray 67, 69
Skoda 44
Soissons 37, 74, 84
Somme 31, 36–38, 49–50, 52, 57–58, 62, 66, 68, 74, 93, 98–100, 180, 190
Somme, Canal 68, 99
Spanish Civil War 41, 43, 45–46, 155, 184
Spears, General Sir Edward 168-69
SS *Manxman* 90, 129, 133
SS *Princesse Astrid* 90, 129
St Aubin 90
St Avold 38
St Leger 68, 99
St Malo 28, 90, 128, 131, 135–36, 142–44
St Nazaire 31, 133, 136–41, 165, 183, 189
St Pierre-du-Vauvray 73
St Quentin 62, 66, 73
St Vaast 68, 99
St Valery-en-Caux 68, 84–86, 88, 93–111, 114, 159, 179, 187–89, 193, 197-98
St Valery-sur-Somme 51–55, 62
Stanley-Clarke, Brigadier Arthur 23, 53-54, 93, 97, 203
Sturzkampfflugzeug ('Stuka') 44, 57, 62, 72, 181
Swayne, Brigadier John 163
Syme, Lt-Colonel A. 70, 180
Syme's Battalion 69-70, 180

Territorial Army 21, 31, 40, 176
The Times 52, 61-62, 85, 89, 97, 109, 130, 133, 150, 170-71, 177
Thermopylae 197
Thieulloy-la-Ville 62
Tilleul 124
Tilloy 53, 55

Toeu 68, 99
Toeufles 57
Torres Vedras 172
Totes 68, 82, 99
Touffreville-sur-Eu 60
Tours 37, 56, 169–70
Treasury Solicitor, papers 110-111
Treport 57
Tricot 58
Trier 58
Troyes 27, 31, 74, 78, 88
Truppenamt 39
Turin 147–50

United Nation War Crimes Commission 111
United States of America 17, 141, 170, 193, 199
United States of America, President of 147

Valines 53, 55
Valognes 126
Varennes 68, 99
Vascoeuil 70
Venables 75–77, 82–83
Verneuil 124
Vernon 48, 81–82, 84–86, 88, 91, 125
Veules-les-Roses 85, 100–101, 103-105, 107-109, 188, 191
Veulettes-sur-Mer 77, 96–97, 187
Veys 128, 131
Vichy 17, 37, 143
Vickary, Colonel C. 25
Vickers Light Tank 117
Vickers Wellington 119, 148, 150
Vicomte 128
Vierville 131
Villedieu 129
Villers-sur-le-Roule 77
Vire 129
Vitré 131, 165
Vrely 58
Vuillemin, *Général d'Armée Aérienne* Joseph 151

War Cabinet 22, 148, 167–70, 172, 193
War Cabinet, Memoranda 22
War Cabinet, Minutes 22, 148, 152, 167–68, 171
War Office 96, 98, 100, 104, 106, 109, 157, 159, 161, 163, 165, 182, 184
Watkins, Rear Admiral Geoffrey 152
Wehrmacht 25, 31, 39–40, 42, 49, 173, 180, 189, 191, 196, 198
Wehrmacht, doctrine and tactics 39-40
Wehrmacht Artillery 55, 76, 86, 101–6, 108
Weygand Line 47, 50, 57
Weygand, *Général d'armée* Maxime 23, 47, 106, 161–63, 169, 172
Woincourt 57, 60-61
Yonne 37, 74
Yvetot 68, 73, 94, 99
Yzengremer 60

Zoteux 57

Index of Military Formations & Units

BEF Formations/Units

Divisions

1st Armoured Division xiii, xvi, 26-27, 32, 41, 49, 51-52, 56, 59, 64-66, 69-70, 77, 82-84, 88-90, 123-24, 128, 130, 143, 157, 159, 161-62, 180, 190-91, 196-97, 204
1st Canadian Division 24, 98, 143-44, 157-160, 191
12th (Eastern) Division 23, 201
23rd (Northumbrian) Division 23, 201
46th (North Midland and West Riding) Division 24, 157, 202
51st (Highland) Division xiii, xvi, 23-24, 27, 32, 48-52, 54, 57-59, 61-64, 67, 69, 71-73, 75, 77-78, 82, 92-102, 104, 106-110, 113, 114, 157, 159-62, 169, 172, 179-80, 183, 187-91, 193, 197-98, 202
52nd (Lowland) Division 24, 86, 88, 90, 98, 124, 126, 128, 130-31, 133, 135, 142-43, 157, 159-60, 163-64, 172, 191, 203

Brigades

2nd Armoured Brigade 26-27, 52, 56, 61, 65-66, 70, 75-76, 82-83, 88, 124, 177, 204
3rd Armoured Brigade 26-27, 52, 63, 65-66, 69-70, 76, 82-84, 124, 126-27, 129-31, 162, 177, 204
35th Brigade 23, 201
36th Brigade 23, 201
37th Brigade 23, 201
69th Brigade 23, 201
70th Brigade 23, 202
137th Brigade 24, 202
138th Brigade 24, 202
139th Brigade 24, 202
152nd Brigade 23, 51, 56-57, 59, 63, 67, 82, 85, 93, 202
153rd Brigade 23, 51, 54, 56-57, 59, 73, 85
154th Brigade 23, 51, 56-57, 59, 63, 67, 73, 77, 93, 203
155th Brigade 24, 90, 125-26, 128-29, 203
156th Brigade 24, 86, 126, 128-29, 203

157th Brigade 24, 86-90, 124, 126-29, 131, 135, 164, 203

Units

7th Argyll & Sutherland Highlanders 23, 53-55, 59-61, 63, 69, 101, 203
8th Argyll & Sutherland Highlanders 23, 52, 54-55, 60, 93, 203
1st Black Watch 23, 50, 77, 94, 102, 107, 202
4th Black Watch 23, 53-56, 60-61, 63, 69, 93, 102, 202
4th Border Regiment 24, 60, 63-64, 205
6th Cameronians 24, 86, 90, 129
7th Cameronians 24, 86, 90, 129, 203
2/6th Duke of Wellington's Regiment 24, 69-71, 75-77, 81-82, 87-88, 126, 128, 131, 202
2/7th Duke of Wellington's Regiment 24, 64-65, 82, 85-86, 94, 102-103, 108-109, 202
10th Durham Light Infantry 23, 202
11th Durham Light Infantry 23, 202
2/6th East Surrey Regiment 23, 59, 64, 201, 205
5th East Yorkshire Regiment 23, 201
1st Glasgow Highlanders 23, 203
1st Gordon Highlanders 23, 50, 55-56, 94, 102, 107, 202
5th Gordon Highlanders 23, 94, 102-103, 203
6th Green Howards 23, 201
7th Green Howards 23, 201
5th Highland Light Infantry 24, 126, 203
6th Highland Light Infantry 24, 126, 203
2/4th King's Own Yorkshire Light Infantry 24, 69-70, 73, 75, 77, 131, 202, 205
4th King's Own Scottish Borderers 24, 126, 203
5th King's Own Scottish Borderers 24, 90, 126
2/5th Leicestershire Regiment 24, 202
6th Lincolnshire Regiment 24, 202,
1st Lothians & Border Yeomanry 57, 59-61, 64, 77, 94, 100-101
7th Norfolk Regiment 100, 102, 111
4th Queen's Own Cameron Highlanders 23, 50, 56, 94, 102-103, 107, 202
9th Queen's Royal Lancers 26, 57, 60-61, 69, 82-83
2/5th Queen's Royal Regiment 23, 201
2/6th Queen's Royal Regiment 60, 100-101, 201
2/7th Queen's Royal Regiment 23, 201
6th Queen's Own Royal West Kent Regiment 23, 201
7th Queen's Own Royal West Kent Regiment 23, 201
5th Royal East Kent Regiment 23, 201
7/9th Royal Scots 24, 90, 126, 203
6th Royal Sussex Regiment 23, 201
7th Royal Sussex Regiment 22, 201
2nd Royal Tank Regiment (2 RTR) 26, 65-66, 67-71, 76, 83-84, 86, 123, 128-29, 204
3rd Royal Tank Regiment (3 RTR) 26, 204
5th Royal Tank Regiment (5 RTR) 26, 65, 71, 83, 204
2nd Seaforth Highlanders 23, 50, 94, 100, 102, 107, 111, 202
4th Seaforth Highlanders 23, 50, 77, 94, 102-103, 202
9th Sherwood Foresters 24, 202
2/5th Sherwood Foresters 24, 202
10th Royal Hussars 26-27, 65, 76, 82-84, 204
4/5th The Royal Scots Fusiliers 24, 86, 89, 124, 126, 129, 203
1/5th Sherwood Foresters 24, 63-64, 93, 205
1st Tyneside Scottish 23, 202
2/5th West Yorkshire Regiment 24, 202
6th York and Lancaster Regiment 24, 202

Royal Artillery 23-24, 63, 127
Royal Canadian Regiment 24
Royal Engineers 23-26, 59-61, 66, 126, 130
Queen's Bays 26-27, 65, 69, 76, 83, 204

Miscellaneous

1st Support Group 26, 60, 69, 204

Arkforce 93-94, 96-100
Beauman Division 25-26, 32, 56-57, 59, 63-67, 70-71, 77, 82-83, 88-89, 93, 123, 127, 130-31, 180-81
Digforce 25, 205
Normanforce 128, 131–32, 143, 164–65
Vicforce 25, 205

Royal Air Force

1 Fighter Squadron 58
12 Bomber Squadron 58
150 Bomber Squadron 58, 90
73 Fighter Squadron 62, 66-67, 87, 139
501 Fighter Squadron 28, 58, 61, 72
615 Fighter Squadron 86-87

Advanced Air Striking Force (AASF) 27-28, 31, 34, 52, 57-58, 78, 84, 86, 90-91, 125-26, 133, 183-86, 191, 204, 206, 211
Haddock Force 18, 147, 149, 151–53, 156

French Army Formations

10th Army 32, 48-50, 63, 65, 71-73, 77, 87, 89, 123-30, 135, 159, 161-65, 172

IX Corps 49–50, 62–63, 65, 67, 71–73, 77, 82, 92–93, 95, 106, 159

Divisions Légère de Cavalerie (DLC) 59, 68, 76, 82, 90, 127
Divisions Légères Mécaniques (DLM) 50, 89

Wehrmacht Formations/Units

Armies

Army Group A 37-39, 74, 208
Army Group B 37-39, 48, 74, 209
Army Group C 38, 210
4th Army 38, 48, 74, 125, 208
6th Army 74, 208
7th Army 74, 208

Corps, Gruppes & Divisions

XV Corps 39, 48, 209

Panzergruppe Guderian 38
Panzergruppe Hoth 39, 208
Panzergruppe Kleist 39, 62, 209

Divisions & Units

5th Panzer Division 48, 62, 70-71, 77, 102-103, 125, 209
7th Panzer Division 23, 39, 48-49, 59, 62-63, 65, 67, 73, 77, 95-96, 100-103, 107, 120, 123, 125, 132, 179, 209

SS-Verfügungstruppe 39, 209